Friedrich August Ramseyer

Four years in Ashantee

Friedrich August Ramseyer

Four years in Ashantee

ISBN/EAN: 9783741194030

Manufactured in Europe, USA, Canada, Australia, Japa

Cover: Foto ©ninafisch / pixelio.de

Manufactured and distributed by brebook publishing software (www.brebook.com)

Friedrich August Ramseyer

Four years in Ashantee

FOUR YEARS IN ASHANTEE

BY THE MISSIONARIES

RAMSEYER AND KÜHNE

Edited by Mrs. Weitbrecht

WITH INTRODUCTION BY REV. DR. GUNDERT, AND PREFACE BY
PROFESSOR CHRISTLEIB, D.D.

NEW YORK
ROBERT CARTER & BROTHERS, 535 BROADWAY.
MDCCCLXXV.

CONTENTS.

	PAGE.
PREFACE,	v.
INTRODUCTORY CHAPTER,	xi.

CHAP.

I.—WAITING TIME IN ANUM,	1
II.—THE GENERAL FLIGHT,	4
III.—IN THE POWER OF THE ASHANTEES,	7
IV.—BEFORE ADU BOFO,	14
V.—WITH THE ASHANTEE ARMY,	18
VI.—THE MARCH TO THE VOLTA,	26
VII.—FROM THE VOLTA TO OKWANO,	31
VIII.—JOURNEY TO AGUAGO, AND THE HALT THERE,	38
IX.—THE LITTLE ONE GOES HOME IN TOTORASE,	44
X.—TO DWABEN AND ABANKORO,	51
XI.—WITH M. BONNAT IN ABANKORO,	57
XII.—IN ASOTSCHE,	64
XIII.—BEFORE THE KING,	67
XIV.—EBENEZER,	76
XV.—IN COOMASSIE WITH PRINCE ANSA,	97
XVI.—TIMES OF SICKNESS AND FORSON'S EMBASSY,	117
XVII.—THE EMBASSY OF MESSRS. CRAWFORD AND PLANGE,	127
XVIII.—ADU BOFO'S ENTRY,	135
XIX.—YAMS AND CHRISTMAS FESTIVALS,	146

CHAP.		PAGE.
XX.—Prince Ansa's Transactions about the Ransom Money,		153
XXI.—Prolonged Waiting during a Revolution in the Colonial Politics,		163
XXII.—Mr. Plange's Second Embassy,		172
XXIII.—A Critical Time,		183
XXIV.—Seeming Liberty,		189
XXV.—The Reason of the War,		201
XXVI.—In Coomassie amid the Fluctuations of War,		207
XXVII.—We Build for the King,		224
XXVIII.—Judgment Approaches,		243
XXIX.—Brother Kühne set at Liberty,		263
XXX.—The Release of the Rest,		275
XXXI.—The Judgment,		290

APPENDIX.

I.—The Adae,		301
II.—The Weights of Gold in Ashantee,		303
III.—The Government of Ashantee,		305
IV.—A Letter of Prince Ansa,		312
V.—A Word on the Politics of the Colonial Government in the Year 1872,		318

PREFACE.

From the earliest ages onward, the Christian Church at large has ever bestowed the warmest sympathy and the most grateful attention on the history of her martyrs. And well she may do so, for have they not acted as the pioneers of Christ's advancing kingdom, presenting in their example a standing embodiment of the victory of Christian faith and patience over the world?

Nor has the Protestant Church, for her part, been without the witness of numerous martyrs from the era of her first struggles for existence, down to the history of her missions in modern times. And though we do not idolize these martyrs, lest we should detract from the glory of the only Mediator and incomparable Martyr of Golgotha; yet we honour their memory, and we look upon their sufferings and conquests as pledges for that universal triumph of the gospel, which shall eventually be brought about. True, a Church whose foundation was laid by the Crucified, must ever remain a cross-bearing Church: amidst much of strife and tribulation, under the pressure of constant trial, her members must grow and increase, till the day arrive when the first holy cross-bearer, Jesus Christ her Lord and Head, shall appear in glory and deliver His suffering Bride from all evil.

PREFACE.

The following pages tell a wondrous story of Christian martyrdom, although the story does not end with the death of the sufferers. Those martyrs who were permitted to seal their testimony for Christ's truth with their blood, have by no means always suffered more severely than the Christian witnesses whose experiences are recorded here.

We see them enduring a tedious captivity, full of most cruel privations, in one of the darkest territories of heathen superstition, under a sanguinary despotism, the like of which, even in Africa, exists only in places few and far between. With the abominations and fiendish barbarities of such a government daily before their eyes, their own lives in constant peril, and at the mercy of a despot who played with the persons of his prisoners as though they were puppets—in the midst of constant fluctuations between fear and hope, the prospect of release again and again held out, only to be dashed to the ground—till at length their peril reaches its climax, together with the political jeopardy of their tormentors.

At length the judgment which breaks in upon the tyrant is the means of restoring them—though weak and exhausted—to safety, in answer to the unceasing prayers of their friends at home. Assuredly this is no easier martyrdom than the quicker process of laying down one's life on the block or at the stake. The fact, moreover, that these sufferers are still in our midst, only deepens the sympathy which we feel in the story of their captivity.

But the interest attaching to this simple journal of the German missionaries is manifold. It excites not only personal sympathy, such as every Christian owes to the sufferings of a brother. It awakens not merely the attention of the ethnologist, who will gain from it a far deeper insight into the political, social, and religious life of the Ashantee nation than any traveller has hitherto been able to give—but it must command the interest of all who desire the extension of Christ's kingdom, more especially of English Christians.

The most recent events in the history of Ashantee are a tangible confirmation of the repeated experience, that a kingdom which resists the spread of gospel light, and refuses to recognise the day of its visitation, is ripening for internal decay, convulsion, and dissolution. The latest news (see "The Evangelischer Heidenbote" (Calw), Dec. 1874), make it a matter of certainty that the kingdom of Ashantee is doomed. Kofi Kari-Kari, a weak, vain, deceitful monarch, is apparently unable to recover the effect of his defeat. His rôle appears to be well-nigh finished, his chiefs and allies are leaving him, and he has already been compelled to admit the independence of his most powerful vassal, the king of Dwaben.

May we not believe that God has permitted one of the most powerful kingdoms of Western Africa to be thus terribly humiliated, in order that a free entrance may be opened into that land for the Gospel of Peace? The unbroken power of Ashantee has hitherto—with few and rare exceptions—withstood the influence of the gospel, and would have continued to render the establishment of new missions fruitless, if not impossible. The yoke of despotism is now broken, and the agglomeration of tribes once held together by superstition and fear, is beginning to be dissolved into its constituent elements.

The nationalities hitherto enslaved by Ashantee are seeking a closer alliance with England, and wish to be admitted into the protectorate. The south-western boundary of the Ashantee kingdom is opened, and not only this but the tribes there situate (Okwau and Dwaben) have expressed a wish for missionaries to come to them. Does not all this reveal the hand of God opening the gates to the messengers of His kingdom? Can we imagine a political situation more favourable to its extension?

These questions demand an answer from Christians on both sides of the channel. What better one can be given by those of England, than the practical conclusion: *Now that the weapons of our country have pierced the heart of Ashantee, and laid Coomassie in ruins, should not the Christian compassion and the vigorous faith of Englishmen seek to raise this unhappy nation from the dust; not to new death, but to true life in the light and liberty of the gospel?*

Wherefore not? Germany and Switzerland, through the instrumentality of their Basel Missionary Society, are ready to help in a second campaign against Coomassie. For more than forty years this Society has been working on the west coast of Africa; gradually pushing forward its stations to the boundaries of Ashantee. How considerable have been the results already attained, how wholesome the influence already exercised upon the population, may be seen from the official recognition of these facts by Sir John Glover, during the late war. Hence we cannot doubt that side by side with the English Wesleyans, the Basel Society is primarily called of God to carry on this work.

In concert with the liberated captives, the Basel committee has already drawn up a plan for the advancement of the mission foreposts in a westerly direction, so as to take possession of the new territory. One of the captives, Mr. Ramseyer, whose health permits him to return, has offered to found the new mission in Ashantee; and three Basel missionaries have already preceded, and are awaiting his arrival at Kyebi (not far from the frontier), and are meanwhile preparing themselves for their work. One of the principal keys of the land, viz., the language spoken throughout Ashantee (Tschi) is already in the possession of the missionaries, who have finished and printed (or are now printing), not only a translation of the Scriptures, but also the most necessary books for schools and churches.

Thus has this new and peaceful campaign against Ashantee *been already* inaugurated. Germany is ready to send into the field the needful, well-qualified soldiers, in the shape of thoroughly educated, persevering, hard-working, frugal missionaries—some of whom have, as we have said, been already dispatched. The indispensable fund for carrying on this holy war amounts to £7,000 for starting, and £700 annually for supporting the new stations. Is it asking too much if we look for assistance in raising these sums to English liberality? Assuredly it must be of the greatest importance for the English protectorate in West Africa—even from a merely political point of view—to change the kingdom of Ashantee from a wily and cruel enemy, into a peaceful and civilised neighbour.

The Committee of the Basel Missionary Society has already issued an appeal to the Christians of England, which has been supported with large-hearted generosity and true Christian charity by the Church Missionary Society—a body which has always shown the utmost regard for the moral rights of other societies, and in this case too has abstained from the least appearance of an attempt to take possession of territory which has been already occupied by the English Wesleyan and Basel Societies.

May this noble example be followed by Christians throughout England, and may they show by the warm support accorded to this new mission (which many of them feel to be a national duty), that they attach far more importance to the extension of Christ's kingdom than to the spread of any one denomination. May the following pages sound, in their artless but touching tale, the voice of the Lord, knocking at the heart's door of Christian England, and asking help for benighted Ashantee. If there be any one who can read a journal such as this, without becoming a friend and supporter of missions to the heathen, let him earnestly ask himself the question whether one who has no compassion for the sufferings of a Christless humanity, can have any true love to the Lord whom these sufferings brought down to take our flesh.

"Behold I have set before thee an open door, and no man can shut it" (Rev. iii. 8). Let us not be blind to the truth in the present case. Inwards, beyond Ashantee, and indeed partly in Ashantee itself, the false prophet is at work, and more of the tribes of inner Africa are constantly being subdued to his creed. This open door may soon be closed, if we neglect to hear God's message, and do not hasten to set up in those regions the standard of the True Prophet.

THEODORE CHRISTLEIB, D.D., Ph. D.
Professor of Theology and University Preacher.

Bonn, Prussia, December 20th, 1874.

INTRODUCTORY CHAPTER

BY THE

REV. DR. GUNDERT, CALW, WÜRTEMBERG.

WE are indebted to peculiar circumstances for the following pages. Two missionaries suddenly found themselves in a position to observe closely the still unbroken national and political life of a pure African race; to live and to suffer with them in a very important and critical period of their history—probably indeed the turning point. But in this case the usual state of things was reversed. Europeans, whether travellers, merchants, residents, or missionaries, when they cross the path of, or come in contact with the negro, commonly do so from a position of superiority. They look from above, but these men saw all from below; the white man was the slave, the negro the master.

Those who wish to know the state of things which really existed in the now fallen Ashantee kingdom, its forms of government, and the individual, social, and political life of this interesting negro people, will find in this journal important and dependable disclosures. Of course, they are scattered through the narrative; for a connected summary, or a polished description of the country has not been attempted here.

To the attentive reader it will be clear that the real journal, viz., that which was written simultaneously with the events, only commenced when the writers had ink and paper sent them. They both made use of the long

INTRODUCTORY CHAPTER.

period of detention in Coomassie to write down the events of each day, at the same time recording their remembrances of the first year of their captivity. That the names of places scarcely occur at all is to be accounted for by the position of the unwilling travellers. The following statement may help to throw light on the circumstances which led to their being taken prisoners.

The Gold Coast extends from the Asini river to the mouth of the Volta, and includes from three to four degrees of longitude. It is traversed through the middle by the Prah, and inhabited by negro tribes who mostly speak a dialect of the Tschi language. On the western side of the Prah are the Asini, Wasa, and Denkjera; on the other side are the Fantee, Abora, Akem, Asen, and Akwapem; and towards the Volta are the Akra, Adangme, Krobo, and Akwamu. Twenty-five forts were built from time to time, in which European merchants formerly carried on the slave trade. The chief of these forts, Elmina and Cape Coast, two miles apart, have belonged (since 1637-1661) to the Dutch and English. These exercised little, and certainly no good influence on the surrounding negroes.

At length the Asantees, or as they are called in the Coast dialect, Ashantees, appeared on the scene as a conquering power, and in endeavouring to force their way to the sea, came into collision with the British. The latter fought a hasty battle with the king, Tuta Kwamina, January 21st, 1824, and suffered a disgraceful defeat. Two years later, September 19th, 1826, this was avenged by a complete victory at Dudowa, after which the experienced governor, George Maclean, arranged the terms of peace, which guaranteed the independence of all the tribes (with the exception of the Asinis in the west and the Akwamus in the east), and placed them under British protection. Two Ashantee princes, Kwanta Bisa and Ansa Owusu, were sent as hostages to England,

INTRODUCTORY CHAPTER. xiii

whence they returned in 1841 as baptized Christians, and accompanied a Wesleyan mission to Coomassie.

In 1580 the English territory was made more compact by the purchase of the Danish settlements, and by an exchange with the Dutch in 1867, when a tax of a shilling a head was imposed on the inhabitants of the protectorate; but very little was done for the improvement of the people. The Wesleyans established a mission in the west, the Basel Society did the same in the east, and these were the chief efforts made for the elevation of the negro population. In 1863 a fresh war broke out between the English colonial government and the king of Ashantee, which led to a disastrous campaign, the British troops falling victims to the climate rather than to the enemy. Captain Pine pleaded for means to make a vigorous attack upon Coomassie; but he obtained only a few West Indian troops who were encamped in the bush during the rainy season, where numbers of them died. King Kwakoo Dooah said truly, "The white men bring many cannon to the bush, but the bush is stronger than the cannon."

In May 1864, an order was sent to discontinue the war; in consequence of which unfortunate proceeding the Ashantees lost all respect for the British power; and Parliament found it necessary to appoint a commission to investigate thoroughly the condition of the British territory on the Gold Coast. Many strongly recommended the abandonment of such an unhealthy, profitless colony, while others as strongly advocated a more energetic management of it; between these two extremes of opinion the commission thought it desirable to adopt a middle course.

It recommended that the government should be left more and more in the hands of the natives, and that the British should carefully avoid enlarging their territory or making any fresh treaties with the tribes on the Coast, in order that the protecting power might, as soon as it was possible, without breach of honour, withdraw entirely. It happened, as might have been foreseen. "The weakness and incapacity of the local government made every progress impossible," as Lord Grey truly stated. No attempt was made to train the natives to self-government, or to make them capable of defending themselves; the weak policy which only aimed at avoiding all dealings with Ashantee, and which, even when roused, persevered in inactivity, inevitably led to war with this proud people.

The Basel Society had, in the winter of 1839-40, sent out their first missionary, Ries; he had gone to Coomassie and attempted to carry forward his work in Ashantee.

But later on circumstances arose which led the Basel Society to enlarge their field of operations on the Volta, and this was done without an idea that it was possible to come into connection or collision with the eastern boundary of Ashantee. Thus in 1846, the missionary Klauss crossed the Volta and began to found a settlement at about eight miles distance from the river, on high ground near Anum. A steep healthy hill, covered with grass, rose about 200 feet above the plain on the north of the town. Here, after much difficulty, a house was at last finished and a school commenced, while regular mission work was carried on amongst the people; an agent in connection with the mission also bought up cotton, which was sent down the Volta to the coast town Ada.

But from the beginning there were many political hindrances to the prosperity of the new station. To the south of Anum, on the Volta, live the Akwems, who have long been on very bad terms with their neighbours. In the year 1867, their enmity took so active a form that Anum became almost cut off from the rest of the missionary territory, and could only be reached by a long and circuitous route.

In 1869, the Akwems and the Anglos, a tribe who live

further to the east, formed a secret alliance with Ashantee, and the latter power sent an army across the Volta to seize upon territory just outside the British protectorate. It was believed in Coomassie that the English would not raise any earnest objection to this, and the plan was, after winning great victories, to push on with increased strength to the Gold Coast. This expedition led, in June 1869, to the destruction of the two mission stations Anum and Wegbe (or Ho). Whilst the residents at the latter place were able to escape in good time, retreat was impossible for the Basel missionaries. The Swiss, Frederick Augustus Ramseyer (with his wife and their infant son), had been in Anum since December 29th, 1868. He had worked on the Gold Coast since 1864, so that he had much African experience. The Silesian Johannes Kühne had been in Africa since 1866, but he had only joined Ramseyer as a merchant two months before they were made prisoners. We will now proceed to their own narrative.

MISSIONARY LIFE IN ASHANTEE.

CHAPTER I.

WAITING TIME IN ANUM.

AFTER the arrival of Mr. Kühne on our station, Anum, his predecessors, Mr. and Mrs. Schönhuth had, by order of our Committee, to leave this place for their new field of labour at Christiansborg; but in war time it was no easy task to find men for the transport of Mrs. Schönhuth and the baggage, because an order from the camp, which was pitched near our town, made it imperative on all the men to join their ranks, as a glimpse had been caught of their enemies, the Ashantees. There was, however, no time for delay, and by vigorous effort we induced four men to assist us, so that Mrs. Schönhuth was safely conveyed to Ho, May 20th, 1869.

Alarming rumours were rife on all sides, while negroes, painted and armed to the teeth, were constantly seen leaving the camp and ascending our hill. The appearance of these fellows was really terrific, with their caps of dried skin surmounted by blood-stained goats' horns. They vaunted their heroic deeds on such of their Ashantee enemies as had come within their reach, and a band of twenty of them demanded a reward for having kept watch for us on the Wolta river. But the Almighty God had been our sole protector, and we firmly refused their unreasonable request.

We scarcely believed anything we heard, and concluded that as there was still a mixed population of young and old left in the town, the danger could not be imminent. We also hoped that the apparent attachment of the Anums to us and our surroundings, and the kindness we had shown them on various occasions, would prove some security, and we suspected that the enemy desired us to forsake our station only that they might plunder it to their hearts' content. We therefore firmly resolved to stay and abide the consequences. No idea of imprisonment or captivity in Coomassie ever occurred to us, believing we had really less to fear from the Ashantees than from the people around us. The king, however, suggested our depositing our property in Ho, though he assured us there was no real danger; this we were willing to do, but how to accomplish it was the question, for most of our servants, and even our nurse, had already fled. Our brethren in Ho, who were equally anxious with ourselves to remain at their post, begged me to send my wife with the little one to them for protection, and I would gladly have accepted their kindness but for her determination to remain with me.

The thing which caused our chief uneasiness was a cloud of smoke which we observed rising behind the chain of mountains near us, and which advanced continually in an easterly direction. Sometimes it was so dense that we thought it must arise from the burning of a village; then it became so faint as scarcely to indicate camp fires; and anon it faded into a thin blue mist. Our negroes could not explain it, yet it was obvious that our king was removing his camp into close proximity to us, so that it was now within an hour's walk of Anum, and there was no sign of breaking it up. By this time all business was suspended, except that a good deal of cotton was still being brought to us in exchange for cowries, and nearly a hundred bales lay ready for dispatch; but the king would not supply the men to take them down the river.

The clerk and the catechist remained faithful, although very uneasy from the general excitement; still, none of us supposed we had more to fear from the enemy than the extortion of a war tax, or the partial plunder of our goods. Our neutrality had been recognised by the king of Akwamu, an ally of Ashantee, who had twice permitted Mr. Schönhuth to pass through his territory, and it was well known to every one that we, as missionaries, not only had nothing to do with war, but that Mr. Schönhuth had once obtained the release of an Ashantee prisoner at his own cost, and sent him back to his friends.

I regarded my wife's decision to remain beside me in the hour of danger as an indication from God that we were not to separate, and subsequent events strengthened this impression. Most wonderfully was she upheld, both in body and mind, during the weary years of our captivity, and again and again did she revive my drooping faith, throughout our lengthened wanderings.

Thus, amid alternating hopes and fears, the first week of June passed away, yet the cloud of smoke was still seen travelling eastward, and the question sometimes flashed upon us, "Could the Ashantees be advancing on Ho?" Meanwhile we could obtain no reliable news, but if an engagement should occur, it would certainly necessitate flight; for where would a combined resistance be more easy than from the summit of our hill, surrounded as it was by a high wall, and only ten minutes' walk from the town.

CHAPTER II.

THE GENERAL FLIGHT.

WE were awakened at day break, on the morning of 9th June, by a loud knocking, and on opening the door, several soldiers announced to me, in the king's name, that a battle was at hand, that the town would soon be deserted, and we could expect no mercy from the bloodthirsty Ashantees. " Would we like to escape?" After some deliberation we decided in the negative.

Scarcely had they left us when our boys asked leave to join their mothers, who were preparing to flee. We could not refuse them, for our other servants had already gone, except two whom we had rescued from slavery, with our catechist and our clerk. By the afternoon a few stragglers alone remained in the town, and the king was trying to establish his camp in its deserted area, for a battle was expected in our immediate neighbourhood. A merchant who attended our services, visited us, and advised us to retire to Ho. "The Ashantees will not injure your persons," said he, "but they might easily carry you to Coomassie. I will, however, meet you again in the hour of danger, seeing you decide to remain." Still later we had a visit from a relative of the king, assuring us that he had not ordered a flight, and regretting that our servants had left us, though we hoped we should see them again the following day. Thus warned, we deemed it prudent, after dark, to bury two hundred dollars in the garden, and hide our rings in the same place.

But the news which reached us on the morning of June 10th, cut off all hopes of a speedy peace. None of our servants returned, and the Christians, who had been faithful hitherto, now begged to be dismissed. "The Ashantees," they said, "were known as executioners, and they might be as likely to practise on black men as on white?" We gave them some money, and a testimonial of faithful service, advising them on no account to mix themselves up in the war. They then collected their few belongings and departed, leaving us in a solitude most solemn and strange, no voices but our own to be heard. We at once proceeded to chop the wood, milk the goats, attend to cooking, and seek for water, which was daily becoming more scarce. A message from the king now informed us of his intention to meet the enemy in Anum, and enquired if we were prepared to face the danger. We prayed for guidance, and replied that we would remove to Ho, if he could spare us men to convey my wife; thus leaving our station and property to the Lord's care. We then besought our Heavenly Father to hinder our going if it were not His will, and rose from our knees peaceful at heart, and strong in His strength. The king's answer soon came, to the effect that Pekyi, with its surroundings (a former mission station four miles from Anum), had joined the Ashantees. We waited for a confirmation of this report, and employed the interval in making a hammock and two small boxes for our projected flight.

In the midst of these preparations, we were startled by soldiers running towards us crying loudly, "run, run, the Ashantees are in the town." The day passed on as we waited in anxious suspense for the sound of a shot, or the appearance of the enemy. As night approached, we ventured to the town in search of water; a death-like silence reigned in its deserted streets, which were strewn with broken fragments, while every house was so still that the bleating of a kid was a welcome sound, and cheered me as I retraced my steps homewards. We kept lights burning and shutters open, trying in vain to obtain a little sleep; the wind, always high on our hill, was especially boisterous that night, and most anxiously did we long for day.

It came at length, and weary and worn as we were with painful watching, we began to prepare our early meal. Milking the goats was, after several attempts, found to be an impossibility, our store of condensed milk we dared not use, for it was our sole dependence for our baby, so we hid the precious tins. Mid-day passed, still the same dreadful silence prevailed; for miles around there was no sign of life; we were alone on our hill top.

Restlessly wandering backwards and forwards we looked and listened; the cry even of a bird startling us. Thus the day wore on, our only employment throughout its long hours being to boil a piece of meat in as little water as possible, for the springs were a mile off, and our precious store was nearly exhausted. Once, indeed, during the afternoon the report of a gun reached us, and then we distinctly heard voices crying, "come, come!" We strained every nerve to catch the answers, but they were inaudible, the sounds died away in the distance, and we were once more alone, with the prospect of another terrible night of watching and suspense. Again we left the lamps burning, and soothed by the sound of a heavy rain, we actually fell asleep, thankful that our most pressing need was thus being supplied.

CHAPTER III.

IN THE POWER OF THE ASHANTEES.

It was a lovely morning; all nature smiled upon our pleasant little station, and the brilliant sunbeams struck rays of hope into our hearts, so that it almost seemed as if our fears of the previous night had been groundless. After breakfasting comfortably, we occupied ourselves with our usual duties.

But while engaged in the verandah, my wife observed the glitter of arms among the tall grass bordering the footpath which led to the town. A troop of warriors soon appeared, greeting us civilly in their own language, but at the same time pointing their guns. We advanced, calmly enquiring from whence they came. "We are friends from Coomassie," said they, and beckoned us to approach. They took our offered hands, and when we assured them we were missionaries, having nothing to do with the war, but quietly remaining when all others had fled, they withdrew their loaded guns, adding that "we were quite right," and begging us to accompany them to their leader, who was close at hand and wished to see us; meanwhile, they would guard our station, which might otherwise suffer from his pilfering crew.

Having really no choice, we, at their suggestion, arrayed ourselves in our best to do the chief honour, took a little refreshment, and followed our guides. I pocketed a few presents, and my wife took two tins of milk, the baby's bottle, and a warm woollen rug—why, she hardly knew, as we were told we should soon come back—but alas, from that fatal moment we beheld our much-loved home no more.

We formed a singular procession, headed by a half-clad soldier, armed with gun, bowie knife, and a long leathern whip under his arm ; next myself, carrying our babe, then my wife and Mr. K., three soldiers bringing up the rear. We were soon met by hundreds of painted negroes, who, despite the efforts of our leader to turn them back, rushed up the hill shouting the name of Adu Bofo. It was easy to see that their aim was the spoliation of our house and property; yet they did us no harm personally, and were even outwardly polite, acceding to our request to point their muskets away from us. In the company of this riotous crowd we at last approached the town. Its silence was broken now—the Ashantees had indeed taken possession. They fixed on us their glaring eyes as they vociferated in triumphant tones and noisy songs their own heroic deeds. We sought in vain for their captain, though they assured us he was near. Alas! on the very spot where I had so often stood proclaiming God's message of peace, all was havoc and confusion; débris of all kinds was scattered about the streets.

We were driven forward under a blazing sun, passing burning houses, whose scorching heat increased our sufferings terribly. For four hours the merciless march continued, and we were urged onward faster and faster, till, on our strong remonstrance of such continued effort being required of a woman, they promised us a sedan chair to carry us back to Anum in the evening. A few yams, and some milk for the little one was our food until we reached Pekyi, a town which was said to have surrendered to Ashantee unconditionally, yet one house alone remained entire among smouldering ruins. Our enquiries after the captain were answered by the command to march on, "but only a very little further." Some food was also offered, which we pocketed, for fatigue and excitement deprived us of all appetite. A company of naked prisoners were just then led past us, bending under the burden of their chains. How we pitied them; yet the close surveillance under which we were, and the exultant tones of the men contending together for the honour of having caught us, increased our fears that we were prisoners too. These fears were soon sadly confirmed, for on looking up we caught sight of a long line of soldiers, heavily laden with our own household goods; so that we at once perceived the deception which had been practised upon us, and realised our helpless condition. The assurance of our gracious God that He would never forsake us alone sustained us in that moment of agony!

At one o'clock we again set forward, with no heart to resist and no care whither we went. We passed village after village in ruins, till suddenly called to halt in the presence of a little fat man with piercing eyes, who was haranguing the bystanders. He gesticulated wildly, rose from his seat, stretched himself to his full height, and pretending to act the part of an executioner, declared that he was a man of great power. I addressed him, begging him to pity the alarm of our terrified child, and relating to him our sad story, to which he listened with a patronising smile, declaring he knew well we had nothing to do with the war, and that he would accompany us to Adu Bofo, which in truth he afterwards did; thus somewhat reassured we left the village.

Our road now lay along the beautiful Pekyi mountains, and had our baby been willing to leave my arms one of our guides would have carried him for us. It was past sunset when, half dead with fatigue and exhaustion, we were once more permitted to halt in a village full of Akwamu soldiers, who flocked around us, laughing and mockingly exclaiming, "Oh! the whites; good evening. sirs, where are your heads?" and from one shelter to another they followed, assailing us with abusive taunts. At length they were tired, and began to prepare for the night, by lighting large fires around which they lay, leaving us only space enough to sit in a crouching posture.

They had given us some wretched meat, which we could not touch, but tried to appease our hunger with a little parched corn and a few half-cooked beans, bestowed on us by a pitying woman. Half choked by dense smoke and heat, we dragged through the wearisome hours of darkness, and slept at length from sheer exhaustion, but were soon aroused by the attempted escape of another prisoner, who lost his head in the struggle that ensued, which episode caused much merriment among our guards.

No words can describe the languor and disgust with which we rose as the day dawned, and watched our selfish keepers eagerly cooking and devouring their morning meal, without a thought or care for our wants. At our earnest entreaty they at length vouchsafed us a very scanty breakfast, while an exultant crowd again gathered round the "humbled whites," and amused themselves by offering us a portion of our own stores of food, which, when we took, they immediately snatched away.

The moment had now arrived for our appearance before the king of Akwamu, whom we found seated in the middle of the village, among a crowd of councillors and officials. He presented a sorry appearance, hanging his head in shame and embarrassment, which was easily accounted for, as no doubt he partly realised himself for what we knew him to be—an arch-traitor.

The silence was broken at length by the question as to what we knew of Dompre, the enemy's general. We gave such information as we had, and then seized the opportunity of pleading our own cause, as missionaries who had placed confidence on the respect due to our acknowledged neutrality. He calmly begged us to make ourselves easy; assured us there was no ground of complaint against us, and that we should speedily be restored to our home—a promise as false as it was fair. On our return, our ears were saluted by the welcome sound of English words, which, though barely intelligible, were evidently meant to express comfort and sympathy. It was a young man who addressed us with, "never mind, never mind," and a few other enigmatic and disconnected phrases, constantly repeated. He was applauded as a prodigy by the surrounding crowd, who listened in wonder to his flowing words; we, however, gathered but one idea from the whole harangue, and this certainly was a cheering one. It seemed that Adu Bofo was expected to arrive almost directly, and we counted much upon his appearance on the scene, though these hopes were soon to be sadly disappointed. In the meanwhile our new friend, Thomas Kofi, could not render us any practical assistance, as his entreaties on our behalf were disregarded, and it was decided that we were to set out for the camp.

It was Sunday morning, and by ten o'clock we were again on our way, with no prospect before us but a renewal of the cruel driving haste, the burning sun, and the vain entreaties for water to relieve our parching thirst—it was just a repetition of the past day's miseries. In our extremity we lay on the ground, trying to drink from a wayside pool, so great was our need. Even this was forbidden. At noon we passed soldiers cooking their dinner, and we once more implored our cruel guards to take pity, and bestow on us a drink of water. They were unmoved, until suddenly remembering my pocketed cigars, I offered them, and the bribe prevailed, so that we were allowed to drink to our heart's content. Not only was this indulgence thus procured, but a gourd was filled, and carried by our leader to supply our future need. Holding painfully on for another hour, we fell in with our yesterday's hero reclining under a tree. Of him we resolutely demanded food, and that so persistently, that the astonished bystanders threw us some boiled maize, which we eagerly devoured, though the gift was accompanied with taunts and jeers. Our poor babe, too, was once more permitted to drink his milk in peace.

At this juncture, Mr. K. twice sunk on the ground from pure exhaustion, and this procured us a brief respite, during which we lay and rested, thinking how differently our brethren were employed on that calm Sabbath day. But the cruel command to rise became every moment more imperative, and we were forced to obey, though our hearts died within us as we perceived that our path lay over a high mountain, and our powers of climbing were almost gone. We slackened our pace in prospect of the terrible effort, and saw our own property continually carried before us by one or other of the endless line of followers that accompanied our march. Our guards soon became furious at the delay, roughly seizing my wife's umbrella, because " it hindered her in running," and otherwise maltreating her. I determinately resisted this barbarous handling, and prevailed.

On reaching the summit of the mountain, panting and breathless, we were commanded to halt, for the quick ears of our leaders caught the sounds of fighting some miles ahead, and distinguished troops in apparent pursuit. Great excitement at once prevailed—shouting, hurrying, and driving; with leathern whip of elephant hide in hand, the commander flew from place to place rallying his scattered forces. Our precious property was thrown into the bush, as the men with shouldered guns passed on to the fight, not one being allowed to lag behind.

From a field of maize we watched the hurrying, clamouring crowd, occasionally catching the sound of distant firing. Suddenly a crash was heard close by, a whiz of muskets, and a cry of war, causing us to bend before the whistling bullets. We soon, however, saw that this was simply a clever trick of our own company, an artful device to deceive the enemy who were in conflict in the far distance; and when it was over they again drove us from our resting-place. Our aching limbs would scarcely move, but remonstrance was useless; they were in haste to reach the camp, and in silence, almost in despair, we pursued our miserable way, feeling that death itself could bring us nothing worse. Sometimes we were staggering through tangled grass ten feet in height, then over a boggy plain lay our painful journey, our distress increasing by falling rain, and still more by compassion for the miserable creatures whose corpses or wounded bodies lay in our path.

Insulted and abused by the soldiers, who threatened to eat us when we reached Coomassie, our miseries intensified, until night closed upon us, and we ended another day of bitter suffering in a village where we were permitted to halt. It was a horrible resting-place, full of slain, so that we had to pick our way over the gory earth; and when my wife stumbled from weakness, her dress was covered with stains. The soldiers were hastening to inter the mangled corpses, and from every house around us sounded the doleful lament of the women. It was evident the Ashantees had been sorely discomfited, and we feared the consequences, but were sustained by remembering that the very hairs of our head were all numbered.

CHAPTER IV.

BEFORE ADU BOFO.

DRIVING long poles into the ground, over which they stretched some branches, some soldiers were busy setting up a rough encampment outside the village. The darkness was so dense that we could distinguish little of the busy scene beyond the fitful light of a blazing fire, around which gigantic forms moved among the shadows, their labours being accompanied by a tremendous noise, caused by the blowing of horns, which thrilled our shattered nerves most painfully. They had driven us into a large hut where one of the king's sons was sitting, and here tired nature claimed her due, and with my boy in my arms I sank upon the ground utterly exhausted, only longing to be left lying there in peace. But we were once more hurried on, till at length our goal seemed to be attained, and we suddenly found ourselves in the presence of the great commander, to meet whom we had been so deceitfully allured from our homes three days before. He was dressed entirely in white, and sat in state, while our savage escort, on bended knee, related the story of our seizure.

I tried in vain to speak. My attempt was met with contempt and cruel indifference, while our inhuman captor, rising, began to tear off my wife's dress, and bore it away in triumph. A few hurried words of command from Adu, and we were ruthlessly driven to a small hut, where a fierce fellow advanced to meet us, brandishing a long, bright knife, and seizing my arm, attempted to drag me away. I forgot my weakness in the thought of wife and child, and sturdily resisted his efforts, whereupon he turned on Mr. K., and instantly both were lost in the outer darkness. We will give the description of the cruel scene that was enacted in our brother's own words.

"First," said he, "I thought of my loved ones far away, begging the Lord to comfort them, and asking for myself that I might be kept faithful even unto death, for I thought the end had now come. It was, however, ordered otherwise, and I was dragged into the presence of an inferior chief, who sat in front of his dwelling, while two attendants supported his arms in a horizontal position. I was also permitted to sit down, and thus observed that the great man was suffering from several frightful wounds. In feverish excitement he turned upon me, vowing that I should lose my hands if I had had any part in the fighting. They now tore the ragged coverings off my swollen feet, which were forced into heavy irons secured by a ring; all remonstrance, of course, being useless, and my pockets were next rudely searched and emptied. Seeing Mr. and Mrs. R. approaching, I made an abortive effort to convey to their keeping their woollen shawl, as a covering for their babe, but it was snatched from my hands. Strange to say, a string of coral beads, found within my hat, was restored, being probably regarded as a rosary used in prayer according to the Moslem fashion. Two of my pockets were also overlooked in the general search. This ordeal completed, some bread soaked in water was bestowed upon me, but fatigue and anxiety had banished hunger, and when left alone, I fell on the wet ground in a sleep that might rather be called the stupor of exhaustion. I could hardly realize my position on awaking. The noisy horns still sounded wildly in the distance, while the light of a clear moon shone calmly over the blood-stained earth."

While Mr. K. was making these painful experiences, we took a hasty farewell of each other, having no hope of life, and inexpressible peace was granted us in the solemn prospect of entering eternity. We no longer felt distress at the prospect of leaving our helpless infant, but were able to rejoice at the thought of the glory that awaited us in our Father's House. Hearing myself called, we turned into a hut close by, and there found our poor brother loaded with fetters, but still alive; and as we were now also in irons, we concluded that our execution was postponed, and lay down to rest, after partaking of a scanty repast. We slept in spite of the wild music that sounded around us, and the slight protection afforded us from the pouring rain by our sheep skin and my coat.

The news of our capture had spread through the neighbourhood, and we were aroused before day-break, by an eager throng who came in hot haste to view the wonderful spectacle of three white persons and a child conquered and chained. They crowded round us in the greatest amazement, handling us most unceremoniously, as if we had been animals, exclaiming now and then, "These are not men, they are spirits; they have heads like horses, they will soon be killed!" One tall, thin, grey-haired man, ornamented with coral beads, iron rings, and fetish cords, stepped up to Mr. K., and stared ferociously at him for some minutes; but his gaze being met with unshrinking calmness, he at length slowly retired, making some remarks to various attendants, from which we gathered that there was no intention of bringing us to trial.

When we had painfully crawled back, on hands and knees, to our brother, who sat by the hut of the wounded chief, some food was supplied us, and a few poles being

THE CAPTIVES IN IRONS.

struck, skins were spread upon them to shield us from the heat and the crowd. After a short time a group of men approached, bearing aloft a large coloured umbrella, under which Adu Bofo advanced to visit the chief. I made an attempt to draw his attention, and again urged the sad story of our betrayal and wrong. But though he took my offered hand, and acknowledged the truth of my assertions, he assured us, with stony composure, that being his master's slave, his only course was to send us to the king, and thus we recognized the terrible fact, that Coomassie was to be our ultimate goal.

We entreated him at least to restore us to the Akwamu King, who might send us to our brethren in Krobo, promising that they would reward him liberally, whereupon he pondered, and pretended to comply, for which we thanked and blessed him most heartily. Our irons were removed, and we were provided with a roof of banian leaves. But before long a procession of soldiers was again formed, and the camp was ordered forward, while we, scarcely able to move, and stung by pangs of the keenest disappointment, were forced to keep up with the rest. Mr. K. most kindly supplied my poor wife with one of his shoes, which were fortunately small, she having lost hers in the muddy path, and thus we recommenced our dismal march under a fresh escort of guards.

CHAPTER V.

WITH THE ASHANTEE ARMY.

June 14-24, 1869.

HAPPILY we were not compelled to advance rapidly, being in the midst of a company of soldiers who were often commanded to halt; so on we went, now on high ground, then wading through long grass or primeval forests. Twenty steps on either side of our column, two other lines were marching in the singular style peculiar to the country, and many a headless corpse which lay in our path, showed that we were going through the scene of yesterday's conflict. The frizzy hair of one of the heads, made it apparent that it had belonged to an Ashantee, the hasty retreat of whose enemy had compelled him to forsake the bloody trophy. A few yards away from this disgusting spectacle sat a man preparing a goblet out of a human skull.

After two hours of such marching, we were permitted to halt for rest, surrounded by a vociferating crowd. Mr. K. here contrived to pass some of his underclothing to poor Mrs R., and this became her principal dress for seven months. He also spared part of his linen for the little one.

To an Akwamu chief, dreadfully disfigured by a wound, I offered my hand, which he refused; but gazing at us intently, he beckoned to a youth in uniform, and covered with amulets like a Fetish priest, who, to our surprise, addressed us in tolerable English, evidently learned of our brethren in Akra. This giddy fellow cut short our questions by turning his back on us with a rude laugh. "I am hungry," said he, "I must be off." At length we were released and taken to a small house, where some sympathising people brought us corn, pounded yams, and goat's flesh, the latter of which we could not eat on account of its high flavour, though later on hunger compelled us to accept many things infinitely more disgusting. At my wife's request, we were supplied with water, a great comfort for our baby; but in the evening our fetters were again fastened, and we were thankful for a block of wood as a pillow, when we lay on the bare floor. We knew that under such hardships our babe's nourishment must soon cease, and what should we do then? We could only say, "The Lord will provide."

The morning of June 15th dawned. We were released from our fetters and led to a little hut in the wood, roofed with palm branches, and about five feet square; this was our resting-place for four days. Here the king's son came to question us as to our possessions. We answered him truthfully, and assured him we had buried no cowries, which made him very angry, and when I did not at once understand his questions he shook both his fists in my face. This discipline being over, a woman was brought who was willing to nurse our baby, but her husband soon forbade it, and we learned how we had been deceived when told that we should have no difficulty in finding a nurse, for this was the only woman who had an infant with her. Alas! the sufferings of my wife and little one pressed more heavily upon me step by step; one of the king's sons, however, gave him a dress.

Our food consisted of boiled yams, water, soup, and occasionally a little roasted corn. Once we obtained a pound of meat, the half of which we smoked and dried to make it last the longer; our fingers had to do the duty of spoons and forks. During these four days our comfort was not increased by hearing, as we did on two occasions, the peculiar beat of a drum and the report of shots, which were answered by a terrible scream from the multitude. It was evident that fresh prisoners were being executed, and that even Anums were not spared.

On the evening of the 18th of June our attention was arrested by unusual sounds; we listened and heard the report of distant shouting, of drums, and of cries of alarm. The principal men around us hastily seized some ammunition and marched off. It was evident that Dompre had made one of his daring sallies, for a sound of continuous firing seemed approaching, and we were desired to come forward. As we did so, Adu Bofo, advancing, commanded us to enter the nearest shed. Here we beheld the booty they had taken; leather trunks, coverings, kitchen utensils, and children's clothing, heaped together in fearful confusion. To attempt to sit was useless, to lie down impossible, for new faces surrounded us and exultingly fastened on our chains afresh.

It was a pale, clear, moonlight night, enabling us to distinguish a crowd of soldiers gathering within the fence of the majestic bamboo house inhabited by Adu. Out of it he emerged, attired in a dirty yellow jacket, hung round with charms to protect him from danger; this was his warrior's dress! From his seat or throne he gave his commands, during which the distant firing made it evident the camp had been attacked. Rising, with his long pipe still in his mouth, and attended by his guards, he marched with a triumphant step to the scene of conflict, his guard following. Thus left comparatively alone we had leisure to observe our surroundings, and noticed among the other guards one who, with a consequential air, paced up and down before us, occasionally uttering a few words. He was a fierce looking fellow, armed with a large sharp knife, which we felt assured was to decapitate us should the combat turn out ill. As the night passed away the sound of firing became more distant; the troops were probably pursuing; so we ventured to rest our weary heads on the wreck of our property and actually slept, dreaming of happy days gone by.

The morning of the 19th broke, and made apparent the excitement around us. Preparations for war were imminent, and our fetters were removed. We were then led through ranks of armed men outside the camp, where the Akwamus, headed by their prince, stood ready to start; a council of war was held, and after some hesitation it was decided that we should return to the camp. Several prisoners passed us, and among them, to our surprise, we recognised the familiar faces of Palm and his wife from Accra, who, at the same moment, caught sight of us, and pointed to the chains on their feet. We could only sadly realise our helplessness, and rack our brains with wondering how they also had fallen into the hands of our enemies. It was evident they had not been taken in battle, as in that case Palm's life would not have been spared.

We were conducted by another official to a new hut, built for us near Adu Bofo's head quarters, and this time our fetters were fastened on long before evening, and we wore them through four weary days, on the third of which, however, I succeeded in freeing my poor wife from their burden. Thus another Sabbath of our sorrowful captivity went by; deprived as we were of the comfort of our bibles, we found it a hard and bitter struggle to resign our minds to this terrible dispensation.

Our supply of food grew scanty, but at ten o'clock they brought us boiled yams, and in the evening pepper soup with maize, and a bit of skin floating in it, was set before us. This repast left us so hungry that we crawled round in our chains to beg a little more, but without success. Often would we dream of our brethren at the other stations, and picture ourselves among them; but these visions of peace and plenty only roused the sharpest disappointment when we awoke, while our anxiety for our babe grew apace.

My wife held up bravely, and her faith was rewarded by the unexpected receipt of two of our own tins of milk from Adu Bofo; these would last us a fortnight, by the end of which time we fully trusted to be set at liberty. We also met with much kindness from a son of Adu's, named Apoku, who paid us frequent visits, and showed his sympathy by cheering words, which gave us much comfort, though his influence was insufficient to effect our release. "You shall go, only be patient," he would say to us again and again. And so we waited on through unspeakable privations and endurances, hoping and longing for the decision that should put an end to our trial.

At last this seemed to be coming, for on the afternoon of the 23d we watched the assembling of a crowd, whose liberal display of bright coloured umbrellas portended a grand discussion. Our chains being removed by the command of Kwating, we were led forward with beating hearts into the semi-circle, eagerly questioning within ourselves whether the expected message had really arrived from our brethren.

There sat the Akwamu king, his son on the left, and on the right Bofo, with officers and servants; while the foreground was covered with a collection of household stuff, the spoils from Anum. Friend Thomas, in his office of interpreter, asked us, with a proud display of very queer English, whether those were our possessions, and on our answering in the affirmative, proceeded to inquire if they were all we had. We replied that they were only a small proportion. "What is missing?" said Thomas.

We could not give a list, but explained that much of the station property was not our own, being merely entrusted to Mr. Kühne for sale by the directors of the mercantile establishment of our mission, and that though we missed many of our own things as well, we could only verify them by the books and inventory. "Where are they?" said Thomas, and again we had to assert our ignorance.

All this time he spoke so unintelligibly that I was obliged to arrive at his meaning by questioning him in Tschi; as, for instance, his pronunciation of "never mind," sounded much more like "noble man;" and the difficulty was not decreased by his high estimate of his linguistic powers, which led him to hammer out the few English words he knew, with fierce and stubborn decision. Meanwhile our two cash boxes came to light, and at their command, I drew out my keys and opened the first of them which rested on the knees of Adu Bofo, whose eyes glistened as he caught sight of a string of beads. These were instantly hidden in the folds of his dress, while the silver dollars charmed him exceedingly, and he displayed them to the Akwamu king with cordial expressions of delight. The latter simply nodded his approval, seemingly indifferent to the whole concern.

Adu Bofo now rose, and offered to return my keys, which I declined, seeing, as I told him, I had no further use for them. I was next called upon to unlock my private box, but being minus the key, this was impossible, so they had to be satisfied with a list of its contents and directions for finding the key. They then wrapped both boxes in a table-cloth, together with a case of dessert knives and forks, a dozen silver spoons—our wedding presents—and two cases for shot. We were then dismissed, our hope again dashed to the ground, and we returned to our chains. By way of compensation for our disappointment, a few men followed us, carrying a present from Adu Bofo, consisting of three chairs, a large woollen quilt, our baby's pillow, two shirts, two window curtains, three sheets, a velvet band, and my wedding gloves; the latter I sent back as useless to me in my present predicament. A pair of large cloth shoes, which we vainly attempted to exchange for smaller ones, completed the list of these gracious presents, and of course we tendered our prompt thanks to the donor.

Soon afterwards, the general sent us a jar of arrowroot and another of meat extract, with an order to take out the contents and return the pots. By this time we had become so confident that we should speedily regain our liberty that I actually committed the immense folly of returning the offered food. Alas! with what gratitude we should have hailed a similar gift later on. However, as it was, we all now lay down under our soft woollen counterpane, feeling quite hopeful and contented, and firm in the faith that we should soon be free.

It was a wretched night, however, for at twelve o'clock a clap of thunder aroused us, and the rain came pouring through the leafy roof—which was only intended as a protection from the sun—not only soaking us, but streaming through the hut in a flood, and obliging us to take refuge upon the chairs. I tried to shelter the baby by holding over his head a wooden dish, while K. dragged himself along, chains and all, into the more substantial hut of our neighbour. For two hours we sat crouching on those chairs, till the rain ceasing, we once more rolled the soaked counterpane around us and fell asleep. At dawn, we left our miserable resting place, and as we dried our garments by the camp fires, we observed signs of removal, and heard whispers of a march to Coomassie. Our alarm was great, for our chains and coverings were put up for despatch. Our questions were not noticed, so we demanded an interview with Adu Bofo. Our irons were removed, and we were led towards the council, but "he had not time to attend to us," and we were obliged to return. Our visit had, however, made him uneasy, and about ten o'clock he came to ask what we wanted. "Freedom," cried we, "freedom; especially for the sake of our suffering baby. Full well do we know our innocence in reference to this war; full well do we know that we cannot long survive in our present condition." We also spoke of ransom, which we knew our brethren would gladly give.

With an ironical laugh, peculiar to himself, he turned to his followers, sarcastically remarking, "He promises much money if we take him to Krobi;" then, fixing his eyes upon us, he continued, "You must first go over yonder, eat a little and rest, after which I will take you to the coast." He then dismissed the people, and left us to guess whether he intended to convey us to some hiding place, or to Coomassie. Thus, after ten days bitter experience of this wretched camp life, we had to resume our onward journey, whither we knew not, but strong in our Master's assurance, "Lo, I am with you always, even to the end of the world."

CHAPTER VI.

THE MARCH TO THE VOLTA.

ON Thursday morning, the 24th of June, we quitted the camp and resumed our old order of march, conducted by a guard of soldiers. After passing a pond on the road filled with headless corpses, we ascended a hill, whence we saw long lines of persons likewise under guard and moving in our direction. There were men, women, and children from Tongo—all prisoners like ourselves.

With very brief intervals of rest we walked on through the day; once we crossed a stream, whose cool, fresh water, for the time, quenched our burning thirst. Though shallow, the current was strong, and I felt most grateful to one of our guides for carrying my wife across, though he grumbled sorely whilst he did so. Night at length brought a short and welcome reprieve, and we sank to rest in a half deserted village, whence we were again driven at daybreak. Though the same dreary prospect was before us, we were somewhat relieved, as our road lay through plantations of corn and yams. Our path was clean and well kept, and led us to a thriving village, where we even enjoyed the shelter of a roof. We were now taken into the presence of the resident chief, before whom we passed in single file, offering the usual salute, and, this ordeal completed, we stood, while the chief with his elders and councillors paid us a similar attention. Carriers then displayed the spoils from Anum, which were duly examined and removed, by the command of the prince, to be stored in safety. It afterwards transpired that Adu Bofo intended to bestow a proof of confidence upon this individual by leaving the booty in his charge; but in 1871 the general, on his return to Coomassie, led off the same prince and his people as captives, and when we again met them they were in the most wretched and dejected condition.

On returning to the village we chanced to discover three of our boxes, which seemed to have escaped the general examination. Wondering what was to be their fate, I begged leave to search for a boot, as my poor wife, being now completely barefoot, was at the mercy of the sharp stones. A reluctant consent enabled me to commence a search among a confused mass of medicines, clothes, a thermometer, and a violin, all of which had been ruthlessly thrown together. I at length thankfully drew out one slipper of my own, and we were glad to tie it on before hurrying up a rocky hill the next morning.

Under other circumstances we should have felt richly rewarded on reaching the summit of this eminence, where a magnificent panorama burst upon our view. Before us, as far as the eye could reach, lay broad and verdant plains—a garden of beauty, bordered in the far distance by the winding silver thread of the Volta. For a moment we rejoiced in hailing the river as an old friend; then, with a flash, the conviction was forced back upon us, that if we crossed the Volta, it would only be on our sure and sad way to Coomassie. So we stood in silence, each of us reading in the other's eyes the reflection of our own sorrowful thoughts; and thus the vision passed, while we turned to encounter the stern reality of the descent.

And, oh! what a descent it was, leading us down among rocks that were almost perpendicular! My feet seemed to touch the head of the person in front, while we cautiously clung to our footing, and crept on with slow, painful movements; when, after three-quarters of an hour's sliding, straining and balancing, we again stood safely on even ground, though with wounded feet and trembling knees, we felt deeply sensible that a special Providence had watched over our way.

Our inexorable guards now urged us rapidly forward over the beautiful plain, but no words can paint the thirst of that fearful mid-day heat. While we could, we kept wet cloths wrapped round the head of our infant, but the supply of water failed us at last, and then all hope seemed gone. Once, in a slight hollow of the road, we came upon a little muddy pool, and this we lapped up greedily, like Gideon's warriors. It was past noon when we reached a small cluster of trees, where a short interval of repose was granted, while yams and a little water were placed before us, being the first food that had passed our lips that day. Our journey then took a north-westerly direction in the course of the river, which we could not yet see.

The shadows were lengthening before we staggered through the streets of a village, Asuaso (called Dschome on the map), and once more looked upon the broad waters of the fair Volta, gilded into splendour by the rays of a setting sun. Close beside its high bank lay our night quarters, where our fetters were fastened, and as Asuaso joined Ashantee, provisions were preremptorily demanded by our people, and we thus obtained the gift of a hen with some corn, in addition to the usual yams.

On Sunday, the 27th of June, arrangements were made for our transit across the river in two canoes, so slight in structure that any movement endangered our safety. Our gallant leader, fearing to risk his own life, sent *us* on first, while he calmly stood contemplating the perilous undertaking, and when all the rest were safely landed, he finally ventured to follow, after which we resumed our journey into the unknown regions before us.

Here we will make a slight pause, in order to introduce some details of the company in which we travelled. The first party was composed of old Ageana* and his staff. He was a bald, grey-bearded man of sixty; surly, discontented, and feared by all. He appeared always angry, except when under the influence of drink, when he boastfully related wonderful histories of himself and his ancestors; at other times he made no friends, and his behaviour to us was gruff and savage in the extreme. Himself a slave of Adu Bofo, he, in his turn, owned numerous slaves, and a great collection of wives. His son Kwabena —a faithful copy of his father—was a confirmed drunkard, though only eighteen years of age, and his rude arrogance and covetousness added a good deal to our discomfort. His relative, Opoku, the inseparable companion and chief councillor of Ageana, was an aged man, and an adept in cunning craftiness, deceit being stamped indelibly on his every feature. He was a person who well knew how to carry his point, and when flattery was unavailing, the expression of his rage became truly awful. A few slaves completed this first party.

The next group ("our soldiers") was formed by three warriors, each about thirty years of age. Adu Kwaku, a hairy little man of sanguine temperament; Bobie, a quiet, phlegmatic fellow; and Angfwiri the youngest, a man of ambiguous character, who said very little, but always contrived to keep in old Ageana's good graces, which made him an object of envy to the others. They all presented a very singular appearance, having twisted their long hair into small tufts, which they regarded as peculiarly handsome. They were rough and rude at first, but as time wore on they became our best friends, and

* The *g* in this name is pronounced hard.

treated us with as much consideration as was possible in our forlorn condition. Each soldier was attended by a lad, and this trio of boys brought up the rear of our procession. In the centre of this company we marched as slaves, daily enduring a fresh torrent of abuse; the old leader himself taking special delight in trying to extinguish our hopes, while he drew lively pictures of the state of things in Coomassie, and assured us that "our heads would be cut off there." Later on, however, it became evident that the king had no intention of injuring us, so that we could again breathe freely.

And now, as we look back upon the terrible ordeal, we can thank God for so ordering our way that we learnt to know the Ashantee people not as our inferiors in power and position—as is usually the case with missionaries in their relations to heathen tribes—but as masters and superiors, seeing that our lives and welfare depended on their mercy and pleasure. Thus I trust we gained a new and more complete stock of information and experience for our future work.

CHAPTER VII.

FROM THE VOLTA TO OKWANO.

It was on a sad Sunday morning that we lost sight of our beautiful river, and plunged, in a westerly direction, into the unknown regions beyond. A thick fog, which gradually turned into heavy rain, corresponded with our cheerless feelings, as we plodded over a path so narrow that the tall wet grass on either side soaked our poor ragged garments through and through, and filled us with dread as to the effects of this exposure on our little boy. Ageana hunted us forward with abuse, and seemed to look on the bad weather as a fault of ours. Every petition for rest met with the reply, "Duom, duom!" (forward) "No rest will be given before evening." However, in the afternoon a halt was made, when we suddenly came upon some empty huts, seemingly built for the accommodation of travellers; and we were able to lay our tired darling to rest on a bed of leaves while a fire was lighted, at which we dried our clothes. My petition for the use of a few of the articles in our own trunks was disregarded, though seconded by the pleading of our soldier guards, and after a scanty supper of boiled corn—our only meal that day—our irons were secured.

The next morning was brilliant, but our early walk through dripping foliage drenched us completely. After partaking of a small maize loaf we pursued our way through tangled woods, treading the marshy soil with grateful appreciation of the shade afforded by trees; but as our path was constantly crossed by wide ditches and long drooping branches, we grew more stiff than ever, by dint of stooping, climbing, and leaping, and emerged on the open plain less able to bear the burning rays of the sun. Still this was a red letter day, for two rare luxuries awaited us. Beside a spring one of our soldiers found a quantity of snails, which were hailed as a prize and made into broth; and never was food more welcome than this repast proved to us in our half-starved condition. Nor was this all. In a clear brook, two feet in depth, we were actually allowed to bathe—for the first time in our captivity. In grateful relief we forgot for the moment our chains, and soon sank into a deep, refreshing sleep.

The weary plain was crossed at length, and on the first of July we saw in the distance a glorious range of mountains, and stood on the banks of a fine river, some eighty feet in width. As this was to be crossed, I plunged in to try the depth, and finding it reached my waist, I asked that my wife might be helped in making the passage. As this was contemptuously refused, I was myself forced to carry her over, a feat which I am thankful to say was accomplished in safety, while Ageana, to our surprise, took charge of the little one. On landing, we found a row of camp huts, built in the beginning of the year by Adu Bofo, on his march to Akwamu, and here Kwateng met us with the caravan, and I extorted a reluctant consent to our abstracting a pair of socks out of one of our trunks, my wife being by this time nearly barefoot. Three soldiers superintended this search. I also ventured to ask Ageana for the loan of one of the chairs with which Adu Bofo had presented us, and which he had appropriated while the others were left behind, but his savage reply was, "leave it alone!"

Our ears were now saluted with the glad news that if we pushed on rapidly, we might hope on the morrow to

reach a town, and find abundance of food, the mere thought of which invigorated us, though knowing the difficulty of carrying supplies, we had refrained from murmuring at the scanty fare that we had hitherto shared with our captors. The Ashantees being a hardy race inured from youth to the severest simplicity, are able to march day after day at a quick, steady pace, with short intervals of rest, and a modicum of food. They lie down to sound sleep at night, after a light supper of corn, waking refreshed and strengthened to resume their way at sunrise.

Our route led us toward a range of blue mountains, which called up sweet and sad associations of our distant home. The rocky ground echoed to our footsteps, and on reaching the first elevation the high outline stretched far away to the right, ending abruptly in a square rock some two hundred feet in length, which curious conformation riveted our interest, and turned out to be the shrine of the great Fetish of Okwao.

We now crossed the high plateau, and prepared for a fresh ascent, toiling onward wearily, as no food had yet passed our lips that day. In two hours a brook was reached, beside which we found seated several members of our own party enjoying a meal of bread. Famished with hunger we expected a respite and some refreshment, but to my intense and bitter indignation this was contemptuously refused. Even now my strongest feelings are roused when memory recalls the blustering urgency of Ageana, as he roared his command, "Duom, duom" (up! forward), not even permitting us to taste the water at our feet, or to fill our calabash. Though we obeyed, I can fairly say that my blood boiled with anger, and for some hours we endured agonies of suffering.

At about three o'clock in the afternoon a pause was made for a few minutes, and a small roll was thrown us, after eating which we entered the deep shades of a primeval forest. Still suffering from the keenest pangs of hunger, which had been only augmented by the cruel fragment supplied, our strength was unequal to the strain, and we repeatedly staggered and fell, our feet refusing to move at our bidding, spite of the repeated injunctions of our guides to rouse and exert ourselves as our goal was near.

At this critical juncture a messenger of God's providence appeared in the shape of one of the soldiers who came to meet us at a bend of the road, carrying some maize cakes, every crumb of which we devoured with avidity, and being thus strengthened, half an hour more brought us to the plantation on the outskirts of the town. Here we again fell in with the captives from Tongo, and to our delight saw large quantities of maize being carried off the fields. Kwateng soon brought us a small supply of palm wine, which revived our fainting powers, and with thankful hearts we entered the clean, well kept street of Tafo, the capital of Okwao, which boasted five or six hundred inhabitants.

Our reception was superior to anything we had hoped for; indeed the people vied with each other in kindness, and no rude jesting escaped their lips as they gazed at us in wonder and pity.* We were shown into a small room in the centre of the town, which seemed to have been specially prepared for us, and the kind owner, unwilling to subject us to the annoyance of inquisitive bystanders, soon removed us into one which was more spacious. We were now prepared to show ourselves to the people of influence in the town, who consisted chiefly

---

* The average of our daily march was about thirty English miles, sometimes more, at other times less. I can regard it as nothing less than a miracle, when I think of my delicate wife's endurance of this continued physical effort during so many weeks.

of women, the wives of officials gone to the war, all painted white, and richly decorated with gigris and fetish charms, worn for the sake of their husbands, for whom they also made a daily procession through the town, invoking the protection of their gods. After exchanging the customary civilities with this group, in the midst of which sat an honoured priest, we were led to the chief, a small man whom we found enthroned on his doorstep, with his goodnatured wife beside him. He testified his gratification by warmly pressing our hands.

Scarcely had we regained our rooms, when gifts of food came pouring in from the hospitable people on all sides; boiled maize, cassada, and an enormous dish presented by the men of the town. Gladly and thankfully we proceeded, for the first time in twenty days, to satisfy our hunger, and fully enjoyed the good mutton broth and well seasoned fufu. The priest an old man, sent palm wine with yams and bananas, while to complete the feast, a present of pine apples arrived from the wife of the chief. These were however returned by Kwabena, the surly son of our leader, and upon the kind woman urging the acceptance of her gift, he himself made off with the welcome supplies, and also appropriated portions of the other food, informing us, with his usual politeness, that he would take care of our provisions.

On this memorable evening, the first glimmer of light broke in upon us, for we had at length met with some sympathy and humanity, and not least from the priest himself—indeed we afterwards learnt that such conduct was characteristic of this class. And now hope whispered that perhaps the worst of our journey lay behind us, and that some civilized towns might be in our forward path. But for our helpless babe of nine months we still trembled. Could he endure much longer the want of proper food (for the milk was almost gone), and the hardships of such travel as ours. Alas! in the evening, the momentary gleam of sunshine, which had brightened our toilsome way, was clouded, for our fetters were once more fastened, though the observers looked on us with pity, evidently believing we were innocent sufferers.

Very early in the morning we found ourselves again on the march, and had already left the town behind us, when we were overtaken by a messenger from the kind chief who had so befriended us, and despite the anger of our conductor, he felt compelled to let us return to the outskirts, where the chief stood waiting our approach. To his enquiry as to how we could leave him without a parting word, we replied, that being prisoners we had no will of our own. He then refreshed us with a draught of palm wine, and with thanks and blessing we bade him farewell.

Our journey this day was through woods, which sheltered us from the heat, and lessened the distressing thirst. We were gradually ascending until noon, when we arrived at a town whose name, Abetifi, signified the "Tops of Palms," and thus, whichever way we turned our eyes, nothing but palm trees met our view. While arrangements were pending for our introduction to the chief, we stood outside the town, and Ageana with two soldiers entered. He was not flattered by his reception, and returned crestfallen, while to us the kindness of the people was great, and for some reason not apparent, we remained among them three days.

This rest was the more welcome as our babe was suffering from fever, and Mr. K. had a deep wound in his heel produced by the heavy irons, and causing him intense pain in walking. The good people, high and low, alike vied with each other in ministering to us, and most deeply did we feel their cheering attentions. The priests visited us repeatedly, always exclaiming, "These must be men of God."

Just at this time a comforter was sent us, in the shape of a young man who modestly presented us with four bananas on a wooden dish, and begged us not to be too sorrowful, "for," said he, "if it be God's will, and with the gracious approval of the king, you will soon be back in your homes." These words soothed us, coming as they did from a native of Ashantee, who had, it seems, spent several years working for our missionary brother, Mr. Mohr, at Akuapem. We felt almost as if we had met with an old friend in talking with him; his name was Yau, and his whole manner and bearing bore the trace of his association with christian customs and people.

But the journey had to be resumed, and our next resting-place was Abene, the residence of the Akwari king, who was absent, but both priests and people showed us extreme kindness, filling our little room with stores of provisions, which taught by previous experience, we carefully guarded. In the evening we once more enjoyed the luxury of a bath, in a small river which ran through the town. Thus again were our griefs alleviated, and though we dared not ask a question as to the distance we still had to traverse, we ventured to hope such happy experiences would continue till we reached Coomassie. Alas! while indulging in these blissful dreams, we heard to our dismay that our next nights would be spent in the bush, and our hearts again sank at the thought of this new trial for our tender child; yet even then, the assurance of our Heavenly Father's loving care was our support and stay.

CHAPTER VIII.

JOURNEY TO AGUAGO, AND THE HALT THERE.

7-28 July, 1869.

OUR next journey lay through well-watered palm forests, where our sufferings from hunger made the few pine apples we had brought with us a most valuable help. About five in the evening we found our burden-bearers resting in an old camping ground, which sight aroused the rage of Ageana, so that the poor tired creatures sprang to their feet, and started afresh with their loads. One woman venturing to complain of its weight, was irritated to the last pitch of endurance by the storm of abuse poured forth on her. She returned a volley of angry words, seized her load, and made off to the woods, where she was followed in pursuit by our entire company. Thus left alone with Ageana, we were accused as the authors of this mischief, for said he, "it was your things they were carrying," an assertion which was utterly false, for with the exception of the chair he had appropriated, and would never even lend us, they had nothing of ours at all.

Unripe bananas boiled in their skins were now set before us. After trying in vain to eat them we sank down on the damp ground—a few leaves our only protection, a stone our pillow—and thus, with our irons clasped round us, we once more fell asleep till the morning, when we pursued our journey still fasting, so that for twenty-four hours not a morsel passed our lips. Our people had cooked themselves a savoury soup before our eyes, from a squirrel which they had shot, and had also eaten corn and ground nuts to the full; but it was evening before we obtained our pittance. At this place we observed some huts roofed with branches of banana, and thus knew that a plantation was at hand. Might we light a fire in the night, I asked of our hard-hearted leader? It was permitted, but still we were sorely tried; our last drop of milk was gone, and though our darling babe had cut some teeth, and hunger made him devour some of our coarse food, we knew he could not long be supported thus. Towards noon the next day, however, a man passed us carrying two large pisangs (a native fruit) and Ageana begged them for the child. They were reluctantly yielded, and one was baked and eaten by the little fellow with great enjoyment, whilst we treasured the other for the morrow. After some further marching, the crowing of a cock greeted our ears, and we soon entered the town of Aguago, whose young chief came out some little way to bid us welcome. Being considered too early an hour to offer us palm wine, gin was brought instead, which however we refused, to the delight of Ageana, who eagerly appropriated it. Corn, bananas, and a dish of fufu, were set before us, to all of which we did full justice.

The houses in this place mostly consisted of only one room open in front, the entrance being formed by a few steps, polished daily with an oily red earth. We were taken into a small yard surrounded by four of these apartments, each of them about five feet by six, so that we barely found space to lie down in the one allotted to us. Ageana took possession of the second, and the slaves of another, while the fourth served as a kitchen.

All the luggage was now unpacked, and it soon became evident that we were to stay here, as the event proved, much longer than we wished. A few days passed and then we observed that the wily Opoku, Ageana's chief adviser, was preparing for a journey, in which he was accompanied by two of our soldiers.

It now transpired that they were bound for Coomassie, and would be back in a fortnight. Conjectures were useless, but our imagination was busy. Sometimes we apprehended that we were to be detained here until the return of the army, or that this might be the preparation for the final stroke. Then the thought of our helpless infant lying beside us so pale and quiet was too agonizing to contemplate, and we could only look to the strong One for strength. In order to supply the lack of milk, we tried to persuade our sullen leader to procure some eggs. Of course, he would not buy them, but at length we prevailed on him to go to the chief, who gave us his own store, with the permission to beg more in the town. Most touching it was to see how eagerly our poor little one swallowed this nourishment, and very heartily did we thank the Lord.

Our life was now very monotonous: as soon as we dared to stir in the morning, we roasted a ripe red fruit for the babe's breakfast, and then strolled about or sat under a tree. Our appearance at first excited much curiosity, and the people flocked around us, but we had no heart to notice them. At eleven o'clock they brought us fufu in a broken dish that resembled a dog trough, and we completed our meal with bananas, which we were allowed to pick freely in the plantation. To make up for this indulgence our regular supplies were curtailed, and a bit of meat as large as a nut was given for three. Ageana had bought the leg of a boar for two shillings, and every day for three weeks, cut off the supply he thought fit for the soup, and after directing his attendants to take it to "the slaves," troubled himself no further.

We crouched in our wretched room during the hottest hours of the day, and most thankful indeed should we

JOURNEY TO AGUAGO.   41

have been for a gospel or book of psalms. Later on, always attended by a keeper, we sallied forth to the brook to try and do a little washing, but as we did not possess a single article of toilet use, our attempts were very circumscribed, and we were shockingly tormented with things we cannot name. However, in the eyes of our persecutors, we were supposed to be treated very fairly. We had now worn our clothing incessantly for six weeks, and our only method of bodily refreshment consisted in dipping our linen in water as frequently as possible.

Ageana's nightly revels interfered with our evening meal, which was rarely provided, though we were required to present ourselves regularly for the fastening on of our fetters, after which, crawling as best we could to our narrow quarters, we usually strange to say, slept soundly. Our breakfast hour was one of severe trial, on account of our babe, who was often prostrate with fever, requiring comforts impossible to obtain. We had not even the use of the common fire, which was claimed and engrossed by the entire company; when I besought mercy in the shape of a little gold dust, to procure some eggs, I was derisively told by Ageana he had none to throw away. With tears in my eyes, the babe in my arms, and his mother by my side, I went from house to house pleading for help; many were touched, and some bestowed on us the delicacy we so much desired.

One afternoon being thus employed, we encountered two messengers of the king, one of whom on hearing of the cruelty and injustice we suffered, offered payment for four eggs, causing our very hearts to bless him. It was about this time that we chanced also to meet a petty chief, who had visited his brother at Akem, and become acquainted with our missionary there. Hearing that we too were missionaries he believed us to be good people, and many a time a gift of fruit or eggs reached us from him; truly did we pray that this cup of cold water might not lose its reward. We were now less strictly watched, and allowed to walk up and down the yard unattended by a slave. Still it happened one morning that—breakfast being late and hunger pressing—my wife took two bananas which no one in a plantation village would have noticed; but Ageana saw it, and springing from his chair abused her till she wept. Her tears increased his indignation, and with violent curses he repeated the threat of cutting off her head. When I said, We shall have a word about this in Coomassie, his son screamed with rage, and extended the threat to us all. Again, when we begged our soup without pepper, which caused Mr. K. much suffering, it was ordered to be made so hot that, spite of our hunger, we could not touch it. The rage of the old man was then extreme, and the water in which some fruit had been boiled was given us in its place.

While we stayed here the natives often called me "Seese." This we discovered to be a variation on the name of our missionary brother, Süss, which, strange to say, seemed familiar to all the Ashantee people. They had probably made his acquaintance at Gyadam, and he appeared universally beloved and respected, so that I was honoured in being taken for his brother. Mr Kühne's name they could not pronounce, so he was usually called "The long one," or "the white one," to distinguish him from me.

One night we woke under the dreadful sensation caused by the bite of hundreds of ants, with which we were covered. Helpless in the darkness, and with our feet chained, we could only crawl away and find refuge among the cooking utensils, where we remained until the morning. But a still worse trouble was the loss of our rug, which had remained behind; thus we had no protection from the cold ground, and palm wine being here very cheap, Ageana indulged in his favourite vice, and after boasting of his greatness as he sat on our chair, he would cross over to us, and say, with tipsy sympathy, "if you are hungry just come to me, and say, Father, we are hungry, and you shall have all you wish." In his sober moments, all sympathy vanished.

Spite of all our loving care, our dear child daily faded away; his once rosy cheeks were pale and hollow, so that our hearts ached when he fixed his brilliant eyes on his mother's face as we took our food, and seemed almost to say, "Have you nothing but this empty bottle for me?" He never fretted, but sat as if he knew the whole case, and was resigned.

On the evening of July 25th, Opaku returned from Coomassie, finding Ageana as usual intoxicated; yet he was soon seen running about and crying, "The king thanks me," from which we inferred he had had a message of approval. From our soldiers we learned that we were to be cared for and conducted to a town, and that two small packets of gold dust, part of which was intended for us, had been divided by Ageana among his own party. We were left in uncertainty as to the king's commands concerning the future, and could only commit ourselves to the heart of our loving Saviour, and rest upon His assuring words, "It is I, be not afraid."

CHAPTER IX.

THE LITTLE ONE GOES HOME IN TOTORASE.

EARLY on the 28th of July we continued our journey in a south-westerly direction. We passed through a fine timber forest, and after three hours march, reached the village of Amantra, whose chief received us kindly, and was touched by our request for eggs for our sinking child.

As we rested in the open square, we were visited by the whole population, and upon our gratefully accepting a red pisang, the people ran to their homes to fetch us corn, bananas, bread, and even a small piece of bacon,* which, though no larger than a walnut, we carefully divided. Our old savage would not let us stay here, seeming to grudge us the friendly offerings of the people, so we were driven on till we reached a group of huts, where plenty of palm wine could be procured, which was always an attraction to Ageana.

I begged to be permitted to go back for a promised supply of eggs, urging the responsibility that rested upon him, of sacrificing our babe's life for want of suitable food. This rendered him furious; he rushed about like a wild beast, and at last seized a chain and secured me with it, while my poor wife sat by weeping. Brother K.

---

* I may here remark that pork cannot be recommended as safe eating in Ashantee, seeing that pigs are permitted to wander about and search for their own food, which (in Coomassie), very frequently consists of slaughtered human flesh !

finally took him in hand, and the chain was removed. We then heard from a slave that two eggs had been offered to a Fetish at the spring, and if we were not afraid of the idol, we might fetch them. Under the escort of a lad, I at once went and succeeded in finding them; it is true they had been laid on the top of some oil and yam, yet my wife rejoiced at the treasure.

We were now told that our next march would be a long one, and as we started on it very hungry and with scanty supplies, the prospect was dreary enough, but the forest still protected us from heat, while a mountain stream crossing the path, slaked our thirst. It was afternoon before we were allowed to halt for refreshment, and after fighting our way for some distance through tall stiff grass, our guides discovered that they had missed the track; as it was now impossible to reach Sukoree, we rested for the night at a small plantation village, where after the longest day's march we had yet made, an unexpected joy awaited us. We had eaten our usual spare supper, and had requested some stock yams for the child, which were refused, so we took leave to help ourselves from the abundance growing around. A violent storm drove us to a hut for refuge, and as night had fallen, we lay down to sleep unfettered. After a while, Ageana came up shouting, "white men, are you asleep?" "Yes," we replied (for "da" in Ashantee signifies both "sleeping" and "lying down"). Upon this he left us, and for the first time for seven weeks we had the delight of resting our weary limbs unchained.

As we approached Ashantee proper, we were struck by the increasing fertility and richness of the well-watered country. In the vicinity of every important place the roads were good, and sometimes for miles together, suitable for traffic. Near the entrance of each village, we noticed jars, sticks, corn, and eggs heaped up as an offering to the Fetish; and the houses, whether scattered or in groups, were mostly surrounded by palm and banana gardens in picturesque variety; sometimes they formed a street, intersected by lanes and by-ways.

Retracing our steps on the following morning, we soon found the right path, and reached a large village, where some women pitying our suffering babe, supplied us with eggs. At the next place, which was surrounded by banana woods, the head man came forward to greet us, and as usual, gave us our quarters in four rooms surrounding a square court; Ageana of course chose the best. The name of this village was Totorase, and we stayed there ten days—days of deep grief they proved!

The next morning, July 31st, two slaves were despatched to Coomassie to announce our near approach (and as we subsequently heard), to tell the king of the critical state of our child. As long as he had played or seemed amused, they believed that we were hypocritically trying to obtain dainties for ourselves, but now when it was too late, they became impressed with the true state of the case, and all except Ageana endeavoured to supply him with better nourishment, and were even willing to petition the king for a milch cow.

The young queen of Sokoree, who now visited us, richly adorned with gold and fetish cords, showed us a good deal of sympathy. She offered her hand to each, and afterwards kindly sent us some eggs, while the people supplied us with fruit; but these comforts came too late to save our darling. His little wasted frame, sharp features, and sunken eyes, will long remain as painful pictures in our memory, and often it seemed as if he were asking, "how long."

Each morning after taking his egg, we carried him to the brook, and many a silent tear fell into the stream as we bathed him. Then we would saunter up and down the beautiful banana gardens, singing simple hymns, such as " I want to be an angel," " My Father waits for me in Heaven," &c. How we shrank from the thought of parting with our little treasure, increasingly dear as he faded away, and earnestly did we plead that he might yet be spared to us ; still we found comfort in the words which lifted our hearts to the better land. Happily no severe pain tried the fragile, worn-out body; weakness and intense thirst were his chief sufferings, making him perpetually crave for drink, especially at night. One day, the sun shining very strongly upon our garden walk, we turned aside under the bananas, and the guard missing us from the usual place, reported it to Ageana, who at once ordered his son to fasten on our irons. Fortunately Bobie the other soldier appeared, and when we explained that we had only sought shelter for the child's sake, he succeeded in getting our chains removed, but we were peremptorily forbidden ever to take such a liberty again.

Meanwhile, the little fellow's weakness increased, and the end was evidently at hand. At times he lay quite still, but painful restlessness succeeded. Kind people came constantly to inquire for him and offer sympathy, while the queen brought eggs and tried to comfort us with the assurance that if we saw the king, the child would recover. When I begged some palm oil for a night light, telling them he was dying, they still tried to console us saying, " No, no, he must not die ; the king will not allow it." Oh ! how hard it was to suppress the bitter feelings which would rise against those who had murdered this innocent babe by their cruelty ! To our surprise he lived till morning, when his eyes brightened ; he ate an egg with appetite, and even began playing with the buttons on his mother's jacket, which he had long ceased to notice. This was only the last flickering of the flame, he gave one more look of silent intensity, as if he wished to say, "good bye," and all was over. Precious child, into whose brief span of life so much of suffering was crowded! Thou callest to us, "do not forget Ashantee;" and thy grave is a token that the healing Cross shall one day reach that far off land.

When the people heard us praying they came to the door of the room, and looked earnestly and sadly at the corpse. After vainly seeking for some boards to make a coffin, I begged our visitors to plait two baskets of palm branches, one to serve as a shell, the other as a cover, and here the precious tiny form was laid, covered with his ragged clothing. Brother K. picked some flowers to put in his hands, and according to the custom of the country, a few mats and two yards of calico were sent by the princess, a mark of sympathy which gratified and soothed us in our grief. At four o'clock we laid him in a peaceful grave, under beautiful banana trees, the usual burying-place for children, only two hundred paces from our house.

I had told the chief that I should be glad to see the villagers at the grave, hoping to have the opportunity of saying a few words to them; but none of them appeared, whether from fear or other reasons I cannot tell. Even our own people who followed me at first as I carried the burden, soon halted and looked on from a distance. Only two slaves stood beside us. When I had gently deposited the little basket in its last resting place, I prayed in German for grace and strength in this hour of darkness, after which the slaves who had dug it, filled up the grave. Oh, that when the trumpet sounds to call thee from thy quiet rest, many who are now in heathen darkness may rise with thee to the resurrection of life!

According to another custom of the country, the chief now sent us a large pitcher of palm wine, and the people used their utmost persuasions to make us drink, but we refused, and sat down behind the house, pleading for help to be enabled to say, "He hath done all things well." After an hour of quiet grief (during which Ageana had been drinking with his friends, probably celebrating a kind of "wake"), we were summoned to meet the soldier who had gone to Coomassie for the cow, and had returned accompanied by an ambassador, wearing a large round gold plate on his breast. They were followed by two soldier boys bearing six ells of coloured cloth, a third with a sugar loaf in a brass plate on his head, and a fourth with a stately ram. The king sent us greeting, and was grieved to hear of the illness of our child; a milch cow could not be found, but the cloth he said would form a bed, and the ram and sugar would be useful; he had also sent some gold dust, in value about nine dollars, of which Ageana took possession. He hoped we should be easy and have patience, for in a short time we were to appear before him, and be permitted to return to our own home.

We replied briefly that "the things had come too late." The ambassador then endeavoured to comfort us by assuring us of the friendship of the king, and his wish that we should be sorrowful no longer. His kind words found their way to our hearts, and the prospect of returning to our work and to our brethren, prevented our sleeping much that night.

On Sunday, August 8th, we arose in a changed position; no longer slaves, but directing as masters the disposal of our presents. The sheep we told the people to kill, and distribute among the whole party according to rank. "That's right," they answered, and then went off to the slaughter, spoiling our Sunday's quiet by urging us to be present at the cutting up. As may be supposed, little remained for our own share, but we had the thanks of many, and were now for awhile important persons. Ageana in his new character of servant had become very obliging, offering us the gold dust, which we however desired him to keep, to purchase for us what we needed, regretting our folly when it was too late. The sugar was also left in his care, and the cloth alone remained to us.

In the evening we visited our little grave, scattering a few fruit stones on the mound, hoping by and by to plant some small shrubs to mark the resting place of our first born, and we meant often to repeat our visit, though in this we were disappointed.

The Ashantee observances on occasions of death and burial are precise and prolonged. We will briefly sketch them.

When a rich man dies, his wives break out into cries of lamentation, and then proceed to wash the corpse, adorn it with pearls and gold, carefully paint it, put on its best apparel, and then leave it as if asleep. Delicacies of all kinds are presented by friends, and the dish the man most enjoyed when living is prepared from slaughtered sheep and fowls. His property is then placed round him, and his pipe in his mouth. The wailing is occasionally interrupted to permit his wives to press food upon him, or to enquire his wishes,—the men meanwhile eat and drink outside. The length of the wake depends upon the rank of the deceased, and friends supply the needful expense. On the second or third day the corpse, in a basket coffin, is taken out through a hole broken in the wall for the purpose, for it may not pass through any door; and followed by its jewels and other property, it is placed in the middle of the village, amid firing and doleful songs. In the case of prominent persons, human sacrifices are offered, to accompany the departed on his long journey to the spirit world, while food and palm wine are placed on the grave for a set time (but eventually only once a year), and thus the wake ends. With men of high rank, the ceremony is sometimes repeated a second and a third time.

CHAPTER X.

TO DWABEN AND ABANKORO.

THE king's messenger was preparing to return to Coomassie, so we charged him with thanks for the royal gifts, and with a request for a comb and scissors to cut off our hair, for reasons too unpleasant to mention, incident on long neglect, and which prevented sleep.

Our stay at Totorase was now suddenly broken up, and we were informed, to our great delight, that we were to start for the capital. We paid a farewell visit to the little grave, feeling that since our darling was gone, we need no longer dread the hardships of the way. We were also under the protection of the king's friendly messenger, who treated us with respect, while our guides ceased their arrogant and abusive demonstrations, and Ageana himself did not dare oppress us, though he grumbled more than ever. The road was good, and in an hour we reached Sokoree, a custom-house station of Ashantee proper, where it is necessary, for all travellers from the interior, to obtain official permission before proceeding further. The princess of the place, who sent us a present of palm wine, had gone to the next village, Afiguase, where we found her after three quarters of an hour's walk. The usual ceremonious salutations being over, we were permitted to experience a great deal of kindness at her hands; and our friend, M. Bonnat, who visited her a few weeks later, was cared for by this kind woman as if he had been a relation of her own.

We met with many plantation villages in this fruitful plain, where corn, rice, pisang, maize, yams, and ground nuts abounded. About four o'clock we approached a large town named Dwaben, and prepared ourselves for a noisy reception. We soon reached a noble avenue of trees, such as I had never before seen in Africa, and under their glorious shade we entered a fine wide street, with whitewashed, and two-storied houses. Of course we were speedily surrounded by the entire population, the youthful portion of which especially, hailed us with riotous excitement, spite of all the remonstrances of the royal messenger.

We had already met with some specimens of the savage female army, who in time of war dance twice a day through the towns of Ashantee, with howls and shrieks uttered for the benefit of their absent warriors. Our appearance in Dwaben was the signal for a grand flourish on their part; no sooner did we appear in sight than these white painted figures rushed forward to meet us, leaping and gesticulating like maniacs, and brandishing their knives amid unearthly yells. One of them waved her sword full in the face of my wife, and then swept onward, screaming fearfully.

In contrast to this frightful exhibition, we were cordially received by the older men of the town, who came to shake hands with us, and offered palm wine to the detriment of Ageana's sobriety, who soon declared, with drunken solemnity, that we must stay here all night, as he could not bear to forego the honour of exhibiting his prisoners. However, the benevolent messenger interfered in our favour, being unwilling to expose us any longer to the diabolical tumult that surrounded us, and our leader was at length compelled to yield after a hot altercation, which ended in our being presented to the king of Dwaben.

This potentate ranks next to the king of Ashantee, of

whom he is a relative, Dwaben being the second town in the empire; and though not so rich as his rival, the subjects of this prince are more numerous. The story goes, that long ago a king of Ashantee had two sons, to the younger of whom (the child of a slave), he left his gold and the throne of Ashantee, while the elder inherited his sword and the throne of Dwaben. At a later period, the throne of Ashantee was once saved by a king of Dwaben, who intended, and almost succeeded in obtaining it for himself, but finally fell a victim to the fortunes of civil war, and was compelled for a long while to take refuge at Akem. Rivalry and ill-feeling has not yet entirely died out between the tribes.

Dwaben appeared to us better built and more imposing than Coomassie, and it is also more cleanly kept. The buildings are quite picturesque, with their leafy coverings, and many a pointed roof appears among the rows of houses. The Dampans (small halls which open on the streets), are raised four or five feet above the level of the ground, and ornamented with pictures and rough frescoes, done in white earth, on a background of reddish brown clay.

A messenger of the prince, distinguished by a gold sword, from which hung a large golden shell, now conducted us to the palace, a richly ornamented building, the broad gateway of which was surmounted by some gold sandals. We entered a large court surrounded by arched galleries, whence many curious eyes peered down upon us. Several hundred courtiers were arranged in a semi-circle, and in the centre of the display sat the king, under a large tent umbrella, profusely ornamented with gold and triangular amulets.

His majesty was a large stout man, with a number of golden rings on his arms and legs, otherwise his appearance was simple, and he made on us an impression of greater dignity than the minor chiefs of the Coast had done. We passed before the first group of court heralds, who wore caps of monkey skin; and then before the sword-bearers and various inferior chiefs, after which, raising our hats to his majesty, we retired and tasted some palm wine, while Ageana and our people indulged in deep potations of this beverage. After thanking the king and answering a few simple questions, we were allowed to depart, and the royal messenger succeeded in sheltering us in a quiet plantation village for the night, whence on the following day we proceeded to Abankoro.

Here we found a troop of women who were dancing and singing wild songs, which increased in vehemence on our approach. They naturally took us for prisoners of war, and swung their fans in our faces with the maddest gestures; but the wife of the chief, who represented her husband in his absence, welcomed us so cordially that we forgot this unpleasing reception, little dreaming however, that Abankoro was to be our abode for six long months, for we were now only a moderate day's journey from the capital where we had hoped soon to be liberated.

Abankoro is a well-built place, having a large street which resembles a square, laid out with shady trees; a contrast to the poorer quarters, where the huts are pitched about anyhow. Elevated on four poles at the end of the village we met with a Fetish house, inside of which a globe shaped mound of white earth marks the burial place of a python snake, to which offerings of palm wine are presented, being poured into a hollow at the top of the grave. A carved human figure with a cloth cap and sword in hand keeps watch in front, and a picturesque group of palm trees forms a charming background to the scene. While staying here I once met with a large snake, upon whose life I was about to make an attempt when a timely warning informed me that the creature was considered sacred, as a descendant of the enshrined python.

The quarters allotted to us were close by, and our opposite neighbour was an Odonko negress, distinguished like the rest of her race by several semicircular scars, reaching from the temples to the corners of the mouth. This woman had two children whom, to our frequent consternation, she used to summon home with piercing shrieks from the dangerous street. In another court lived a quiet wine dealer, who was almost the only male in the place, for with the exception of a few cripples and invalids, we had met hitherto with scarcely any men. The wife of the absent chief was the principal authority, and a stout cunning little woman who turned out to be the Fetish priestess, acted as her adviser. Our soldiers lodged at the end of the village, so as to be as far as possible out of Ageana's way, seeing they disliked him most heartily.

Before leaving us located here, the royal messenger granted us permission to walk about and also to visit the stream daily, which we felt an unspeakable privilege, our sufferings for want of water to wash in having been indescribable. We were all tormented by a painful eruption of blisters, which gradually made its appearance all over us, attributable doubtless to the unusual diet, which our keepers persisted in peppering to such an extent, that we often preferred starving to touching it. The soldiers supplied us with a medicine which afforded some temporary relief, but it was months before we succeeded in overcoming this disease. Ageana continued to provide us with only one midday meal, which was irregularly supplied, and though the soldiers sent us occasional presents of fufu, it was almost impossible to persuade them that a morning or evening meal was at all necessary.

We were at first permitted to go alone to the brook, but after a while it occurred to our guards that this was very unbecoming conduct on our part, and thenceforth one of the boys always accompanied us. The days passed monotonously, and we almost despaired as to whether the king ever meant to send for us at all, for our guards appeared to have settled down permanently.

One night after we had retired, we were surprised by a number of people suddenly crowding into the court, and staring intently at us by the light of a dim lamp. It transpired that they were the attendants of a prince who was passing through Abankoro, and who called upon us the next morning, richly dressed in silk and gold. Upon his return journey a few days later, we implored him to furnish us with a comb and scissors, which he promised to send; though a long time elapsed before his messenger arrived with a little soap wrapped in leaves, an old comb, and a small pair of scissors. How thankful we felt when we could thus at length rid ourselves of the burden of hair, which we had had no opportunity of combing for ten months! It is needless to add, that when Kwabena ordered us the next day to give up the scissors, we stoutly resisted his demand, and hid them away most carefully.

CHAPTER XI.

WITH M. BONNAT IN ABANKORO.

ON the 27th of August, a white man, accompanied by two soldiers, suddenly entered our yard. He was sunburnt and in rags. He greeted us in French, and we were indeed pleased to hear his sympathising words, " Madame, je vous plains !"

We soon learnt that our companion was a merchant from Ho, where he had been taken prisoner by the Ashantees, after the missionaries Hornberger and Müller had escaped. His captors beheaded his two mulatto assistants, who had been educated in Europe, then seized, stripped, and tied him to a tree, when he was kept all night, and witnessed the plundering and burning of the station, saw the Ashantees tear the books, chop up the harmonium, and throw away the coffee and flour. When the bell fell from the burning chapel, they lifted and brought it into the camp of Nantshi, Adu Bofo's first officer, and thither M. Bonnat was also taken.

The people of Ho made an attempt to recover their town, which so enraged the Ashantees that like angry children, they destroyed all the mango and palm groves in the neighbourhood. M. Bonnat at first expected to proceed direct to Ashantee, but his attendants decided to settle near us, and when they noticed Ageana's treatment of us they began to imitate, and at last even excelled him, so that our poor friend would have been really starved had we not shared our pittance with him.

Our old leader had bought a little salt and some yams with the money we had entrusted to his care in Totorase, but very soon he declared that it was all gone, and in reply to our demands would rage furiously, exclaiming, " salt, salt, do you suppose I shall go to Akem, and fetch it for you on my head." The broken wooden bowl which held our food usually contained very thin pepper soup, in which a few balls of fufu, and very occasionally a tiny bit of meat were to be found. This was the day's provision for three people, and rather than beg some of the slaves' food of our hard-hearted leader, we preferred to appeal to the pity of the people around us.

Some of the good-natured women kindly gave us now and then some fruit, but of course these gifts were irregular, and there were days when we learnt what starvation meant. We were therefore much cheered, on the 7th of October, by the welcome news that the king had sent both us and M. Bonnat, a sheep and a sua of gold dust. Of the latter we should have heard nothing, for Ageana simply pocketed it, had it not been that the soldiers claimed their part of the booty, as they helped to provide us with food. There was a hot altercation, and the matter being referred to Coomassie, the old man was forced to give up half. M. B.'s portion was given to his keeper, who squandered it in a fortnight, and then told his prisoner that he had no money to buy a little salt.

In comparing our adventures we soon learnt the history of our new companion. Born in the department of Ain, he had early in life longed to see the world, and therefore joined a Niger expedition in 1867. His ship was wrecked in the first storm at sea on the coast of France. Provided with another small vessel they reached the west coast of Africa. Here M. B. separated from his countrymen and began to trade, with the assistance of his mulatto servants, going further inland until he at length reached Ho. Here he purchased a quantity of cotton in exchange for cloth and powder, and intended to send his goods to the coast. The Ashantees were however approaching the place, and the missionaries urged him to join in their flight, which he refused to do, though he retired to the mission-house with his servants, so as to avoid being involved in the affairs of the town.

On the 25th of June the sound of drums approached, and red umbrellas were seen glancing in and out among the coffee trees; while the closed doors and shutters of the house were soon pierced by Ashantee balls. M. B. was now dragged out of the window, and his two men were beaten, tied together by the neck, and executed. The next morning he was found by the general Nantshi secured to a mango tree where he had passed the night, and rebuking the soldiers, Nantshi ordered food and clothing to be given him. His own clothes having been stripped off the previous day, he was now clad in man's and woman's dress. Plenty of food was provided, and he was permitted to take what German books he liked from the library. He chose one called "The way of the Cross," the pictures in which were a comfort to him, though he confessed to us that like the child in the story, he often wished to cut off a portion of the cross which he was himself called on to bear. During the sally of the Ho people four of his captors stood over him with long knives, undecided whether or not to kill him, while the bullets whistled about the hut where he was guarded. It was however finally resolved that he should be sent under strict guard to Coomassie. He believed that he owed the indulgence of never wearing irons on the journey to the report of our blameless conduct.

M. B. brought with him a scrap of butter, which imparted a great relish to our roasted pisangs, and he knew also how to extract vinegar from the half rotten bananas which were sometimes given us. We soon became great friends, and he brightened our dreary life with all sorts of clever inventions. One day he joyfully led into our presence a young man who had addressed him in English in the street—this was a Fantee from Coomassie, whose master, a prince Ansa, lived there. Whilst we were talking Opoku entered, and sharply asked what the stranger was doing here, whilst Ageana gave orders to have him placed in irons. Opoku now hurried off with a soldier to Coomassie, but returned rather crestfallen the next day, and the old man who seemed to think he had done a very fine thing, was ordered at once to set his prisoner free.

On the 21st of October, brother K. met another man who spoke English, and who had come from Cape Coast, and had brought letters and some champagne for the king. From this, the first news which had reached us from that quarter, we concluded that some negotiations in which we might also be interested were in process between the king and the European officials. This idea received confirmation when on the next day a greeting reached us from his majesty, accompanied by the present of an ox. I should however add, that this ox had refused to approach any nearer than the next village, and was thus condemned to be slain there.

It also appeared that this obstinate animal had not possessed several of the organs with which oxen are usually endowed, for the fore-quarters which reached us in a basket next morning, were painfully shorn of their natural proportions. Ageana appropriated one leg, gave another to M. B., and a third to us, while the fourth he put aside, remarking that he would buy salt with that, the rest was distributed between the wife of the chief, the Fetish priestess, and many other "friends" whose multiplicity we had never guessed before. Our landlady claimed the head as her share, but finally ceded the tongue to us.

As Ageana and the soldiers could not eat beef, they only wanted to obtain favour by giving it away. Every Ashantee avoids eating some particular kind of food in honour of his Fetish, thus one touches no beef, another avoids snails, and a third cannot taste fish, &c. Many drink no palm wine on Tuesdays, others refrain on Fridays, all being regulated according to the taste or rule of their respective idols. The king for instance denies himself beef, and takes no palm wine on Tuesdays; and our old man being unable to enjoy our store, cooked it most unwillingly, and managed to spoil a good deal of it.

However, in his reports to the governor, the king boasted of the splendid liberality with which he was treating us. He also appeared to have heard of our obstinate eruption, and so far pitied us as to forbid our being employed in menial work.

One November night we were aroused from our sleep by tremendous knocking, and the entrance of some mysterious looking men from Coomassie. They carried lighted torches, and whispered among themselves so as to excite our suspicions of a cruel death, but we soon noticed that Ageana's wife was weeping, and felt sure her tears would not fall for us, so we dismissed our fears, and found in the morning that it was the death of the district chief, which had thus been announced, and six days later his funeral festival was celebrated. Two slaves were brought from Coomassie, with ropes round their necks, and with a knife stuck through the cheek of each to prevent noise and cursing. Eight other unfortunates were killed at the same time. This incident will give some idea of the sad way in which our life was varied.

The people around us in Abankoro would not, or perhaps could not, give us any idea of the fate intended for us. The few words we sometimes caught of what they said, only misled us, and they would answer no questions. Our food was so insufficient, that we were glad to cook wild cabbage, and eat it without salt. We could sometimes pluck a little fruit in addition.

It was now December, in the middle of which month a wind called the Harmattan began to blow. Had we been at home we should have welcomed the agreeable temperature thus produced, but with only a thin cotton sheet as a covering, we suffered so severely from cold, that we were repeatedly attacked with high fever.

We had complained to the king of the lamentable state of our clothes, and that our boots were just a few tatters of leather. Oh, the sadness which filled our hearts, as in this piteous plight, we saw the glorious festival of Christmas approaching! The natives, who keep an annual celebration at this time, had already held it; and during their wild festivities, a death occurred. A coffin was brought through our village, followed by the victims led in chains, who were to be sacrificed in honour of the departed. With feelings of deep grief, we sat under the shade of the trees, thinking of the blessed time our friends at home, and our brethren at the mission station, were enjoying. Had we in those dreary days only possessed a copy of God's Word, how we should have hailed it as an ever present friend. As it was, we solaced ourselves by repeating verses from the Psalms and the Prophets, and yet we often felt so poor—so lonely!

But after all, we too were to have our Christmas gift. On the evening of December the 24th, a procession from a neighbouring village approached, bringing us a large supply of yams, bananas, bread, etc., a most welcome and grateful surprise. Nor were we forgotten at the New

Year, for on January the 6th, 1870, a soldier, accompanied by a royal messenger, returned from Coomassie, with a few articles of clothing from Sokoree—a shirt and trousers for K., with a boot and slipper, and much the same for my wife. She also received two needles and some thread, so that she could now appear dressed as a woman; and Ageana advised her to hold her dress up higher. She became the object of universal admiration, and the improved appearance of our entire party in our new costumes gave rise to the boastful exclamation among our companions, "The king gave it them!"*

Our stay at this place came to an unexpected termination in this way. Salt is rare and expensive in Ashantee, a handful costing four pence, and it is not generally supplied to slaves. We had found it necessary to enter on numerous altercations with Ageana, who wished to force us to do without it, which we persistently refused at the risk of being starved, and begged to refer the matter to the king. Two messengers were thus dispatched to court, who after a month re-appeared, bringing not only a load of salt and a fine ox, but also bearing a message that the king ordered our removal to another village. Full of apprehension and wonder we prepared for the change, which was most unwelcome to our guards and the villagers. The ambassadors however enforced instant obedience, and we hastened to depart, Ageana complying with the royal command with evident reluctance, in which we could not share.

* It may be a matter of surprise that we were enabled to keep count of time. This is explained by the fact, that the Ashantees reckon with weeks of the same duration as ours. We always noted the first Sunday in each month, together with other events of importance, by scratching memoranda with scissors upon an empty milk can, which was our drinking vessel, and the only utensil in our possession.

CHAPTER XII.

IN ASOTSCHE.

ON the 15th of February we once more recognised in our forest home the well known sound of "Forward." Our sullen old leader was alive again, and we prepared for a march, longer or shorter as the case might be.

After an hour we reached an irregularly-built village of some size, where we were introduced to the wife of the chief and some aged elders, one of whom showed us into several good houses belonging to himself. An ox was soon slain and distributed with some salt, which act of generosity was deeply felt and acknowledged.

Our position was here much improved. Not only did the villagers try to outvie each other in kindness, but the son of the chief took a lively interest in "the white people," and stood our friend when needful. Presents of fruit, eggs, rice, and onions were brought us from five different villages, and an excellent dish of fufu was daily supplied from the elders' table.

In Abankoro there were only women, and our old leader could abuse us to his heart's content; here there were plenty of kindly-disposed men. Our soldiers who had feasted luxuriously in their former quarters besought us to return, but we assured them we were perfectly contented as we were. One of our privileges we greatly valued—we were allowed to live separate from our escort, and were permitted to distribute for ourselves the presents we received. Our hearts were also made glad by the frank way in which these villagers assured us that we should be taken to Coomassie when Adu Bofo returned; though if we asked when the army was expected they invariably replied, "In about two months."

It was here that the first opportunity was offered us of showing kindness, by befriending a little orphan boy about five years old, whom we observed creeping about unnoticed and reduced to a skeleton. He could not speak, and was regarded as an idiot; but when he saw my wife bringing him food, he would cry for joy. Our kindness to this little sufferer astonished the people. "They are God's children," was the exclamation, which opened the way for me to tell them of His love—not quite in vain, for one woman actually went so far as to wash the poor little dirty fellow more than once—an act of singular compassion in an Ashantee. At length death put an end to the sufferings of this touching type of vast numbers of neglected little ones, who thus perish in this dark land!

In due time we were not only allowed to bathe twice daily, but to walk about freely. On one of our excursions we noticed a small piece of paper not larger than our hand. The sight filled us with delight; it seemed more precious than gold. It had come from Europe—it had been manufactured by white hands; and, oh! could we not employ ours, thought we? The idea gave us fresh spirit, we cut palm branches in the wood and wove them together, and in due time our handicraft had made such progress, that we had mats of our own manufacture to sleep on. But spite of these little encouragements our depression was often great. Brother K. grew fearfully thin, so that our soldiers procured medicine and better food for him—but his appetite was gone. They went to tell the king, and returned with a promise, never fulfilled, of eggs and chickens to tempt the sick man.

One day as we sat weaving our mats, an ambassador from the court appeared, with three sedan chairs, and orders that we were to proceed immediately to Coomassie, to the great astonishment of our leaders, one of whom called out "The king loves you much."

Old Ageana was thunderstruck that the chairs should be sent for *his slaves*, and tremblingly faltered out—"The king wishes it, you must go to him."

To us, who had resigned ourselves to the agonizing thought of being destined to adorn the triumphal entry of the returning conqueror, this was indeed a wondrous surprise. It was in vain we tried to imagine what had caused the change, and deeply touched, we could only render thanksgiving and praise to our gracious God.

Early in the morning of April the 22nd, we put our few things together, took leave of the friendly villagers, and mounted our sedan chairs. M. B., for whom none had been sent, took his place on a bearer's shoulders, a mode of travelling common to chiefs, and even kings in this land; but he found it so tiring as to prefer using his own feet the best part of the way. When however we passed a village, he had to mount, that it might be seen how the king honoured his white men. We dined and rested in our old quarters at Abankoro; and now times had changed with us, we were greatly admired as elevated people.

Our afternoon ride was along a beautiful road, and towards evening we were near Coomassie, but were carried aside to a little village, in the centre of which, under a large shady tree, a group of mahomedans were sitting, in their picturesque fashion. Descending, we entered a house, where we were evidently expected, and were informed by the owner, that the king had ordered dwellings to be given us. We were then conducted by a side path through bushes, to a little clearing on the borders of the forest, where we found two miserable fresh grass huts, as our future quarters, and yet we were only half-an-hour's distance from Coomassie.

CHAPTER XIII.

BEFORE THE KING.

A VIOLENT thunderstorm during the night, depriving us of sleep, and obliging us to sit close together in the centre of our lonely hut, greatly chilled the sanguine hope of the past day.

But in the early morning the arrival of a sheep and yams from the king shewed us he felt some interest in us, and as we had fasted long, this was indeed a welcome gift. Two bottles of sweet liquor came later on in the day. Our next incident was a visit to an adjoining village (Duru by name), where a number of chiefs, richly attired and covered with ornaments, waited to receive us. We made our obeisance to this semi-circle of dignitaries, and then sat on chairs provided for us. The whole company at once rose to return our salutations, on which our people humbly remarked, "This is the nobility of Coomassie." This introductory ceremony completed, the grandees went into a house, and commanded us to follow. During their long conference, we stood waiting till they permitted us to be seated. We were then addressed by one of them in the following words:—

"Adu Bofo has sent you to the king. He says you are good men—translate to us this letter." He then produced from a cloth, in which it had been carefully wrapped, an open German letter addressed to us, endorsed on the outside, "Shew this letter to no one, or it will cost the bearer his life." It was from David Asante, a native missionary educated at Basle, and as we thought of the messenger we shuddered.

The contents ran thus—

"Much beloved brethren,—We have taken all possible pains since your captivity to effect your deliverance. Twice have we sent messengers to the Ashantee camp offering money for your release, but in vain. I have been sent to Begoro, on the frontier of Akem, to try and come into communication with you, as up to the present time we have only heard of you by reports. I give the bearer a pencil, paper, and scissors, that you may write; or if that is not possible, send some of your hair, as an assurance that you are still alive."

Further on signs were mentioned, through which we were to make ourselves understood to the bearer without words; but he had either been captured, or from fear delivered the letter to the king. We thought it best to keep simply to the truth, and translated the letter verbatim. After hearing it they rose, and giving us their hands, permitted us to return to our seclusion in the wood. But who can describe the feelings of our hearts upon hearing from those so dear to us after a silence of ten months. We now understood why we had been brought so near the capital, and we perceived that the mention of ransom had made a deep impression; for, as the courtiers remarked, "the king loves money."

After an interval of two days, we were summoned to the village to receive a present of food from the queen mother, which was followed by another ox from the king. In acknowledging these gifts, I sent them word that our supply of salt was exhausted, and we immediately received another load, so that we were now, by comparison, living in comfort. We afterwards heard the reason of this unusual liberality. It seems Adu Bofo was just then in a very embarrassing position, and it was thought we might favourably influence the British Government. On the 3rd of May, an assembly of chiefs was convened, and we were desired to answer David's letter with the pen and paper he had sent, but were told that our letter must take the form of an address, now going off, to the "King of Europe." After much perplexity, we ascertained that the Dutch governor of Elmina, was the person to be thus honoured.

The sense of our epistle ran thus:—"According to the laws of the Ashantee country, the king has no power to set prisoners at liberty till the general who captured them returns." It was furthermore mentioned, that "news had reached Coomassie of the general's way being stopped by a force that had been sent from Akra, Krobo, Akem, and Akwapem, to hinder his retreat. The king had despatched reinforcements to his aid, from several different districts, and it was now demanded of the Dutch governor, that he should request the English commandant to allow the general to retire without fear of hostile attack; otherwise, our release would be refused." We were commanded to send with the letter, a lock of our hair, however unnecessary it might seem to us.

As it was intended that our friends should read this letter, we asked leave to give them some personal tidings, and were told we might communicate to them the loss we had suffered in the removal of our dear child.

The next episode in our experience was a message to prepare us for a speedy introduction to the great king, but in the evening of the same day, we were informed that a pair of gold sandals having been stolen from the palace, the feelings of his majesty were too much excited to permit him to give us audience. A few days later, however, a chamberlain arrived at our abode prepared to accompany us to the presence of this mighty potentate. My wife being very poorly was allowed to mount the chamberlain's chair, while we walked by her side. The distance was in itself very short, but they delight to conduct strangers by circuitous routes. Men bearing swords hurried up and down the broad avenues of palm trees, with an air of great importance, while drums were beaten, and horns blown. The melee was indescribable; mahomedans in their long robes were strutting about, minutely inspecting us as we passed onward to the beautiful square in front of the king's villa (called Amanchia).

Here in the middle of a brilliant circle, shaded by noble palms, sat his majesty of Ashantee, fanned by pages, and surrounded by interpreters and chiefs. A crowd of about three thousand people were seen assembled at a distance. Each chief was shaded by a bright coloured umbrella, some twelve feet in diameter, the points of which were ornamented with carved and gilded elephants, pelicans, apes, and human heads; both the king and the chiefs had numerous attendants. The scene was really imposing and very picturesque, and from time to time was animated by sounds of wild music. We were presented while waiting, with two jars of palm wine, and three bottles of gin, after which two fresh sword-bearers appeared on the scene.

One of these in full uniform was a wonderful figure. He carried the royal sword, in a sheath made of leopard's skins, while hung around him were the rest of his majesty's arms—his cartridge-box, knife, personal ornaments for his neck, arms, and feet, and his cap, with a beautiful, fan-shaped tuft of eagle's feathers, each article glittering with gold. This official was to conduct us into the immediate presence of his sovereign, so we formed a procession. First walked a few of our people, then Mr. K. and M. Bonnat, my wife and I followed, and a few soldiers brought up the rear. We stepped along the semi-circle, bowing as we went to the king in the centre, and removing our hats (even my wife's). These salutations were responded to by a friendly nod.

Our march finished, we sat and received in our turn the greetings of this high and mighty assembly. All rose, the horns blew, the jubilant cry resounded louder than the drum, as the grandees approached us with measured steps. The inferiors preceded, then the great men shaded by their umbrellas, and surrounded by their pages, saluted us as they passed by, each raising the hand. In front of the principal chiefs marched boys, adorned with elephant's or horse's tails, and carrying drums made of the trunks of trees, and horns adorned by human jaws. A few of them had elephant's tusks hollowed out, and emitting a sound surpassing all others in strength and clearness, each musician trying to honour us by producing their loudest and shrillest tones, as they passed us. The chiefs were arrayed in silk, or the brilliantly embroidered cloth of the country; every individual wore his handsomest jewels, especially his massive gold plate on his breast, his carved seat being carried on the head of an attendant, who was followed by soldiers bearing his arms.

After a number of such personages had passed, the great monarch himself approached. He was heralded by some eighty individuals, each wearing a cap of monkey's skin, adorned by a golden plate, and each holding his seat in his hand. Then came the dwarfs and buffoons in red flannel shirts, with the officials of the harem; there were also sixty boys, every one of whom wore a charm sewn up in leopard's skin, with written scraps from the koran, which were highly valued; this train was followed by five tastefully carved royal chairs, hung round with gold and silver bells, and richly ornamented with jewels, but all black, being stained with the blood of human sacrifices.

Next, under an enormous silk sunshade, appeared the actual throne chair, encased with gold, and with long golden pipes carried behind it, as well as various wonderful vessels and articles of vertu. A peculiar music was heard rising above the sound of the horns and the beating of the drums. This was produced by some thirty wild-looking boys, each of whom swung, as he marched, a calabash half-filled with stones. This din was anything but agreeable to a European ear, though the performers kept marvellously good time.

Still larger umbrellas and fans now approached, preceded by a corps of a hundred *executioners* dancing, whose ages varied from boys of only ten years to grey-headed old men; all wore leopard skin caps, and had two knives slung from their necks. The dismal death drum, whose three beats were heard from time to time, closed the procession.

Now the music became wilder and louder, the ivory horns sounded shriller, the screaming and howling surpassed all description. Led by an attendant under a magnificent sunshade of black velvet, edged with gold, and kept in constant motion, the royal potentate appeared. Boys with sabres, fans, and elephants' tails danced around him like imps of darkness, screaming with all the power of their lungs, " He is coming, he is coming. His majesty the lord of all the earth approaches!" The boys then retired that the king might be able to look well at us, and enjoy the intensity of his happiness. Golden sandals adorned his feet; a richly ornamented turban was on his head; his dress was of yellow silk-damask; his hands and feet glittered with gold bracelets and bangles. Half a dozen pages held him by the arms, back, and legs, like a little child, crying continually, " Look before thee, O lion! take care, the ground is not even here."

Kari-Kari is a man who really impresses you, still

young and of middle stature, but well built—his face, though somewhat marked with small-pox, bears the stamp of a powerful, yet beneficent king, and his whole appearance gives the impression of a soul capable of great deeds. There was no look of cruelty, and I no longer felt anxious about my wife. He remained standing before us for a few moments, in some degree of astonishment, for I suppose we were the first white people he had ever seen; in our patched and torn garments, which a beggar in our country would have disdained, and with our toes peeping through our shoes, we encountered the gaze of this mighty monarch, who at length waved his hand kindly to us, and passed on, his long procession of attendants following.

At this juncture, we were told to stand up and thank the "nena," or queen-mother, the most influential person at court, for presents she had lately sent us; she was protected from the sun by large fans, embroidered with coloured silk held round her by court ladies, and wore a gorgeous dress, with a silk scarf thrown over her shoulders. She was a stout energetic old lady, and returned our greeting with a good-natured smile. The procession, after lasting an hour and a half, ended with a number of officers and others; and we departed more light-hearted than we had arrived. The excitement had done my wife good, her indisposition had disappeared, and we all looked with new hope to the future. We tasted the palm wine, but found it so strong that we divided it amongst our people, and the "friends" who crowded around us.

On May 25th, we received from the king a couple of sheep, and an old pair of Dutch military shoes, accompanied by a pair of boots for Mrs. R., of English make, and the finest leather. They had been presented by the Wesleyan missionary Freemen in 1842, to the reigning sovereign, and inscribed on the soles in gilt letters were the following words:—"To his Royal Highness, Quakoo Dooah, King of Ashantee, West Africa." They had never been worn, and though time and insects had made their acquaintance, they were still in serviceable condition.

Thus had a covering for my wife's feet been prepared for her thirty years before, and this circumstance gave us a fresh assurance that our God would still provide for her.

I will now describe the king's return visit:—We were one afternoon summoned to the chief of Duru, and on entering the courtyard, after politely saluting him, we observed a man of sallow complexion, in a shabby European dress. He rose, offered his hand, and said to us in English, "That we had no doubt often heard of him, that he was sorry to find us in such a position, that he was himself detained at Coomassie, but daily hoping to be allowed to return to the Coast." He added, "that he and the brethren in Coomassie had for a long time mentioned us in their prayers." This was not all said consecutively, but in the course of conversation; and while we were wondering whether he was an English envoy or an agent of the slave trade, he told us that we were in the presence of the king. The latter had observed us from the ante-room of the chief, and was so amused that he laughed aloud. Chairs were then brought us, and the king asked us how we were, and in what manner we had been taken prisoners.

He looked serious when we told him we had been put in irons, and seemed not to know that we had been plundered. A word escaped him which sounded like "they shall repent of it;" before we took leave we asked him if he could let us have a Bible through "the prince," as we had now been without the Word of God for almost a year. Great was our joy when by permission of the sovereign "the prince" promised to send us a copy of this precious volume.

BEFORE THE KING.

The king did not speak much, but remarked that we were not quite white, which was true enough. We explained this as the effect of exposure to the sun, and opened our dress that he might see the white skin beneath. After he had left, we naturally thought much of "the brother," or "the prince," who had spoken English to us, and wondered who he was. Judging by his colour, we thought he might be an ambassador from the Dutch governor of Elmina; anyway, that would be proved if he really sent us an English Bible.

To our great joy, after three days, the much longed for treasure was placed in our hands—a New Testament with the Psalms, accompanied by a few old numbers of Wesleyan missionary notices. The bearer was a young christian from Cape Coast, and who can imagine the delight with which we grasped the coveted volume, or how we thanked God for that, which we now knew so well how to prize, yea far better than before we had been so long without it.*

* In an old treaty of peace between the British government and the king of Ashantee, it was stipulated that the heir to the throne should be educated in England, but as the heir then living was too old to learn, two of the king's nephews, Ansa and Kwantabisa, came in 1836 to England in his place, Ansa being then twelve years old. These princes were well educated and treated with the honour due to their rank.

In 1841, they returned to Africa with a pension, granted to them by Queen Victoria, of £100 a year each. Kwantabisa died at Cape Coast, but prince Ansa received his allowance till within three years. For some time he had been engaged in the Wesleyan mission, and was finally ordained as a missionary. In 1867, he was sent by the colonial government to Coomassie, upon the news of Kwakoo Dooah's death, and he had there been detained till now.

This was the beginning of our acquaintance with the converted Ashantee prince, John Owusu Ansa, a man to whom we owe the deepest gratitude, and who seemed to have been expressly sent to Coomassie, to prove a messenger of grace for us during our long trial.

CHAPTER XIV.

EBENEZER.

In the joy of our hearts, and in deep thankfulness for His mercy and grace in looking on our afflictions, we gave to our nest in the wood the name which signifies, "The Lord has helped us." Drawbacks and disagreeables were not wanting, but our position was now endurable; we were well supplied with food by the king, though, through the many who had to share it, our own was still but a meagre portion. Our attendants had become civil and obliging, and the visits of the grandees impressed them with an idea of our importance.

We will here describe one of these visits, which occurred on the 20th of May. Its hero was no less a person than Bosommuru, a chamberlain, who on his entrance desired our people to retire, and produced my confiscated watch, with a piece of embroidered cloth, seeming to think the two had some connection; perhaps on account of the price-ticket attached to the cloth. His object was just to get an explanation of the watch, not as one might have hoped, to return the article to myself.

With the usual vicissitudes attendant on a condition like ours, in the hands of a barbarous sovereign, we shortly after this suffered a sudden diminution in our supplies, our soldiers declaring that the purse was empty. This being reported to his majesty, twenty-seven dollars were forwarded in gold dust, and soon after he paid us another visit, the object of which appeared to be simply a friendly call on his white men. He took his place on this occasion in the centre of the village, on a bench formed of palm branches, under a roof of leaves, with about sixty people sitting before him.

Forgetful of courtly etiquette, for "necessity has no law," I took this opportunity of laying aside my coat, and, with an exclamation, "Oh king! I pray thee look here," I showed him my uncovered back, and the remains of my tattered shirt. The Ashantee custom of giving presents liberally at the outset to gain a good name, had caused reports to reach us from the coast, that we had been overladen with gifts. We had certainly received another ox, but the present was accompanied by a swarm of bees, in the shape of a motley crowd, furnished with knives and sacks, to cut and carry away the spoil, so that we had difficulty in securing a moderate portion for our own share, and could hardly spare enough to dry some slices, and make a few sausages well seasoned with pepper for future use. Later on, a year passed without any gift whatever.

I have mentioned two huts erected for our use. One of those was occupied by our keeper Ageana, the other by ourselves. M. Bonnat at first slept in the village, but spent his days with us. In due time Ageana built a third hut, and allowed M. B. the use of the one he forsook, which was then shared with Opoko. The latter worthy was afflicted with a contagious eruption, so M. Bonnat contrived a wall of rushes, and in his own division was kept our dried meat and sausages. It was a dainty apartment for a store-room, and alas! it was open to thieves, who carried away so much as to alarm us.

Upon this, M. Bonnat's diplomatic talents came to our aid. He actually succeeded, though not without some painful resistance, in inducing Opoko to find other quarters, and make room for Mr. K. in his place. Having proceeded thus far in separating ourselves from our black attendants, we set to work to construct bedsteads with sticks and palm branches, forming string from banana fibre. With a little wooden hook, which I had cut as an implement, my wife made a pocket, a hat for herself, and a cap for me, while I succeeded in manufacturing a worktable for her, and a dining table for general use, from plaited rushes. The ingenuity of M. Bonnat greatly aided us in our various manufactures, which gave a deep interest to our secluded life.

As we had now the privilege of a daily ablution in a neighbouring stream, our health quickly improved, but our clothing alas! as rapidly decayed, and indeed was in the last stage of existence, when a quantity of common calico arrived, out of which M. Bonnat and my wife managed to construct a woman's dress, and a suitable garment for the other three of us.

On July 6th, the king again called, his retinue accompanying him, some of them carrying a brass dish, on which was his fetish, as a protection from evil spirits. He took his seat under the palm tree, asked a few questions, and spoke with the people about us and our dress. Prince Ansa was with him, who brought us a letter from David Asante, and petitions from Mr. Ramseyer's family, and from the senior missionary, Wiedmann. We read and translated these papers, which were all open— though this had already been done by prince Ansa, who was desired to write in reply, that we should be set at liberty as soon as Adu Bofo returned. At our request we were each of us allowed to enclose a small pencilled note in the king's letter.

Although the question of our liberty was still in abeyance, we could perceive that the king's feelings were friendly, though we continued to be treated as under suspicion. One of the pencils sent by David was left with us,

AT EBENEZER, NEAR COOMASIE.

but not a scrap of paper, and private conversation with the prince was impossible. We however managed to note the most important facts on the fly-leaf of our Testament.

Two days later we were again instructed to write to our brethren, David and others, telling them they might send to the king umbrellas, salt, liquors, silk materials, &c. This we gladly agreed to do, only reminding his majesty that Mr. Wiedmann was not a merchant, but would procure the goods if money were sent, and this we promised in our letter should be done. We added a word of petition for necessary clothing for ourselves.

On July 12th we were again before the king, as he sat under the palm-trees, when the cry of the eunuch sounded in the distance, announcing the approach of the royal wives. The men disappeared in an instant, and we stepped aside, knowing the penalty incurred by any man who even by accident sees one of these ladies;* but we were soon recalled, and beheld fourteen women, surrounded by little boys, sitting on the right hand of the king. Some of them were very beautiful, others ugly enough. They were not grandly dressed, and their only ornaments were rows of coral beads. They stared at us with unfeigned curiosity, while the attendant cried out constantly, "Ho! Ho!" Their heads, like those of other Ashantee women, were closely shaven, with the exception of a tuft of hair on the left side and a few small circles round it.

Our usual petition for salt was preferred again on this occasion, and on the 24th of July we received a beautiful present of fruit, vegetables, flour, sugar, &c., &c., from the ladies. On the 25th a load of salt arrived, with an intimation that,

* On one occasion a Wesleyan missionary met the wives of the king accidentally on his morning ride. He was at once dragged from his horse by the eunuch and shamefully treated. He complained to Quakoo Dooah, who ordered the execution of the eunuch, as the missionary was a white man and a stranger; but on the missionary's intercession he was handed over to corporal punishment instead.

as it was so costly, it must be sparingly used. Upon this we mentioned that the half was always claimed by our guards; thus provoking the wrath of Ageana to such a fearful degree that I took up a thin piece of wood and wrote a few words with my pencil to Bosommuru, begging him to come and say a word to the old man, who, on seeing us hand the writing to the bearer of the salt, thought it best to cease his abuse.

The king himself came over in a few days, and was not a little surprised, like the South Sea Islanders, that a piece of wood could speak. He ordered Ageana to be called, who at first denied the offence, but at length pleaded guilty, and received a severe rebuke, with orders that for the future he and his people should treat us well. He was glad to get off so easily, and his outward conduct improved, though he gave no evidence of real kindness of feeling. I then told the king of the wretched condition of our huts, causing us to be drenched by every shower. A court official was sent to inspect them, and the village chief was ordered to repair them, but they were not made water-tight.

On the 14th, Bosommuru, through whom we had communication with the court, brought us a letter from the missionaries, Schrenk and Eisenschmidt, with a chest containing some personal necessaries, and a most welcome supply of paper. A present for the king, which had been enclosed, never reached us; a piece of stuff too, which had been sent for ourselves, so pleased him that he sent to enquire the price, and we thought it best to give it, whereupon we received a sheep in return, and a sua of gold dust, which, alas! were taken possession of by our people.

There was one remark in the letter of our brethren which distressed us, namely, that they would not be able to continue this connection with us from Begoro. We concluded they were acting thus, under the direction of the British governor. Still, as a decided improvement had taken place in our position, we tried to hope that all would be well when Adu Bofo returned, and we were now at liberty to go to the village whenever we pleased. On one of these visits, Mr. K., accompanied by our soldiers, observed in a yard more than a hundred prisoners from Krepe, men, women, and children, all living skeletons, and infants on their mothers' backs, starving for want of their natural nourishment.

In the afternoon we were summoned to the presence of the king, who had come to visit these prisoners. Arraying ourselves in court attire, viz., the under drawers which Mr. Schrenk had sent us, we hastened to present ourselves, and were pleasantly received by his majesty on his usual seat beneath the palms. The prisoners were assembled in groups on the open space, surrounded by baskets of maize, corn, native bread and yams, which they devoured with their eyes, as loaf by loaf it was distributed.

As we gazed on this mass of misery, my wife noticed a poor, weak child, who was commanded in angry tones to stand straight. The little fellow tried to obey, and painfully drew himself up, showing the shrunken frame in which every bone was visible. This reminded her so vividly of our own lost darling that she burst into tears. The king inquired the reason, and on hearing it, remarked, "this does not concern you; God will give you another child;" yet perceiving the sight distressed us, he permitted us to leave, and in the evening sent us some palm wine to restore our spirits. With what thankful hearts did we compare his considerate treatment of us with the misery of these poor creatures now about to be separated from each other. We could only hope they would find merciful masters.

The king mentioned this occurrence to prince Ansa, expressing his surprise at my wife's emotion. "We black people," replied the prince, "have hard hearts, and can behold misery unmoved; it is not so with the whites; such a spectacle wounds them deeply." Soon after this, we one day carried our fufu to the poor imprisoned children, but found to our disappointment the king already in the village, engaged in separating the prisoners. Our soldiers sprang forward to drive us back; we hid behind a hedge, and entreated them to take the food themselves to the children, whereupon the dish was shown to the king, who uttered an exclamation of surprise, but desired that our wishes should be fulfilled, and soon after sent us a sheep with his compliments.

After this prisoners continued to arrive, just living skeletons. The sight of one poor boy touched us deeply; the thin neck was unable to support the head, which drooped almost to the knees. I spoke to him repeatedly, and offered him food; at length he gave me a look I shall never forget; just said, "I have eaten," and the head hung down helpless as before; all hope seemed gone! Another of apparently higher rank coughed as if in the last gasp of existence; he was as emaciated as the others, but had been allowed to retain some beads and a brass ring; we gave him some snail soup, and promised to bring him a daily supply of fufu.

Another object of our compassion was a young child so weak from want of food as to be unable to stand. It was touching to see how the little thing jumped on its mother's knee as my wife approached with fufu and ground nut soup. Alas! it was but little we could do to ameliorate the miseries of these wretched groups, but that little called forth their most grateful thanks.

On the 26th of August we again received a sheep and a sua of gold dust, and for a few days our diet was improved, but we soon fell back into the old routine—snail soup and dried meat. On the 28th we were summoned to an audience, and anticipated special news, as we were to carry our chairs, which always denoted something important. On arriving at the leafy chamber where the king awaited us, we saw some boxes addressed to us. We naturally supposed they were from our brethren, but to our surprise the king handed us a letter from his excellency administrator Ussher, expressing the hope that, in virtue of his treaty with the king, he should soon welcome us at Cape Coast; meanwhile he had sent us a few needful articles.

On opening the boxes we were deeply affected at their contents, which consisted of stuffs, soap, metal plates, knives and forks, preserved meats, ham, cheese, tea, sugar, biscuits, and, above all, writing materials; with a quantity of gold dust, in value £22, quite a fortune in our secluded life. Three umbrellas were also found; one had disappeared on the road. There was besides a valuable present for the king, consisting of three boxes of champagne; we too had our share of wine, some of which we offered to his majesty. He took four bottles, which he drank in company with his chiefs, till the whole party became very merry. Our people were commanded to appear before him, and he swore, with uplifted hands, that whoever took anything from us would lose his head. This was said so solemnly that Ageana, though he tried to speak, became dumb; and being roughly pushed aside, had quickly to retire.

After the king's departure, Bosommuru begged for a second translation of the letter, though prince Ansa had already read it; we of course complied. This done he gave us another letter from Major Brownell, which informed us that he had conducted the embassy to the Ashantee king as far as the Prah, and would remain there until we came. How joyfully we embraced this prospect of deliverance, feeling that He, to whom nothing is impossible, could easily bring it to pass.*

Returning to our humble home, we gratefully thanked our heavenly Father for His interposition on our behalf; and in the gladness of our hearts, we prepared a present for the king, consisting of four metal plates, some sugar, soap and pomade. For prince Ansa we set aside a pair of shoes, which he greatly needed, some tea, sugar, writing materials, and other valuable things. After dispatching this business, we sat down to try the cheese; oh how delicious it was, and how gladly did we cast aside our wooden plates!

Prince Ansa called on us as soon as permitted, to offer his thanks, telling us the shoes were more valuable to him than a crown of gold. He encouraged us to hope that a mission might soon be established in Coomassie, the king being now so favourably disposed towards Europeans. The schools which the Wesleyan missionaries had tried to form, failed for lack of children; if the king favoured their establishment it would be different, and by helping the missionaries, he would gain the friendship of Queen Victoria. He had already received a very kind letter from the administrator, in which he had petitioned for our freedom; and the present of a piece of green stuff, embroidered with gold, sent him by our brethren, had also delighted him.

After about three quarters of an hour, his attendants intimated to the prince that his visit must end; he immediately rose, and expressing the hope to be allowed soon to repeat it, wished us farewell, recommending us to cultivate the friendship of Bosommuru, who possessed great influence; and we sent by him the present of a brush for the latter, which he had long desired.

* Later on we heard that one of the messengers from Cape Coast had told the king that the governor accounted us for great people, and would pay any sum that might be demanded for our liberty.

In the beginning of September we entered on a new phase of affairs in our domestic arrangements, and for the first time, after eighteen months, we drank tea and read by lamp light, instead of retiring to bed at dusk. It was also now our frequent privilege to minister to poor captive children, as they passed through our village with their parents. To one of these covered with scalds we offered food, but the little sufferer could not open her mouth to eat it.

One morning, before we had completed our scanty toilet, we were desired to hasten to the presence of the king, who wished to see us, on his way to a yearly festival in honour of his father, as he called the Fetish. We managed to emerge in time to see the red umbrella enter the village, under which sat the king in his sedan chair, fully arrayed. The bearers were ordered to halt, while he saluted each of us separately, evidently desiring to make an impression. On his arms were gold and silver ornaments in various devices, from his green velvet cap hung broad lappets, to which were suspended gold and silver amulets; his dress was of damask, and a rich golden-tinted silk covered the sedan chair. It was a marvellous, but most miscellaneous, display of the ostentation and gaudy show of an African procession: the crown jewels, in baskets, chests, and tin vessels, ornaments of every variety, fans of peacocks' feathers, coloured leather, staves straight and crooked, with gold and silver knobs, and even articles of furniture—with antelopes' feet, elephants', cows,' and horses' tails, contributed their share to the show.

By the side of each bearer walked an official in plumed hat, while for music there was the continual beating of drums ornamented with human skulls, mingled with the shouts and screams of the multitude; the fifers and drummers being clothed in Danish and Dutch uniforms.

The royal camp bedstead, covered with leather and ornamented with glittering steel nails, appeared to be of British manufacture. Overseers marched by in fragments of European costume; one had a scarlet coat, but no trousers; another wore a long dressing gown, reminding one of a German university professor; one of the generals was in a brown velvet dress and sash, another had proudly donned a field marshal's hat and white cockade, while to the lot of a third had fallen a woman's under garment, in which he found it somewhat difficult to walk.

A band of three musicians in Dutch costumes followed, whose cymbal, clarionet, and European drum added considerably to the inharmonius noise (perhaps because their instrumënts were out of tune), but the effect was startling: these brought up the rear of the procession, and although their music was discordant and barbarous in the extreme, it had a certain imposing effect even on a European; while on the Africans it produced the wildest excitement, causing them to tremble.

One of the slaves in a sort of frenzy knocked off the hat of brother K., whereupon he administered summary justice, though in the presence of the king, giving the man a smart box on the ear; thus impressing on them the fact that we no longer meant to be treated as children. This sharp practice had the desired effect, for he came afterwards humbly to beg pardon, and promised to call us in the evening when the procession returned, that we might see the first part which had preceded the king. Fifty sheep had been sent in advance for feasting and for sacrifice; whether human beings were killed or not we never ascertained.

At five o'clock our chairs were placed in the street; but we had scarcely taken our seats, when a cry of the eunuchs, who are mostly dwarfs, warned us to escape; my wife, however, remained, and received a friendly salutation from eight of the royal ladies, dressed in red native cloth, and richly adorned. They were accompanied by numbers of children, the girls carrying yellow, red, and green damask cushions; the boys, who were sons of executioners, and being trained to their father's profession, wore caps of leopard skin, and carried gold handled knives. After this interlude we left our hiding place, and witnessed the remainder of the procession, which was less regular and imposing than that of the morning.

Amongst the curious things which were borne past us were silver dishes, and the king's dining-table, with feet beautifully carved; the chairs of chiefs; and a kind of flag, with figures of the Fetish. The aristocracy were carried in sedan chairs, surrounded by musicians sounding their ivory horns, and recalling to our memory our first entrance to the camp. It was now dark, torches of palm branches were lighted, and for two hours the procession continued, every person of distinction being honoured by a renewed performance on the drums. The king arrived at last, looking sullen and tired as he lay in his sedan chair, giving one the impression that he felt compelled to endure these noisy exhibitions, to conciliate the people whose chiefs had placed him on the vacant throne. It is only by slow degrees that the strongest sovereign can act independently of them.

Kari-Kari never appeared to us fond of ostentation, though he might have felt some pleasure in displaying his power to his white prisoners; but he usually came to us in a simple style, and the better we knew him the more were we impressed with the idea that his natural disposition was amiable and kind. On this occasion golden suns were carried behind him on high poles, and helmets of the same were conspicuous; so that after the amount of precious metal displayed on this day, we no longer regarded the report of the riches of this dynasty to be exaggerated.

Wearied with sight-seeing, we retired thankfully to our little hut, after seeing the brother of the king and Bosommuru carried by.

What a relief to our feelings was the thought of the following day, which was the Christian Sabbath to us, though in a land of darkness; and we purposed to commemorate it specially by meeting together at the table of the Lord. The present of wine we had lately received enabled us to hold this strengthening feast, for which our souls yearned. One of our boxes, covered with a white cloth, served as a table, and when all was ready, we anxiously awaited the arrival of prince Ansa. It was not till late in the afternoon he could obtain the king's permission to come, when he brought a native christian called Joseph from Cape Coast. How delightful was it again to enjoy the privilege of a christian service, to read together God's word, and unite in prayer and praise with our voices and our hearts.

After the service we conversed with the prince on the subject of our freedom, which he regarded as only a matter of time. He could sympathise with us from his own experience, having been for three years put off with fair promises. "After the Fantees on the coast have been set at liberty, and after Adu Bofo appears, your turn will come," said he, though the general himself has little influence, in spite of his being purse-bearer and keeper of the keys. We then discussed the fate of our property, of which we concluded the chiefs would retain a share, however much they might have grudged it to Adu Bofo. A month later the feast of yams was to be held, and he was expected forty days after. This number the Ashantees consider particularly lucky, and always try to connect with some important event.

We now ventured to invite the prince to breakfast with us, and on Sept. 15th, a special messenger being despatched to accompany him, he arrived at 10 o'clock, but to our great surprise the king came with him on a visit of inspection, escorted by eleven attendants, and carried on the shoulders of one of his servants. It was the first time he had seen our "Ebenezer," and after saluting us kindly, he greatly admired our arrangements, particularly our table constructed of boards placed over boxes, and our hammock of banana fibre.

After he had retired, our late breakfast was served, and we thoroughly enjoyed our good tea, eggs, and preserved carrots, a tin of which we had opened for the occasion. The prince conversed unreservedly, getting us to tell him our history, and relating to us his own sad experience from Sept. 17th, 1867, when he was first brought here, and since which he had been constantly promised his freedom, and as constantly disappointed. We comforted him with the suggestion that his detention might possibly have its bright side, for had he continued in office at Cape Coast, he would most likely have been involved in much trouble. Every Sunday he held a short service with his Fantee servants, in which Mr. Watts, a good Wesleyan catechist who had been detained here eight years as a hostage, took part; and he invited us to the dilapidated mission-house, where some Ashantees were always present, to whom we might speak of Christ.

The prince had himself, through the influence of the Dutch, become an object of suspicion to the king, and though now apparently restored to favour, had to be very cautious lest the people should accuse him of telling us too many secrets. He however believed he should be permitted to unite in our worship on Sundays, the king having told him that the name we had given to our place had greatly interested him. He advised us to propitiate the king's interpreter, Nantshi, by sending him a present of some sugar. From this time prince Ansa came by invitation to breakfast every Sunday and Thursday; by degrees his visits became still more frequent, and his communications more confidential.

We had often doubted whether it were not desirable to send Bosommuru a joint every time we killed a sheep, and we now found that other important people expected similar presents, and that we had already incurred the reputation of being stingy; but as the prince became better acquainted with our affairs, and learned that we had always given our people some of the money which had been sent by the king, and that we had sometimes only four snails or half a fish to make our soup, he was greatly astonished, and advised us to arrange differently, as it was not at all the king's wish that we should fare so poorly.

"You must manage your own housekeeping," said he, "and never give away what the king sends you for your own use. There is often fresh meat in the market, buy for yourselves (I will send you scales and weights for the gold dust, &c.), and have your food cooked according to your orders, keeping all supplies in your own custody." We feared the effect of such a sudden change, but the prince spoke to the people with so much tact, that they showed no open opposition, although not perhaps altogether pleased. We carried out his instructions immediately, cooking yams in the morning and fufu in the evening, and our spoons and plates were washed by the attendants.

The news which now came from the seat of war caused much joy both in town and country. It was reported that the daring rebel Dompré had been killed in battle, and that king Kwadjo Odee of Pekyi, and king Kumi of Anum had been beheaded. Kari-Kari was so delighted that he danced with joy, and all the people shared in the excitement, for it appeared that the war was at an end, and Adu Bofo's return might be expected in two or three months. White garments, the sign of rejoicing, were universal; and many painted themselves with white earth.

Prince Ansa on the contrary seemed depressed. He was expecting to be allowed to return to the coast in October, and yet he could not get an audience of the king He had, as has already been noticed, come here four years previously with a commission from the English Government, but had not been allowed to write any letters in his official capacity for three years. He wished to purchase from us the coral beads which K. had concealed in his hat, but even this little transaction could not be completed without the king's permission; so truly is this a land of fear, where no man trusts his neighbour. The prince had also adopted a little child who would otherwise have been exposed in the bush, but it died notwithstanding his care.

About this time Adu Kwaku left us in order to look after his wife in Purumasee, who was seriously ill after her confinement. He begged a sua of gold from us to propitiate the fetish who was killing his wife, but we told him we had nothing to do with fetish. She died, and we gave the customary presents to purchase mats, &c.; we were glad to hear that the child was living, and would not be buried with its mother, acccording to the custom of the country.

On October 2nd, we were surprised by a visit from a Dutch official, Mr. J. S. Mensa, who had lived in Coomassie since the 4th of July. As he spoke Dutch, he understood a good deal of our German; we also addressed him in English; this excited the suspicion of the Ashantee chief who accompanied him, making him suppose we were English also. After a short time, Mr. M. left us, taking with him a letter which M. Bonnat entrusted to his charge.

The miserable state of our huts, which leaked at every shower, caused us to entreat the king to give us better ones; and we hoped that he would allow us to remove to the town. Bosommuru however brought word that no change would be permitted until after Adu Bofo's return, and he gave orders to the people of Amanghyia to build new huts for us; we were also permitted now and then to write a letter, which was some consolation to us during this long delay.

We one day complained to Bosommuru of Ageana's rudeness to us; he constantly refused us the services of his boys, so we asked if the king would be kind enough to send us two lads, that we might not be dependent on our surly keeper. Bosommuru severely reprimanded the old man, telling him that he was unfit to have the charge of white men, and that for the future the soldiers were to obey our orders exclusively. This reproof made so deep an impression upon Ageana, that he actually begged us to pardon him, and not to deprive him of the honour of waiting upon us. So we tried him once more.

On Sunday, October 23rd, the shouting and screaming in the village, mingled with the beating of drums, announced that the great yam festival had begun. It lasts a fortnight; the first and fifth days the people fast, but only to whet their appetite for drink. The king distributed brandy to all his attendants, and sent us a bottle, which we gave to our people. On the fifth day, a criminal is executed—"sent as a messenger to the late king in the lower world;" then his majesty eats fresh yams ("ode," as the best sort are called), and on this occasion, the people also are permitted to partake of them. The king's mother passed through our village, laden with this vegetable, and at the suggestion of the servants we went forward to welcome her, and to thank her for her kind presents to us. Suddenly the sense of her own importance seemed to impress her, as mounting a high stone she commanded her attendants to form a semi-circle, and we were then called forward to kiss her extended hand. Before entering her sedan chair she promised to send us a further supply of "ode." On the fifth and eighth days of the festival the king gives wine to all his chiefs, for which purpose he expended £48 sterling. This was in addition to his own palm wine, so the street was ornamented with hundreds of vessels, and the mirth knew no bounds.

How different was our position! Brother K. was suffering from liver complaint, had quite lost his appetite, and was dreadfully depressed. My dear wife too had fever, and her spirits were so low that she could with difficulty restrain her tears. We determined to petition the king to allow us to change our quarters and remove to the old mission-house in the city. We were desirous if possible to send in our request before the meeting of the grand assembly, which took place on November 3rd. when the high dignitaries of the kingdom, the princes of Mampong, Dwaben, &c., came together to talk over everything of importance which had occurred in their respective districts since the last feast of yams.

Prince Ansa brought us intelligence of what was done that day. The Major's letter respecting the exchange of prisoners was discussed, but it was decided that if the governor would not consent to exchange the black men without the white (although it was the latter he had especially demanded) they must all remain until the return of the troops. We were cruelly disappointed, and the prince who felt the deepest sympathy for us was exceedingly grieved. "You do not know," he said, "how ashamed I am when I remember the great kindness shown to us in England, and contrast it with what you are suffering now. I can never forget Queen Victoria's kind parting words, as she gave me her hand and said, 'Go, and be a blessing to your country;' every day shews anew what misery war brings upon a land, and how hopeless our prospects are under its influence."

The prince had lately seen a large number of prisoners, amongst whom was a mother with a dead child on her back; and this cruel war still goes on. Maize and corn were sent to the camp, and the leaders who had come home were sent back again. Meanwhile, Major Brownell was detained on the Prah, and complained bitterly of having to keep his seventy Ashantee prisoners there so long.

Brother K. still continued very unwell, and we all felt much annoyed at Bosommuru's behaviour; for the last five weeks he had promised to send us meat, salt, and clothing, but nothing had come. Brother K. adopted what appeared to be the only available means of making an impression, and refused to partake of food until the promised supplies arrived. Upon this, Bosommuru paid us a visit of enquiry, and we had to inform him that white men understood "yes" to mean "yes," but that we had here discovered that promises were worthless, our letters to the king being unanswered, and those to the Coast not forwarded, or we should certainly have received some attention.

The chamberlain manifested displeasure, and half threatened to send us to another village, saying that here we saw too many people, by which he meant to express his annoyance at prince Ansa's frequent visits. However, he ended with an attempt at apology, and begged brother K. to take some food. We were talking over the subject after his departure, when suddenly a large black serpent glided up the wall, which was only made of sugar cane fibre. Brother K. attacked the reptile, and struck it with a knife, but it managed to escape, and we all considered it advisable to decamp to other quarters for the night.

We now lived upon roast bananas, and only enough salt was sent for my wife. The king at length finding that it was not good for us to fast (eating roast fruit is looked upon as fasting here), sent us a sheep and a load of salt. The following day, at the house of the chief Dikurow, we came to an understanding with his majesty. Prince Ansa's tact helped us so much that the king no longer objected to our removal to Coomassie, and he commissioned the prince to have the mission-house made ready for us, the only delay being the necessity of bringing the matter before the council. Adu Bofo would not object.

The appearance of my wife, who was suffering from an abscess, seemed to touch the king. At the same time he confessed to prince Ansa that many people had sought to excite a prejudice against him, but that he was now convinced that the prince had always given him the best advice, and was his truest friend.

We now prepared to bid adieu to our crowded little huts, in which we had settled ourselves as carefully as voyagers arrange their cabins on board a ship. Seven feet by six, and seven feet in height, contained all our possessions; on either side of the door was a narrow bedstead made of palm strips, while underneath them was our store-room, and above a frame for our "bag and baggage." Hooks on the walls supported the fragments, which had once been clothes, while between the beds stood the chest from Begoro, which contained our most valuable things, our clothes and writing materials. Umbrellas, old shoes, and sandals were thrust in above us, under the fragile grass roof where rats, mice, spiders, and lizards found a refuge, and occasionally dropped down upon us. A hen house had been contrived outside, which though often plundered, occasionally afforded us the luxury of an egg.

And here I must not forget to add, that during our last fortnight, our dear prince Ansa rejoiced us with a most welcome present, consisting of a fine sheep, some yams, and two hens. We were soon after enabled to buy another fowl and two chickens, at a trifling price, and the care of this poultry was a wonderful pleasure to us.

In the meanwhile, the prince had prepared for our use two rooms in the mission-house; these were cleaned and whitened, and permission was obtained for our taking possession the next week. Thursday, which we suggested, being considered by the king an unlucky day, our removal was fixed for Monday, it being stipulated that we should go by moonlight, to avoid creating sensation in the town.

We could scarcely believe in the truth of this pleasant change, which was the first of our desires that had been acceded to during our captivity, and we could hardly realise the happy fact. The prince, moreover, stirred our hearts by hints of various great changes now taking place on the Gold Coast. It appeared likely that England would shortly purchase Elmina from the Dutch, the latter retiring altogether from Guinea; the entire Coast thus coming under British rule, it would probably ensue, that a strict system of government would supersede the irregular order of things which had hitherto prevailed; in any case, we rested in the thought that our God would order all things for the best.

CHAPTER XV.

IN COOMASSIE WITH PRINCE ANSA.

MONDAY, December 5th, was a day never to be forgotten in our Ashantee life; after a sleepless night we rose and began to pack; about ten o'clock came the prince's boy to announce the indisposition of his master, who would be unable to join us till the evening; he took one of our packages with him, which greatly excited our people, who did not like the change; declared the elders did not wish us in the town, and in their anger, tried to persuade the king to withdraw his permission. Two of them started for Coomassie; but Isaiah viii. 10, was now exemplified, "Take counsel together, and it shall come to nought."

The prince, though unable to come himself, kindly sent us a number of Fantees to help to carry our few things, and as we accompanied them to the gate to prevent further hindrance, our two soldiers were seen returning more quiet and subdued than we had ever known them before. They allowed the packages to pass without a frown, and at six o'clock the prince arrived. He told us he had been accused of disobeying orders, and bringing the white men into the town by day; he indignantly denied the charge, upon which it was affirmed that the luggage was being carried across; he was highly displeased, and perceived his mistake in having provided us with bearers from his own people, so he at once told our soldiers they must do the rest of the work unaided. This explained the crest-fallen looks we had observed.

When the moon had risen, the prince gave the signal to start, placing my wife in his sedan chair, and following with ourselves just behind her. We soon reached the stream which surrounds the town, and in fifteen minutes more, the old mission-house stood before us. We passed through some fine open streets, but the houses were dilapidated, and the roads stony and uneven, so that the place struck us as inferior to Dwaben. On entering the mission-house, Mr. Watts, the master, and Mr. Lindsay, the constable of Cape Coast, both in European dress, shook us warmly by the hand, and wished us God's blessing. Cæsar, and other Fantees who were sitting with them, we greeted after the fashion of the country, and we were then conducted into another building within the court-yard, where the prince's rooms and our own were side by side. After our miserable grass huts, they seemed to us like a palace, but sweeter far was it to realise that we were with friends and brethren, and we knelt to unite in offering praise to Him who had wrought so wonderfully for us; for until it was actually accomplished, we had scarcely dared to hope this removal would pass so quietly.

But all was not over yet; before the prince had time to report progress to the king, Bosommuru entered, followed by several men with torches, bringing as we hoped, a congratulation from his majesty. But alas! his message was of a different nature: it appeared the king was now convinced it was a mistake to introduce important people like ourselves into the town by night. His elders would disapprove of it, and we must therefore immediately return to the wood till, after counsel with the chiefs, he could give us a public reception. We were thunderstruck; Mr. Watts, who had been longing for our arrival, placed in the strongest light the effect of such treatment on us, and the bad example it would be to the population. The prince expressed extreme surprise, and I broke forth in determined remonstrance.

"The king," said I, "has declared we should get ill if we remained in the wood; if he send us back it is like saying, should you be ill that does not matter. My poor wife has just found comfort again: if we return, our position will be worse than before. Tell his Majesty that it is not because we will not, but because we cannot eat,* we are too deeply grieved; our trouble is too great, yet our innocence is well known. The king must have pity on us and allow us to remain here,"

While high words were going on between the bystanders, Bosommuru consented to take our message to the king, and he had no sooner left us than we once more fell on our knees, entreating the Lord, in whose power are the hearts of all men, to show Himself strong in our behalf in this our extremity; yet we sought grace to say, "His will be done." Our minds were calmed; we took a little refreshment, and patiently waited the effect of our appeal. In due time Bosommuru returned; "His Majesty," said he, "permits you to remain, but will be unable to give you a public reception for the present. You are not therefore to go beyond the yard, and the prince must have all the doors locked, that no one may come in." We were filled with joy; a new life opened before us; and a third time we knelt in thanksgiving to Him who had thus put honour on our weak faith.

Mr. Watts had been nine years in Coomassie, labouring in the service of the Wesleyan Missionary Society, and for the last four had been prevented from communicating with the Coast, and had lived on the little money given him by the king at the feasts. The mission-house was fast falling into decay, the blocked up state of the roads

* To refuse food is the only way in which you can make an Ashantee feel you are really in earnest.

making repair impossible, the roof was in holes, the floors rotten, and the whole place scarcely habitable. The lower storey, being the best part, was used for a chapel and store-house; our rooms were in the right wing, where were also those of the catechist and some workmen.

The kindness of our host was extreme, the prince himself made arrangements for our table, and we enjoyed better food than we had thought procurable in Ashantee. We slept again on bedsteads, though without bedding; my wife's spirits revived, and we were almost tempted to think ourselves stationary. Most earnestly did we pray that we might shine as lights in the surrounding darkness.

But though the prince exerted himself in every way for our comfort, we were obliged to remind the king how much we were inconvenienced for want of money, especially as we were told that the prince and Mr. Watts were soon to leave us to be present at an exchange of prisoners on the Prah, December 20th. We wondered how this could take place, while *we* still remained captives. The whole proceeding was involved in mystery, and we daily needed the grace of patience to sustain our fainting spirits. We took care to obey to the letter the king's orders, so on our first Sabbath in the mission-house we contented ourselves with reading together in our own rooms, much as we longed to enjoy the little service conducted by our kind friends.

The next day, Monday, was fixed for our public reception by the king. Bosommuru came to announce this, telling us at the same time to keep up our courage, as we should probably hear rough words from the unmannerly town's people. Mr. Watts too seemed anxious about us, and considerately had the door guarded to prevent any of the savage Ashantees from entering, knowing their customs and their fearful cruelties. Often did they blunt their knives to increase the sufferings of their poor victims, or cut pieces out of the neck of the man they were about to behead; at the same time they were full of superstition, and would throw palm-wine on the ground, and from the figures it formed prognosticate the future.

At four o'clock, a royal messenger with gold-hilted sword came to escort us to the king. Clad in our best attire, white trousers, &c., we made ourselves look as well as we could. Mr. Watts and the prince could not accompany us, as they had to take their position near his majesty. We were received in the market place by our former chief from Duro, and Ageana with our soldiers all in full military costume; the dresses were beautiful, even Ageana wore silk, and was far too proud to notice us. We were then led for an hour and a half through narrow streets and bye-ways, and at last brought into the midst of a crowd, here we waited a long time in the most intense heat, though happily the prince's forethought had provided us with chairs.

At length the approach of a stately man covered with golden ornaments, and his head adorned with fans of eagle's wings, warned us that the grand event was near; making his way through the throng he led us before the king, but though we were surrounded by the aristocracy of Coomassie, so rough was the scene, that my wife's hat was torn off as she bowed before his majesty. Then retiring some distance, we took our seats under the shade of a large tree, and awaited the saluations from the grandees in return; some were very friendly, while others, among them Opoko (one of the linguists to whom we gave the name of Pharisee), would not take our offered hand; it was easy to see that the chiefs were at variance among themselves. Two men then came and danced like maniacs, with drawn swords, apparently trying to frighten us, while their servants were very insulting, screaming in our faces, and pretending to cut off our heads.

The king's chairs were very curious, and quite new to us. About twenty of them were of mixed Ashantee and European workmanship, and had one or two bells, reminding us of the cow-bells of our beautiful Switzerland; although finely ornamented they were all stained black with human blood. The real throne is a chair of the country, about four hundred years old, so patched with golden wire and plates that the original wood is scarcely visible. An immense umbrella is carried over it, and not until he has taken his seat in this chair is a new sovereign looked upon as king.

As his majesty was carried past us he saluted us pleasantly, and then began a war-dance. He waved his sword most gracefully in every direction except towards us ; he next took a gun, inlaid with silver, with which he went through the same manœuvres, laughing and nodding at us. This the prince explained afterwards, was a great honour. Over him was held the most beautiful of his umbrellas, of red and black velvet, and laced with gold.* He, like most of his chiefs, was clothed in calico, the symbol of mourning, no doubt on account of the war. It was quite night when we arrived at home, by a short road which brought us in ten minutes from the spot which had taken an hour and a half to reach in the morning. As we passed along the people followed, screaming and shouting: "Enemies," they cried, "you shall all be killed! Oh, you fools!" How thankful were we that this dreaded reception was over.

We were told various stories of the doings on such occasions. The following may be taken as a sample of the cruel tastes of this savage people. On one occasion

* It is the same umbrella which is now in the museum at South Kensington.

the British ambassador was being received with great magnificence, when a man dying on a rack was carried past, as if by accident; another time—March, 1869—the messenger of Mr. Simpson was ceremoniously greeted, when the bloody head of a man who had just been beheaded was placed before him. Prince Ansa, who was then present, angrily struck the bearer to the ground.

We had much to learn in this strange capital. On the 18th of December the great Adae or feast was held, when we were expected to go with the prince and Mr. Watts to the hall in Deabo Street, and sit while the procession passed, that we might salute the king. This feast-day occurred every fortieth day, and was followed in eighteen or twenty more by the little Adae. About six days before each, the king retired into his palace, after having drunk palm wine in the midst of all his chiefs, while two men stood by shooting arrows into the air;* on the feast day itself, he appeared in the streets, gave gold dust to the chiefs and strangers, and treated them to wine. Before he left the palace, he visited the two buildings containing the chairs of the former kings, fourteen in number. The bones of these ancient worthies repose in Bantama. Their chairs of state the king sprinkled with rum. This over, he proceeded to the appointed place Mogyawe (meaning the blood dries), his ministers and chiefs preceding him, amid the wildest music.

On this occasion many saluted us, and some even danced before us; a few had iron chains round their necks, which at the end of the dance, they laid hold of with their teeth: the king's sixty fetishes were carried before him. Recognizing us he smiled, and commenced

* At these palm wine festivals, which generally took place at the street called Dweboanda (meaning the flint-stone never sleeps), we, like all strangers, were obliged to be present and pay our respects to his majesty; as a reward we received a jar of the wine.

his war-dance with sword and gun; the executioners making ominous signs, were similarly engaged behind him. We followed to the place of greeting, where a dreadful crowd had gathered, crying out, "They shall all be killed," but the presence of the prince checked their rage.

Having at last succeeded in paying our respects to his majesty, we retired to our chairs to receive the customary presents. The prince had four dollars given him, Mr. Watts three, and ourselves nine, together with a small bottle of brandy, which we gave to our soldiers, who were constantly forcing themselves upon us in hope of obtaining something. Nine dollars for four persons was little enough, and yet it was all we had to live on until the little Adae, twenty-three days later, if our expected boxes from the Prah did not arrive sooner. The day after, we went to meet and thank his majesty, as he returned from his accustomed visit to Bantama, before he passed on to Amanghyia, where he allowed himself a rest of forty days, until the next Adae came round.

From the various accounts which reached us of the king's daily habits, we gathered that, like the Africans generally, he took but two meals a day, and ate but little of the many dishes set before him. Chicken, mutton, and especially pork, are his favourite viands. He eats alone at a beautifully wrought table in the court of the palace, but surrounded by his chiefs. At a distance stands his head cook (a golden spoon attached to his umbrella being the sign of his calling), incessantly stirring with a long fork the contents of the dish of which his majesty was partaking; another attendant meanwhile rehearses in loud tones his royal master's virtues; and when he happens to be in a good humour, he sometimes throws a chicken or a piece of meat to his courtiers, that he may enjoy seeing the scramble which ensues. Each of the king's kra,* about a thousand in number, carries a gold plate upon his breast. All their money and jewellery, as well as that of thousands more, belong to the king; indeed, most of the free people in Coomassie are so connected with the palace, that they bear the title of chiefs, and fulfil a particular office, and when they die their property goes to the monarch. The vassal states pay their tribute in slaves, cotton, silk, sandals, oxen, &c. Thus the king's riches are increasing continually.

A court is held every day but Friday, to which all have free access. A person accused of crime is put in irons until the trial, when he is brought forward before witnesses. If the testimony is deemed insufficient, the accusing party takes his oath; if the accused then swear his innocence, he has to undergo a kind of ordeal; being obliged to chew a piece of odum wood, and afterwards to drink a pitcher of water. If no ill effects follow, he is reckoned guilty and must die, but if he become sick he is set at liberty, and the accuser dies instead. A murderer is beheaded after the most cruel tortures, as described at page 127.

On January 26th one of these trials took place. A rich heathen went to a mohammedan and asked him to bless his fortune. The moslem declined, saying the money had been acquired wrongly, and would soon be lost. A quarrel ensued, and the two men parted vowing never to speak to each other again. Some weeks passed when the rich man's slaves again visited the mohammedan with the same request, *i.e.*, that he would bless their master's wealth. The moslem declared, that notwithstanding his vow the rich man had sent his slaves to

---

* A kind of spies; literally the king's souls; meaning that they are to die when he dies; they are therefore very careful to report to their master anything which might be injurious to him.

him; this the latter denied, and a worse quarrel followed, in which the moslem called his enemy a liar and a deceiver. The Ashantee upon this took the great oath of the king that he was innocent, the other did the same; then followed the test. The Ashantee drank a large quantity of odum water, which caused him to swell fearfully, and he soon became sick. With a cry of joy the whole multitude rushed upon the mohammedan, dragging him to the block, where he was shortly afterwards beheaded.

The following are a few of the laws which were in force in Coomassie while we were detained there, the breach of which was occasionally punished with death.

1. No drop of palm oil is, on any account, to be spilled in the streets.
2. No egg must be allowed to fall and break in the streets.
3. No one may smoke a European pipe in the streets.
4. No such pipe may be carried with a burden.
5. No burden packed in green palm branches may be carried in the town.
6. No one may whistle in Coomassie.
7. Every one is to hide himself when the king's eunuchs call.
8. No work is to be done in any plantation on a Thursday.
9. Nothing is ever to be planted in Coomassie.
10. No pair of cocoah sandals may be worn in the palace. (These sandals are made of horse hide; the price of them is cocoah or sixpence.)

After witnessing such scenes as we have described, our joy and comfort in retiring to the quiet mission-house can be conceived. On Sunday, December 18th, we had the happiness of attending the little service in company with sixteen others, and ten people from the town. Mr. Watts spoke to us from Eccles. ix. 12—"For man knoweth not his time "—and also from Is. xxx. 15—" In quietness and confidence shall be your strength." We needed the lesson, for all around us was unstable to the last degree.

On the evening of the 19th, the king took his seat so near the mission-house that we could not avoid saluting him, and we had the honour of sitting near prince Ansa, and within twenty yards of the sovereign. We supposed he had ordered this meeting for the purpose of drinking palm wine, two jars of which were sent to us. This however was not his only object, for as he sat, about eighteen people advanced in procession before him, laden with presents, a tribute from the prince of Asini; and this occurred only three weeks after Asini had sworn allegiance to the British Protectorate. Several dozens of rum, liqueur, champagne, and some beautiful silk stuff made up these presents. As soon as they had been delivered, about a hundred women, in three groups, appeared on the scene, splendidly adorned and not wanting in grace, with white circles painted round their eyes, supposed to enhance their beauty. The king seemed very happy, and congratulated us on looking well. He promised to send prince Ansa an antelope, which really arrived the next day. During the time of rest, presents of these animals are constantly coming from the surrounding chiefs, who are in return supplied with gunpowder. The prince, who had to make a present, offered a bronze case of lavender water, upon which he received nine dollars in gold dust, and a second antelope.

Christmas came, and found us in a far better position than we had been the previous year. I preached God's word for the first time in Coomassie (from John iii. 16), and felt that I was again at a mission station. How I longed to speak the Tshi more fluently and correctly; however, the people said they understood me. Unhappily, during the service the king's band, sent by his Majesty with congratulations "to cheer our hearts on this festival," interrupted us with their drums, clarionets, and cymbals—an honour we would gladly have foregone—continuing their performance till five in the evening, when we gave them some dinner and a few small coins. I was afterwards attacked with fever, which did not leave me till the beginning of the new year. Notwithstanding my illness, I went with my party to see the king (December 29th) in Amanghyia. The royal messenger, Kwabena, who called us, allowed no time for breakfast, some goods having just arrived; and in consequence of this unnecessary haste we had to wait for the interview two hours in the heat.

The king sat in a yard of the extensive two storied villa; and in front of him stood seven chests addressed to us, which were opened, and an inventory taken of their contents. There were some composite candles which pleased him greatly, and he took possession of half of them. I got an alpaca dress for my wife, under protest, because she really needed it; of ten other pieces of material, his majesty took six, of course the best. They were beautiful he said, and he would give us gold for them. We were to receive a benna of gold dust, equal to thirty-two dollars, but when it arrived, fully an eighth was wanting. Almost all the things we had ordered, with the exception of shoes for me, came. Prince Ansa's wife sent her husband an umbrella; and fourteen ounces of gold dust were given us in a sealed packet.

When I asked the king if I might order some shoes from Christiansborg, he said prince Ansa and Mr. Watts would see to that, as they were going to the Coast next week. The prince plainly said he did not believe it; whereupon the king offered to bet that he would obtain leave to depart on Saturday. He then gave us another sheep and two suas of gold dust, and handed us three letters. Two were from the administrator, who begged us to have compassion on M. Bonnat, and alluded to the Franco-German war, more particulars of which we learned from the accompanying papers. The excitement of the day was too much for me, and violent fever supervened.

Presents had now to be made; first to the king's chamberlain who had opened the chests, next to our former people, who complained that we had not taken them with us to the king; and lastly to the bearers. We closed the year with a social tea and a midnight service; we conversed and prayed most earnestly that we might celebrate the close of the coming year with our friends, and we did not forget to supplicate peace for poor France.

On New Year's day, 1871, came a present of yams, and four dollars, with which some friends had kindly planned to surprise us, but nothing more was said of the prince's departure, so the king lost his wager. We were not much concerned at the delay, for though we knew he would do his best for us at the Coast, we could scarcely imagine how we should get on in Coomassie without him. Not only did our former people cling to us like limpets, but they were commissioned by Bosommuru, to keep the Ashantees from annoying us, so that all our efforts were vain to resist their officious interference.

On the return of the king from his villa, January 5th, 1871, we welcomed him at the usual place of reception, and then saw, among other wonderful things, his Fetish, which he worships every Tuesday. It consists merely of a small box covered with gold and silver, round which the Kitebund dance. After his majesty had received our salutations, he retired into the palace, whence he would not come forth until the little Adae on the 12th of the month.

A tremendous blowing of horns on the night of the 6th

announced, as we thought, a great conflagration; the cause, however, was an eclipse of the moon, which the mohammedans have taught the people to believe can only be removed by their prayers: on this day therefore they were loaded with presents. In the morning we again heard the dreadful sound which betokened an execution—this time that of a thief.

Prince Ansa had made repeated attempts to gain the ear of the king on our behalf, and at length he succeeded in reaching him in his retirement. He first requested that we might be entirely freed from our former people. Bosommuru opposed, but the queen-mother took our part on hearing how ill they behaved to us. He then pleaded for my wife, who had none of the care and comforts she was now specially needing. She was very unwilling to leave me, but I earnestly wished that she might be allowed to accompany the prince to the Coast. The king however declined to let her go on some trifling pretext, but promised that some of our former property should be brought us from Totorase.

On January 12th, the little Adae was celebrated, and the king, again visited the buildings which contained the chairs of the deceased monarchs. Ten sheep were killed and cooked for them, after which his majesty sprinkled the chairs with their blood, "to serve the spirits." We paid our respects in the third court of the palace, and received the customary nine dollars from Bosommuru.

A rumour was set afloat at the court, that my wife was the daughter of Mrs. Bannerman, originally an Ashantee princess, married in the war of 1836 to a mulatto, who was thought to be a deadly enemy of the Ashantees; and it was added that Dompré had lost his life in his enthusiastic efforts to procure her liberty. There had been so much silly talk on the subject, that we desired to know what the king had to say. For the first time in his life, prince Ansa was permitted to speak with his majesty in the presence of his torch-bearers only, who were quite boys.

When this gossip was mentioned, the king laughed and said, "if Mrs. R.'s mother had been an Ashantee woman, she would have had curly hair and a different nose." Ansa then took the opportunity to speak of the shameful way in which we had been entrapped and subsequently treated, but the only reply he received was, "Yes, Ageana is certainly a wicked man, and the soldiers will have nothing more to do with them."

"But what about Adu Bofo?" continued the king, "have they an accusation to bring against him when he returns?" "Very likely," said Ansa, and then asked if Mrs. R. was not to accompany him to the Coast, at which the king laughed, but said nothing.

The prince then asked if it was true that other white men had been taken prisoners, and were coming to Coomassie. The king replied that there was some foundation for the report, but that he had ordered the captives to be set free. We afterwards found that the missionaries, Merz and Müller, of the North German Mission, although on British territory, and under the protection of the allies, had escaped with difficulty, not by command of the king, but by the prompt aid of the negroes of Keta. It was very difficult to reconcile the conflicting rumours, but we could at least rejoice that no more brethren were coming to share our misery.

A strange interruption occurred on the following Sunday (January 15th), by the entrance of Bosommuru as we were commencing our service. Being invited to stay and listen he sat down, but interrupted the prince at every sentence, loudly explaining all for the benefit of his followers. When others entered, he called out "prince, do you allow people to come here like this, when you are worshipping God?" After the service, he announced the cause of his visit, which was to inform us that a new delay had arisen in the transporting our goods from Totorase, no doubt the fault of the interpreter Nantshi, who would have liked to appropriate them. The following Sunday (January 22nd), he came again, when I had the opportunity of speaking before him on our Lord's words, "Go ye into all the world," &c.

The feast of the king's household fetish, lasted ten days, when chickens and sheep were sacrificed; goats were brought for the same purpose, and kept in a hamlet near the town, although they are usually strictly forbidden throughout the whole country.

On the first day the king danced in front of a house near us, the birth-place of one of his ancestors. Prince Ansa declined to be present on such occasions; but on the 20th, when this dance was repeated, his majesty sent for us; Rosa, however, remained at home, being unable to bear the noise. We found the king surrounded by his chiefs, dancing with a quiver on his back covered with gold, and a richly ornamented velvet cap on his head. He sprang backwards and forwards, flourishing sword and gun, and looking continually at us, evidently desiring our admiration. He kept very good time to the music, which was performed by a band in the centre of the group. He dances really well, but wildly, so that some of his people surround him with outstretched arms in case his foot should slip.

But as to his followers, their dance surpasses in savageness everything which can be imagined; if one can fancy a number of men in all possible and impossible positions, flitting about in noisy confusion, and so mingled together as to remind one of a band of demons, you have them before you. Yet they kept wonderfully good time. Still, however frequently one may witness such scenes, there is something not only startling but awful in them.

Nothing more was said about the journey to the coast till the night of January 23rd, when the king sent for the prince and Mr. Watts. Letters had arrived from the English authorities thanking the king for sending back several Fantees, and expressing the hope that he would keep his word, and give the Europeans their liberty as soon as his general had returned. Should he, however, be delayed, it was hoped the king would inform the governor in order that he might hurry Adu Bofo back over the Volta. As regarded Elmina, the Dutch governor denied that the fort had been bought by the Ashantees, or that money had ever been received for it. On this point the king could satisfy himself by sending a messenger to enquire.

It was very painful to him (the governor) to find that the king did not keep his word with regard to the exchange of the prisoners. Again and again he had promised and Major Brownell had waited long and patiently. They had begged the king to recall his army from Akwamu, instead of which he had re-formed it. The governor then drew his majesty's attention to the danger of such conduct, but added that if the king would at once send the Fantees back with prince Ansa, all would yet be well, and peace would be proclaimed throughout the whole territory. If he still refused, Major Brownell would be recalled with his prisoners. Ten days was the longest time which could be allowed to consider this proposal.

The prince strongly advised the king to accept the offer of peace, speaking in the highest terms of the patience the English had manifested throughout, and expressing his sense of shame at the constant vacillation, excuses, and unfaithfulness of his country. He also put in a word for

I

my wife, whereupon Bosommuru interrupted, saying, "The elders will not have it." "What do I care for the elders?" answered the prince. Further experience, however taught us that the opinion of these worthies is of great weight, and we were prevented by it from having an audience of the king.

On the 31st, prince Ansa received his message to the English ambassador—" His majesty regretted not having officially announced to him that he, Kofi Kari Kari, had ascended the Ashantee throne in 1867, and that a messenger had repeatedly started for the coast, but had been driven back by fear of robbers. Some Akems had recently taken some Ashantees prisoners, and even killed them; he would therefore like to know whether Akem was under the British Protectorate."

At the prince's request the interpreters wrote these messages down, but our affairs were not mentioned. Presents of dresses and gold were given to him and his followers, and at his earnest entreaty seventy eggs and four pounds of rice were added for our use. A poor Asen negro, who two years before had been severely punished for secretly selling gunpowder, would then have been killed but for the prince's intercession. Now that prince Ansa was about to leave Coomassie, the chief executioner claimed him as his property, saying, "only Fantees are set free." Again, the entreaties of the prince prevailed, and the poor trembling man was delivered.

The prince invited us to accompany him on his farewell visit to the king. Brother K. was too ill to go, but M. Bonnat and myself agreed to his request. Passing through the seven courts leading to the palace, we found the king in the eighth, sitting under the arcades, which were tastefully decorated—he was almost enclosed by them, and was quite in *dishabille;* six boys stood before him bearing torches. He was very merry, saying to the

Fantees around him, "Go home now, and tell your countrymen to forget the past, and to think of something new and better—peace."

I then addressed his majesty, thanking him for the presents, and added that I had laid my case before the elders, and could not understand why they had not deigned to answer me. I also said I could take no future responsibility, but would rest content, knowing I had done my duty.

His majesty listened patiently, and said I was to make myself easy, as Adu Bofo would soon come back. Immediately after the little Adae, the jaw bones of the fallen enemies would arrive,* and a week or two after the great Adae, the general himself would follow. Then, as soon as prince Ansa came back, we might go to the Coast.

On February 1st, we eagerly began to pack up. The prince had left four of his servants with us—an old, infirm upper servant, who could do little but give orders to the others, a woman but recently confined, from whom we could not expect much; our chief dependence was on Caesar, who looked after the kitchen, and a little girl who was to attend on my wife.

The prince left early on the morning of the 2nd, and Mr. Watts followed two days later with the other Fantees. How heavy were our hearts at this parting. Brother K's health was terribly shaken, and when I begged Bosommuru to send two boys to help us, he said ironically, looking at the poor invalid, "Yes, pray to your God to make him well again." I replied, "our God can make him well to-

---

* Before the return of the army, the general in command sends to the capital, the jaw bones of the slain enemies. His own return cannot take place till forty days after these have been received. While in the camp, we ourselves witnessed the drying and smoking of these bleeding trophies.

day, if it be His will; but it may also be His will to let him suffer longer; at anyrate, all the Ashantees have to say about it is, that they have tortured the innocent, and have caused the death of our child. It is true our God is long-suffering, but He will not always be mocked."

CHAPTER XVI.

TIMES OF SICKNESS AND FORSON'S EMBASSY.

THE departure of the prince inaugurated a new order of things with us, for in him we had lost our housekeeper, adviser, and the manager of our purse. Our sorrow was deepened by the increasing indisposition of brother K., who could only take rice soup and chicken, and who in his depression would sometimes pray he might be released from his sufferings.

The most dreadful of the Ashantee festivals, Bantama, or "death wake," now approached. The king went early in the morning of February 5th, to Bantama, where the remains of his deceased predecessors were preserved in a long building, approached by a gallery, and partitioned into small cells, the entrances of which were hung with silken curtains. In these apartments reposed the skeletons of the kings, fastened together with gold wire, and placed in richly ornamented coffins, each being surrounded by what had given him most pleasure during his life. On this occasion every skeleton was placed on a chair in his cell to receive the royal visitor; who, on entering, offered it food; after which a band played the favourite melodies of the departed. The poor victim selected as a sacrifice, with a knife thrust through his cheeks, was then dragged forward and slain, the king washing the skeleton with his blood. Thus was each cell visited in turn, sacrifice after sacrifice being offered, till evening closed ere the dreadful round was completed.

We had heard the blowing of horns and beating of drums throughout the day, and were told that nearly thirty men had been slain. These alas! were not all, for at six o'clock after the king had returned, the horn and the drum again sounded, betokening that more victims were yet to fall, and far into the night the melancholy sound continued. Two blasts of the horn signified "death! death!" three beats of the drum, "cut it off!" and a single beat from another drum, announced "the head has dropped!" Powerless as we were, amid the fearful darkness around, to hinder such atrocities, we could only sigh and pray that our captivity might bring about a better state of things.

We had now to endure much discomfort, being unable to obtain the merest trifles, such as rice for our poor invalid, and salt which we could not buy, without long delay, while thefts were of daily occurrence in our unprotected premises, even boards and benches being abstracted, neither were the promised lads sent to our help. We heard nothing further of the return of the army; on the contrary, fresh troops were despatched to strengthen Adu Bofo's hands. Kind messages often reached us from the prince, and frequent presents from the Coast assured us that we and our needs were not forgotten by our friends there. When I next paid my respects to the king, a violent storm of wind scattered the people, turning the large umbrellas inside out. I caught cold, and was soon laid low by fever, so that on the great Adae, March 12th, M. Bonnat alone was present. The king's physician was sent to attend me, but his green pepper soup failed to relieve me. I became worse, and longed for European medicine. The report of my increasing illness brought his majesty to my bedside in great haste, and that too at three o'clock, the hour when he usually slept. He was surprised at my unusual colour, and said, sympathisingly, to poor Rosa, "You have, indeed, much trouble, white woman." I seized the opportunity to tell him I had lived too long in Africa; that my illness made a change to the Coast necessary, and I entreated him to hasten our departure. He bade me take courage, promising to send a messenger with letters to my friends. He then paid Kühne a visit, to whom his physician daily brought rice soup, mixed with fish and vegetable.

The excitement of this interview, heightened the fever, so that I feared I might be leaving my poor wife desolate in this barbarous land; but I rallied through God's mercy, though I suffered long from extreme weakness.

Meanwhile, the long expected exchange of prisoners took place on the Prah. Of our party, only M. Bonnat could be present at the reception, on March 20th, of the seventy-six Ashantees. The general joy was so great, that many of the chiefs danced, and the liberated hastened to shake hands with M. Bonnat, while parents and friends thanked the king by a loud shout. The warm heart of the Frenchman sympathised deeply with them, and some day, we trusted a similar festival was in store for us, though it approached very slowly. A letter from the prince stated that the exchange of prisoners had taken place on the 2nd, and one of the returned captives said, that he had not resumed his journey until five days later, so that we knew not when we might expect his return, and our life was more dismal than it is possible to describe.

We had just retired to rest on Sunday evening 26th, when the death horn woke us, and in the morning we heard that the king had danced with his wives. On these occasions, human life is always sacrificed. The best band of music, called the Kete, is stationed at some distance, no *man* being permitted to approach. The instruments are small drums covered with black and red checked cloth, flutes and calibashes of different sizes, in which beans or small stones are rattled, to mark the time. The king seldom dances this Kete dance, but when he does, many shudder who are usually indifferent. On the night which followed this painful entertainment, we were alarmed by two thieves, and though a lamp was burning in K's room, our salt bottle was stolen. Cæsar met in the yard one of the rogues carrying a torch, which he threw down and fled. In the morning we found our saucepan broken, and our only chicken minus a head, which the scamp had bitten off. It was then announced by the town-crier, that any one stealing our property in future, should be killed.

Brother K. was still very weak. His two physicians meeting one day to consult at his bedside, quarrelled so violently that the poor invalid jumped out in a frenzy, and begged to be allowed to die in peace, while I urged his being sent to the Coast as the most effective restorative. When I begged earnestly for chickens, offering to pay for them, the king laughed and promised. His thoughts were occupied with the return of a chief laden with presents, a small race-horse being the most acceptable. He had been sent two years before to Scram, a tract of country to the north, a tributary of Ashantee, and on his arrival danced several times before his majesty.

Brother K. struggled through, by God's help, spite of the non-appearance of the chickens, and at length gradually recovered; but we still had anxiously to wait for news from the Coast, and at the little Adae were not present, though we received the customary nine dollars through Bosommuru.

On Sunday, April 8th, new horrors were perpetrated. The king went to Bantama to repair the roof of the royal burial-place, which had been injured in the late storm.

Every ceremony connected with this building was accompanied by the shedding of human blood, to appease the wrath of the deceased kings. On this occasion the cheeks of three poor boys were perforated with knives on the usual plan, and their hands were bound behind them. This fearful cruelty was lightly spoken of as a very common thing.

Such victims are mostly criminals, but how trifling often was the offence. Every one who used the king's oath, or spoke rudely of the royal house, was laid in irons. If a poor Odonko negro, in a fit of home sickness, tried to escape from his cruel master, he was caught and chained. Thus there were always a number of these doomed creatures ready, for once chained they were seldom pardoned, though it was in the power of the king to set any of them free.

Notwithstanding this severity crime was universal, and the ignorant degraded people sported like children with the king of terrors. If his majesty, who alone had power to inflict capital punishment, remitted the sentence, a heavy fine was exacted, and the nose, ears, or lips of the culprit were cut off. It was by no means uncommon for an executioner to be bribed by a young warrior that he might be allowed to try his hand on the next culprit.

On Easter Sunday, to my great disappointment, no one from the town appeared at our service. The people excused themselves by saying the king had forbidden them to come— he had only forbidden them to *steal* from us. I regretted this misapprehension (if such it was) and invited them again to visit us, especially on Sundays. We were summoned to the palace on Monday morning, and found the king in the court of justice. Seeing us, Opoku called out, "Susse, come and sit here." I went and had Major Brownell's letter given me to translate. He alluded to the return of the seventy-six Ashantee prisoners, stating who had died, adding that others who had run away should be sent back when caught. He then expressed the hope that his majesty would carry out his intention of coming to terms of peace, and permit the missionaries to go to Cape Coast as he had promised. But alas! we were dismissed with a bottle of rum; and our renewed request for lads to help us was simply met by the usual fair promises.

A few days later (15th) Bosommuru informed us that a "European" had arrived at the Prah, sent by the governor to look after us; and he then brought us the long promised "serving boys." Three prisoners of war, Kwabena Mensa, a boy of nine, Kwabena Oposo, a youth of sixteen, and a woman of thirty-five, all sadly wasted and very quiet, had also arrived. They were shy at first, but after eating a palm-oil fufu became cheerful. Bosommuru then announced a visit from the king, and commanded that our court-yard should be swept for the occasion.

A heavy storm of rain was scarcely over when his majesty appeared, attended by numerous followers. He inspected everything in our rooms, and pronounced us comfortably settled; then entering the chapel he exclaimed, "it is beautiful here!" We told him it was the place for worshipping our God, and that we met every Sunday to pray and to read from our books; he listened, but made no remark. We thanked him for sending us the promised servants, which seemingly reminded him of another old promise, for a present of five chickens appeared shortly after.

On April 18th, a meeting was held in the court of justice to receive Mr. Forson, the messenger from the English government. The grandees were quite excited, dancing and drinking as usual. Joseph, the christian boy who had once accompanied the prince on a visit to us, came running from the crowd towards us, and we went forward to join in the general welcome and shake hands with the new arrival. The rooms allotted to Mr. Forson not being comfortable, he and Joseph took up their quarters with us, and though he was not hasty in revealing his plans, he seemed full of hope that he should soon be able to take us with him to the Coast, but we had been so often deceived and disappointed that we were afraid to indulge in such pleasant anticipations. The prince wrote to us frequently, but very cautiously, yet we believed it was through him that Mr. Forson had come to try and negotiate our deliverance. He appeared to be making his way; the king had given him one of the returned Ashantee prisoners as servant, to aid him in his communications with the Coast, and all the released captives appeared devoted to him.

The ambassador was anxious to announce his arrival to his friends at the Coast, and asked us to join him in sending a messenger. To this the king objected; not as he said on his own account, but his large family (the chiefs) did not understand such things; it would therefore be better for us to defer writing.

At the Adae, April 23d, Mr. Forson received the same sum as ourselves (nine dollars), and showed his thorough acquaintance with the customs of the country by distributing numerous presents to all the members of the king's household. The next day he entered very fully into his arrangements and plans regarding us, reading Mr. Ussher's letter to us. It began by thanking the king for every kindness shown us, but at the same time explained that we had nothing whatever to do with the war, and that we were neither British subjects or natives of the Protectorate. Our own governments, particularly the Prussian and Swiss, had interceded for our liberty, and he, Mr. Ussher, was commanded to use every means in his power to effect the same. Mr. Forson had therefore been sent to demand our freedom, and it was hoped the king would send us back with the ambassador. He also read us a letter from Brother Schrenk, in which he requested the release of my wife, and urged the fact that our mission had several times ransomed Ashantees or otherwise saved them, and always cherished the idea of extending the mission-work to Ashantee itself.

Days passed, and we heard nothing. At length a present for Mr. Forson, far handsomer than we had expected, arrived. It consisted of a cow, two sheep, food of all sorts, and £18 sterling of gold dust; but he failed to obtain an interview with his majesty, the same answer being returned to every application—"The king is very fond of you, but has no time." Kari-Kari was just then engrossed with an important domestic transaction. He had elevated one of his wives above all the rest, and had made her a present of six villages, with six hundred inhabitants. More than a hundred ounces of gold dust were given away on the occasion, and the legal arrangements were very important.

We were invited, with Mr. Forson, to visit the king's favourite minister, Sabeng, a man high in office. He showed us his treasure with great satisfaction, and his bed covered with rich European materials; but between the mattress and the bedstead, we observed several golden-handled daggers, while the caps of half a dozen executioners were hanging on the wall. In a yard outside were some seventy Fetishes and charms, and large sheets of paper were covered with Arabic signs, and verses from the koran, &c. The mohammedans have great influence here, though they understand little of Arabic, simply reading and writing a few words like parrots. We understood the meaning of the daggers, when we heard the next day that this polite man not only had human beings sacrificed at a funeral, but had even beheaded one of the poor creatures himself! According to a horrible custom of this horrible country, the sons of the departed kill many of their villagers in the streets, until the king sends a message to stop the shedding of blood.

Mr. Forson still indulged hope of soon taking us away, and we had even begun quietly to make preparations; but the long desired interview with the king, damped our spirits. "As the affair about Akem and Elmina was not settled, and Adu Bofo could not be questioned as to whether and why he had plundered the Anum station, and under what circumstances we had been taken prisoners—nothing could be done until his return. All entreaties were vain, not even Mrs. R. could be set free." After thus using every available means to gain his point, Mr. Forson had to return alone, depressed and disappointed. Another present from the king soon followed; it consisted of gold dust, a coat, and five slaves. Among the latter was a man, valued at £7 15s. 0d., and two women with a young infant.*

Mr. Forson obtained a parting interview with the king, in which his majesty spoke very fairly. Adu Bofo had now received orders to return *immediately*, and if he did not obey instantly, he had better shoot himself. "Both the kings of Akem," continued he, "are acting equivocal parts; they are under your protection, but they let me know how gladly they would ally themselves to me, and surrender the heads of all those who shoot at the Ashantees."

Mr. Forson listened patiently, and then expressed his

---

* In reply to the request that my wife at least might be permitted to accompany Mr. Forson, the king said that it was impossible; but that in order to soften the disappointment, he intended to send her a musical box to enliven her spirits, and what more could we desire? In bitter vexation Mrs. R. exclaimed, "I am not a baby."

surprise that the king had given us such an insufficient supply of money. Whereupon followed fine promises. On May 22d, our visitor left us, and after the great excitement we had gone through, quietness was a relief. He had obtained some honey for my wife from the king, which supplied in some measure the want of sugar, while from the wax we were able to make candles. The prince's boy Joseph was still with us, waiting for the payment of twenty-three pieces of cloth, but detained, as he believed, for other reasons.

Rumours came from all sides; messengers were said to be on the way from Elmina; then it was reported the prince himself was near, or that an Ashantee chief was kept a prisoner at the Coast. It was then said that Adu Bofo's army was returning in a half-starved condition, and it was evident there was something yet to be explained, or my wife's entreaty for chickens would not have met with such prompt attention—four reaching us within a few days.

CHAPTER XVII.

THE EMBASSY OF MESSRS CRAWFORD AND PLANGE.

ON June 5th, a murderer with his hands bound behind him, a knife through his cheek, and two forks piercing his back, was dragged by a rope past our rooms. Others had been thus tortured already in various ways, the vital parts of the body not being wounded. Commencing at mid-day, the punishment increased in intensity till eight o'clock, when the poor wretch was gashed all over, his arms cut off, and himself compelled to dance for the amusement of the king before being taken to the place of execution. If he could not or would not dance, lighted torches were applied to his wounds; to escape this excessive torture he made the greatest efforts to move, until the drum was beaten and the head cut off. Some victims thus lost several of their limbs, or were pierced by an iron rod through the calves of both legs or other parts; and yet murders were far more frequent here than in the British protectorate.

We were taken by surprise on June 17th by a visit from Kokoo, the wife of R. Palm, one of the most distinguished women of Anum. She had been in Coomassie ten days, having been captured by the Ashantees in June 1869. Being afterwards seperated from Palm, she had had no intelligence of him for months—and only knew from us that he was in Coomassie. The king asked her if we had ever supplied the Anums with guns and ammunition, whereupon she told him *we* had never sold weapons.

Falling on her knees before us she entreated us to take

her in. She had not tasted food that day, and amongst the division of prisoners which had taken place, she alone remained behind. I felt how useful she would be to us, having always lived with Europeans, and knowing us so well. We therefore begged Bosommuru to speak to the king, and in about a fortnight she was given up to us, on condition that if we eventually went to the Coast, she was to remain behind. Thus at the right moment, what we so much needed was supplied, and at the same time a box from the coast with needful articles for my wife, arrived. Bosommuru was overwhelmed with astonishment that so much preparation should be made for an expected child.

The long looked for ambassadors now arrived. One of them, a Mr. Plange, sent by the Dutch governor, lodged in the town; the other, Mr Crawford, who had formerly resided in Coomassie as a Wesleyan teacher, occupied the prince's rooms, he being detained by illness, but he sent us a letter, and mentioned how he had been traduced by natives at Cape Coast; and Elmina, on account of his treaty with the king, and especially because of a letter which he had written to Elmina by his majesty's orders.

Mr Crawford brought not only peaceful assurances from the British colonial government, but powder, lead, and other implements of war, which had not been allowed over the border for three years. The governor also sent back to the king the Ashantee prisoners who were in Akem to show him that nothing stood in the way of friendly intercourse. He demanded in return that Adu Bofo should be recalled. Nothing was said concerning us in writing, as no doubt was felt at the Coast that Mr. Forson would take us back with him.[*]

---

[*] At the same time it must not be forgotten that the English Colonial Government always said, "The white men having been taken prisoners outside of the Protectorate, we have no *official* duty to them.

Privately however, the ambassador was commissioned to effect our freedom, and, if necessary, to offer a ransom. The chief, Akjampong, was to be set free as soon as the king had actually sent us off. If he hesitated, the way over the Prah was to be again blockaded.

The next day, July 2nd, was one of great rejoicing. Fifteen letters from our dear ones were handed to us in one packet; the dates spread over two years. Oh! how much they had suffered on our account, and how they had prayed for us in our distant home! They had for some time concluded we were dead, and had worn mourning for us. The king allowed us to reply to these letters; whether he would despatch our answers was another question. That the message of the Dutch ambassador also concerned us we learnt from what passed at his introduction to court, and still more during a visit which he paid us. Mr. Plange was a young man of very pre-possessing manners. He had remarked to the king how "green" we all looked, to which he replied, "he had feared the climate was injuring our health; but Adu Bofo," he added, "is coming soon."

The hope of a ransom evidently influenced the king more than he chose to confess, and he would wish it, he said, to be paid in arms and ammunition, so that to the English it might look like a present, while his people would consider it as a ransom.

Mr. Plange's chief business was to get an explanation from the king about Elmina. Twenty-four ounces of gold dust was the sum which his majesty had been accustomed to receive for himself from the Dutch, on account of the black men whom he sent them as recruits for Java. This sum the king had chosen to call "tribute," which greatly irritated the governor. Mr. Plange, the Dutch ambassador, was therefore to request him to withdraw the word; in

K

case of his refusal to do so, the payment would be discontinued.

To the little Adae (June 29th) the ambassadors were not invited, perhaps to save the usual presents. At the great Adae (July 16th) they received nine dollars each, as much as was divided among us four.

Between these negotiations, a day of rejoicing occurred on July 3rd, when nineteen loads of jaws arrived from the seat of war, as trophies of victory. Mr. Crawford alone was present at this fete; he described the prisoners carrying the remains of the enemy on poles, two chiefs' heads being borne in metal dishes, covered with a white cloth, and one of the bearers being painted on the chest and throat with red and white earth, to signify that he would be sacrificed at the end of the ceremony.

More than two thousand prisoners, mostly women and children, followed; they were accompanied by soldiers, who wore their hair rolled up in a peculiar fashion, to indicate that they were returning from victory. It was said the king had sent the prisoners food before their arrival in Coomassie, it being now so dear and scarce that they were likely to fare badly on their entrance. We were at this time eating maize instead of fufu.

A day of mourning followed on July 6th; the sounds of crying and howling being mingled with beating of drums and blowing of horns; while consolation was sought in large draughts of palm wine. The names of the fallen were called over, rightly or wrongly as the case might be, no accurate list of them having been kept. Everything was streaked with red earth, and Mr. Crawford found the king dancing in the market place, surrounded by red figures. Towards evening the death horn sounded to announce that fourteen prisoners were to be despatched for the fallen chiefs. Next morning I saw vultures greedily feasting on the sacrificed, their heads lying on a heap aside.

On July 18th, the king sent his sword-bearer to summon us to another festival at Atuatu, where we saw about a thousand prisoners from Krepi. Amongst them was every form of misery; the greater number had no other clothing than a rag round their waist. Two chiefs were carried along on men's shoulders, under red and blue umbrellas. The prisoners belonged to two towns which had long since surrendered; but notwithstanding this, these poor people had been dragged from their homes, and were equally divided between these two chiefs.

In passing, the monarch saluted me with his hand, and enquired why he had not seen me for some weeks past. When I explained that I could not leave my wife, as any fright might give her a shock, he laughed incredulously, and said I had better come to see him. The chiefs of Wusutra are said to have been bitterly disappointed by the division of their people, and stood howling in the market place; behaviour which will scarcely be allowed to pass unpunished.

The two ambassadors now wished to leave, but they were made to understand by different signs, that they were purposely detained. It was reported that the king would prepare Fetish, and go to Fantee after Adu Bofo's return, but Bosommuru informed Mr. Crawford that a circumstance had occurred which put a different face on the entire aspect of affairs.

"If a person comes into our kitchen and approaches the fire on which anything is being cooked and roasts a banana, is he not driven away or pierced through?" (an Ashantee proverb). This comparison is applied to Elmina, which fort the king declared belonged to him because, as he stated, his ancestors had paid, ages ago, nine hundred ounces of gold for it! When Akjampong made this statement to the Dutch governor, he was ordered to leave; and because he hesitated and remained a month longer, he was imprisoned. It was evident that the Ashantees sought to prevent the surrender of Elmina to the English. Opoku told Mr. Plange that about a hundred ounces of gold would be demanded as ransom for each of us, *i.e.*, £1440 for the four! Opoku after much delay gave us a bundle of newspapers, and told us there was nothing about Ashantee in them, only European news; he had convinced himself of this by looking into them.

On August 5th, Mr. Crawford came with a serious face; he had been insulted at the palace. The king seemed to have determined to accept the challenge of an Akem chief, Kofi Afua, as soon as Adu Bofo returned. The ambassador was desired to inform his master at Cape Coast, of his situation, and when he attempted to remonstrate, he was told, it was not for him to speak; as if an attack upon Akem was not, in fact, a declaration of war against the whole Protectorate. It was evident that the king wished to place the responsibility of war upon the governor.

At the same time Mr. Ussher, the administrator, gave notice to "his friend," that he was going to England on account of his health; until his return, Mr. Salmon would attend to all business matters, and meet the king half-way. What that meant was not clear, still we supposed that he meant to tell the king negotiations must be transacted on the Prah.

The Ashantee messenger Boating, who accompanied Mr. Forson to the coast, had invited the Wesleyan missionaries to return to the capital, perhaps only to throw dust in the eyes of the English. In consequence of this, Mr. Grimmer a missionary, now enquired whether the king would engage to send the children to school, if they would again occupy Coomassie? We afterwards heard from Basle that it had been proposed there, also to occupy the town as a mission station, in hope of facilitating our release. It would have been indeed a glorious revenge, if our captivity had brought about this fruit.

On August 14th, we were surprised by several visitors. First came Bosommuru, with Mr. Smith, a merchant from Anum, who was seized at the same time as Kokoo, and had been driven about unclad till supplied by the king with garments from our stores. They had sent him to us, because he had spoken of himself as belonging to us (and he had in truth often done business with us), he now stood before us sick and miserable, arrayed in my best black coat, my shoes, K.'s trousers, and my wife's straw hat! He is a prisoner in another house, but allowed to visit us, and when he came next to see us, he brought an old acquaintance whom the king had placed with him, Nils Palm, the husband of our Kokoo! People can imagine the joy of the pair at so unexpected a meeting. Palm had also been provided by the king with a complete suit of clothes.

Then appeared the servant of Prince Ansa, Robert Kwansa, with a letter from his master. And lastly, Asengso, who had once made friendly exertions for us, just returned from Cape Coast, to deliver thirty prisoners who had been held captive at Akem. The release of these and other Ashantees seemed to appease his majesty, and he wrote to the governor that if the chief before named kept himself quiet, all would be well, yet it was desirable that Forson should come again to Coomassie to settle other points.

Both the ambassadors now received their farewell gifts, a peredwane of gold dust each (£8), and two female slaves with a child and clothes. The queen mother and several of the chiefs also sent them presents, and nothing further hindered their departure. Mr. Crawford, however, wished to remain for the expected entrance of Adu Bofo, and of course gained the king's permission.

On June 29th, a box was broken open while we were assembled for prayer, and nine dollars worth of gold dust was stolen, whereupon we discharged the most guilty of the party. Out of our last package, we selected as a present for the king an English New Testament, and when Joseph presented it, he wished to look into it, but was hindered by his people, who said, "It is the Word of God, and had better remain unopened."

CHAPTER XVIII.

ADU BOFO'S ENTRY.

I HAVE already marked in my journal certain red letter days, which were to us like an oasis in the desert. Such an one was September 2nd of this year, when our weak faith was again strengthened gloriously by the birth of a little daughter. Mr. Plange was just leaving for the coast at the very time, and conveyed this happy intelligence to our kind friends there. Through the good offices of Bosommuru, and even the king himself, proper attendance, and a suitable nurse, had been provided, and our old friend, the wife of Palm, was with us.

In the afternoon of the same happy day, there was a grand muster of chiefs to receive Adu Bofo; the ceremony was described to us as very imposing, by brother K. and M. Bonnat, who accompanied Mr. Crawford to witness it. Ten thousand men marched past, while as many looked on; the highest noblemen were those from Dwabeng, Mampong, and Bekwae—the two first pressed the hand of brother K. The stately old prince of Mampong in mohammedan costume had two superb horses with Moorish saddles, and looked, with his flowing white beard, quite venerable; the chief of Tafo was also present. In the evening, Mr. Plange started.

On Monday the 4th, Crawford, M. Bonnat, and Kühne, went early to the market place where the army defiled from seven in the morning until night, during which time, chests containing the bones of the fallen chiefs, each surrounded by the wives of the deceased, were continually carried past. The chief who falls in battle is lightly buried, and water is poured on his grave many times a day, for some weeks. The bones thus becoming clean, are taken out and deposited in a chest, which, on this occasion, was covered with rich damask silk. The women besmeared with red, shrieked and howled fearfully. The chiefs who return alive, are likewise surrounded with women, who, decked in green foliage, dance around their husbands amid songs of joy.

The number of common soldiers who fall, is denoted by small sticks fastened to a pole, and carried by one of the company. On this occasion however, this was omitted, as they did not wish their heavy losses to be made prominent.

Our old friend the general, wore a small round cap, ornamented by buffalo's horns, and falcon's feathers, and was accompanied by his lieutenant, Nantshi. Before Adu Bofo was borne, the stolen bell from Ho, which for years called the people to service, was now rung again as the brightest trophy of the campaign. How the sound went to our hearts! making us long that church bells might soon send forth their invitation to the weary and heavy laden throughout Ashantee.

I went out for a few moments in the evening to get an idea of the review. It was really an imposing sight. The whole market place as far as Bantama, was crowded with people, and between them defiled the soldiers as far as the "Coom" tree, which gives its name to the town; under it the cluster of large umbrellas betokened the presence of the most important personages. As each company appeared before the king, they fired a salute, then turning round, marched back again in a second line to the place from whence they came. The hair of the majority was rough and shaggy, giving their heads the look of Medusas. Their costumes were by no means uniform; some wore blouses English fashion, others donned various pieces of European clothing, but they were mostly in native dress, rolled together under their cartridge pouches. The chiefs appeared in dirty red and yellow coats, ornamented with amulets, and many had caps of antelope skin decorated with feathers, gold plates and charms. The lookers on were mostly streaked with white or red paint, the red were the mourners, not a few of whom stood aside, crying and shrieking.

On September 7th, the report of the campaign was given to the king, and Adu Bofo was then honoured with many presents, and a visit from his majesty, who, accompanied by his chiefs, went to the end of the Market Place, where the army was drawn up. Kühne and M. Bonnat joined him there, and offered their hand to Adu and his officers. The first presents were twenty peredwane of gold dust, £162, three gold bracelets, two large umbrellas, twenty sheep, twenty loads of salt, twenty kegs of brandy, with several other things.

There followed, of course, a day of mourning for the slain of Coomassie, which was kept in every village throughout the land. Three great chiefs (one of them prince Ansa's brother) having fallen, it was necessary to send a considerable retinue after them into the other world, so that the shrieks of the mourners were heard all day, and the sounds of the horns and drums were unceasing. Most of the inhabitants fasted, and were painted red, while so much brandy was distributed that they were staggering about the next day quite drunk. Palm and Smith were living in a yard, where fifteen poor prisoners lay in irons ready to be slain that day. A woman who tried to escape was caught, and with the knife through her cheeks was made to sit in the market place, amidst the taunts of the crowd, till the fatal hour arrived.

The death wake continued over Sunday (September 10th), but the number of victims decreased. One hundred and thirty-six high chiefs had fallen in this war, which gives some idea of the sacrifice of human life that followed. For each of the six belonging to Coomassie, thirty of their people were killed, thirty for those of Sokora, and so on.

Our life of discipline was now varied by a domestic trial, arising from the serious illness of our infant's nurse, which nearly cost the little one its life. When the king first saw it, he was delighted with its strong and healthy appearance, for was it not his property? It now grew pale and thin, and for days hope and fear alternated as to whether it would survive. I tried to feel reconciled to the blow that seemed impending, but trembled for my poor wife. Our days of anxious suspense were at length graciously relieved by seeing this cherished and precious little creature revive again, and we received her as a new gift from our Heavenly Father.

I now paid my respects to Adu Bofo, and he honoured us with a return visit. He was much aged, suffering from his feet, and so intoxicated that he spoke with difficulty, while a convulsive movement affected his whole frame. He gave me a still more unpleasant impression than when with him in the camp. He shook hands with each of us, whereupon Bosommuru told us to thank him. We puzzled our brains to think why, and our silence seemed so to embarrass the chamberlain that we at last broke it by thanking the general for his visit.

It began to rain, so his chair (one of ours), was brought that he might sit with us. He talked about the war, directing his remarks chiefly to Bosommuru. He seemed to have attained the height of his ambition, spoke of his slaves, umbrellas and gold, though he wanted more of that, and hoped to get it. People had often said he would never come home, he was too ill, and suffered from sleepless nights, and that he dreaded the journey back. Why should he have feared? If he had been a murderer, surely the king would not have loaded him with presents!" At length the rain ceasing, he rose and left.

A bright and beautiful Sunday was the 24th of September to us, when under the shade of the orange and mango trees, I baptised our little one in the presence of our people. Bosommuru, whom I invited, remained with thirty of his attendants during the service, and heard what I said. When I sprinkled the forehead of the little Rosa Augustine Louise, he could not conceal his astonishment. Thus was our dear child's, the first baptism celebrated in Coomassie—may many yet follow.

Scarcely had we returned to our room, when a heavy thunder-storm broke upon us, but we sat down with Joseph, and Robert Kwansa, to a social meal, followed by some confectionery made from the flour we had lately received. The mulattos, Smith and Palm, were also present, and the rest of our people received an extra meal, which made them wish that baptisms would occur daily.

I soon after spoke to Bosommuru on a subject which had long troubled me, and asked him if I might proclaim the gospel in the streets. He replied that the king had often wondered why we did not celebrate our worship thus, and that he would like to come and listen when we preached the word of God. So on the 1st October, I held my first open-air service, and about a hundred people, besides Bosommuru and his great retinue, heard me tell of God's love to men, His horror of sin, and how He blessed those who truly seek Him. I made it pretty short, that the hearers might not tire, and trust that God's power came to the help of my weakness.

Meanwhile, our days passed on as usual, whilst at the coast, it was fully expected we were returning with the ambassadors. These latter were detained at Fomana, impatiently waiting for the king's messenger, a cousin of Prince Ansa's (Kwado by name), who had not started before October, taking with him payment for the goods which had been sent here, in the shape of slaves.

British subjects, even Government native officials, did not hesitate to settle accounts thus, quieting their consciences perhaps with the thought that these poor creatures, whom they exchanged on the way for ready money, might thus fall into better hands than if they had remained in Coomassie. The governor however, at last interfered and forbade this questionable trade until the arrival of further instructions from England.

The jealousy that existed among the chiefs made the greatest care necessary on our part, lest we might be the means of causing more intrigues than already existed. A great disturbance had occurred in the palace in consequence of a robbery. The keeper of the king's sandals had during the last two years sold several cast off pairs. The king found it out, and demanded the name of the buyer, to whom he said, " I do not like any one to dishonour my talisman " (referring to the Arabic writing on the sandals). The affair was brought into court, the man was beheaded, and twenty people imprisoned, six of whom were bound in irons, but at length the king, wearied of prosecuting the affair, pardoned the criminals.

On October 2nd, his majesty sent me my violin, with an enquiry how to play on it, so little sense of shame did he exhibit in the possession of other people's goods.

Our little girl excited the deepest interest in those around us, and many a visitor did she receive. One mohammedan presented her with a shilling, a very acceptable perquisite to the nurse and Kokoo.

Meanwhile our open-air service continued to be a great source of joy for us. Deeply did I feel my weakness, but took comfort in the thought that God often chooses " the weak things of the world to confound the things which are mighty." Nearly fifty people came on Sunday, and when I remembered how twenty-eight years before the Wesleyans had preached in these streets without encouragement, I was cheered, and rejoiced that at least the people listened attentively. Meanwhile the sacrifices continued, it seemed as if things would never change, and our feelings were lacerated afresh at this time by the celebration of another of these heathen observances. A great brass basin in the middle of the market place represents the market Fetish, into which, after every campaign, a stone is thrown, thus enabling one to count by their number how many times Ashantee had been to war. On this occasion, a boy from Krepe, his whole body painted white, was led to the basin, and a stone was thrown in, whilst an orator informed the Fetish that in gratitude for his protection during the campaign a slave was herewith —not sacrificed, happily—but consecrated to him. From thenceforth this boy belonged to the Fetish, and waited upon him daily with food, freely supplied from the market.

The clouds of the political horizon did not dissipate, for while Ashantee traders went in crowds to the coast, crossing the boundary as they chose, others wishing to make the same journey, were detained in Fomana, because this or that point was not cleared up. The king summoned prince Ansa, whose advice he greatly needed, but without bearers to meet him, the prince could not defray the expenses of the journey. At length the inevitable effect of such proceedings occurred—the trade in powder and arms was stopped by the English government.

A few days ago, the king rose in anger from his council, and withdrew raging to his room, calling for his Kete bund,* a sign that he was in one of his worst

* For description of this music, we refer the reader to pp. 119 and 120.

humours. The councillors were beside themselves with excitement, and the people on the market place gathered up their wares, and fled trembling into their houses; nothing but absolute necessity made any of them leave their homes that night.*

It was just about this time that I one day found a pair of my shoes offered for sale in the market, and gladly bought them. Soon after, one of the king's sons appeared in a dress belonging to my wife.

I had now the joy of helping a poor starving woman I saw lying in the market place, seeming to have but an hour to live. Accustomed as I was to horrors, so sorrowful a sight I had never beheld. Two of our boys brought her with difficulty into our house, where in a few days she recovered sufficiently to walk with a stick. Her mistress had sent her away sick, with the words, "Go into the bush and die." A musselman who spoke her language, told us she was a Fula, which accounted for her not having been killed, as mohammedan Fulas are not put to death by the Ashantees. A fortnight later she died, thankful for our kindness.

Soon afterwards, another woman in fetters fled to us for protection, whom we succeeded in getting set at liberty, and three days later, a man rushed breathless into Kühne's room, trying to hide himself under the bed. As soon as the poor fellow was sufficiently recovered to speak, he told us that six weeks before he had used the oath of the king, had been found guilty, and placed in the stocks. After many fruitless efforts, he had succeeded in extricating his emaciated hand, and had run to us for protection.

The earlier missionaries had been allowed the privi-

---

* We heard soon after, that the cause of the king's anger had been some tricks which his chiefs had played him, in regard to the succession of the chieftainship of Nouta. In the night, an influential man of that town, and a linguist of Coomassie, were killed.

lege of interceding for the lives of those who fled to them, so we begged Bosommuru to ask the king to pardon this man. The courtier was astonished, but willing to fulfil our request, only remarking that the Ashantee out of whose house the prisoner had come, would have to pay a heavy penalty. In the evening the king replied that "we must not let the man go at present." It was, perhaps, difficult for him to grant an immediate pardon, as many sacrifices had to be offered the following Saturday, when he was going to Kokofu to the funeral of his uncle, which was to be celebrated with great splendour. However quiet this plan had been kept, the poor creature must have heard of it.

He was a singular man. As he lived the whole day in the yard, we proposed to him to help to pound the fufu, not that we needed his assistance, but simply that he might not be idle. To this he replied, "I am an Ashantee, one of the king's slaves. I have never done such a thing." My wife then proposed to give him soap to wash his clothes, but this also he considered unbecoming his dignity. He would not join in our devotions, though he sat a few times with us under protest, and at length he escaped to the house of Palm's master, giving as his reason that he could not understand when we invoked our God. We again pleaded for his pardon, and he was allowed to return to his own people.

By degrees it became apparent that the king's ministers were getting anxious about the results of their equivocating behaviour. They pretended to wish for peace, and yet could not rest without fighting. A vassal of Ashantee, a prince of Safwi, had sent some troops to a certain chief of Apolonia, named Amontiful, who had sought the protection of the king of Kwantiabo. These troops came to the coast, and were beaten by the English allies of Apolonia, and as a chief fell in these operations, his head and the gold plate which he wore, were sent to Cape Coast, which led the authorities there to the conclusion, that Ashantee was secretly concerned in the disturbances there. The king requested our assistance in writing a letter to justify himself to the governor, in which he said that he had sent for this chief of Safwi to kill him, and therefore asked his excellency to send a messenger as witness of the execution, assuring him that this captain had gone to war without orders from Coomassie, for Kari-Kari had always urged the upholding of peace, &c.

We will now describe the funeral festivities of Kokofu. After a number of human sacrifices, the king set off, accompanied by five-sixths of the inhabitants of Coomassie, and about thirty other victims all bound, and with the knife through their cheeks. We were afterwards told that more than two hundred human beings were sacrificed, the king beheading several with his own hand, who were held up before him, that he might not be obliged to stoop. Some were shot in the forest, and forty were killed on the first day. He was enthusiastically received on his return, and we could not escape the horrible entertainment. The slaughterers danced in the faint light of the torches, like people possessed by evil spirits, as doubtless they were, and nearly all were drunk. At the very moment we felt the greatest horror of him, the king not only came and danced before us, but gave each of us his hand. We had always heard that he only did this at private interviews, and now, as he strutted along, adorned with gold, and arrayed in purple, while some supported him under the arms, and others swept away the little stones before his feet, it was an extraordinary mark of friendship.

Another strange thing happened on that same evening. Some eunuchs approached, armed with bush knives, crying "Fwe," "Fwe." Everyone remained sitting, and saw the numerous women of the army, and forty-five ladies of the Seraglio with them, pass quietly by. They were all walking, even those attired in silk, and looked very weary, with the exception of the last in the procession, who sat with her child in a sedan chair, surrounded by the regal state of a chief, sword-bearers, courtiers, etc. Behind her appeared the queen mother, who greeted us very kindly, and the king's brother who had danced before us. Had we not been already so weary of our stay (it was nearly a year since our entrance into Coomassie), this sort of state pageant might have made a great impression upon us; as it was, we were very very sad, and, in many respects, less hopeful than before.

CHAPTER XIX.

YAMS AND CHRISTMAS FESTIVALS.

December, 1871.

AT last the question of sending us to the Coast was again mooted, from the cause we proceed to explain. Adu Bofo had handed over his nephew, Kwame Opoku, two years ago, to the Krobos, as a pledge for us, and he had been immediately sent to Cape Coast. On December 9th, a letter arrived from this same Opoku, which we were summoned to translate. He desired that we should speak to the king, asking that he might be recalled. The governor had told him that after his uncle, Adu Bofo's return, the white men were to be liberated, but as they had not come he was detained. Meanwhile, he suffered from hunger, his daily allowance having been diminished in consequence of the grumbling of other Ashantees. Would the king come to his relief. We took the opportunity of remarking that each of these Ashantees received eleven dollars every three weeks, while we had only nine to divide among four of us.

Bosommuru brought also letters from his relations to M. Bonnat, wondering greatly that they contained no gold, but he was told that in France they trusted the rich king of Ashantee to treat his prisoners honourably. We further complained that the promised salt did not arrive, and that our boxes from the colony were detained, so that we thought of asking the king for a piece of land to cultivate. "In short," said we, "our position grows worse every day, and has become quite unbearable." Upon hearing this, the chamberlain became very angry with Opoku, "who had turned our heads." He remarked that if the king sent us back in about six months, it would not be worth while to begin a plantation, still he would think of it.

The preparation for the yam festival now began in earnest. All the public seats (Dampans) were whitened, the royal seats in the streets entirely renewed. The talk of the day was of what had happened to a nephew of prince Ansa, Kofi Antschi, who had abused a prince because he had carried away his wife, and had also used the oath of the king. He had been for ten days in irons, but escaped in the night, and took refuge with the Fetish in Adjuman. He got off at last, with a fine of thirteen Peredwane, $67\frac{1}{2}$ ounces of gold. A brother of prince Ansa's, who had gone wrong with two ladies of royal blood, fared worse. The king tried for a long time to change the sentence of death against him, to one of banishment, but his counsellors demurred, because the crime was one of a very unusual character, so the prince was to be killed, and his accomplices also. Persons of royal blood were not however beheaded, but shot or drowned, or their necks broken with an ivory tusk.

On the day of preparation for the feast (December 14th), the king went through the town to assure himself of the renewing of the "Dampans." If the decorations had fallen, or the roofs were leaking or patched, no notice was taken, but the top must be well whitened.

The procession was more warlike than that of the preceding year. Behind every chief the soldiers shouted a wild war song, of which we often heard the words, "if you meet him, meet him to his destruction," and they beat time with their weapons held aloft. After the king had greeted and honoured us with a bottle of rum, he stepped across with some mohammedans, who were awaiting him in the market place, dressed in new bright attire. They held an ox, the throat of which was now cut by the king.

On the evening of the 14th, Bosommuru brought a letter from Mr Ferguson, the governor of Elmina, written in German, and addressed to Kühne. It was intended for the king, thanking him for the satisfactory answer brought by Mr. Plange, but begging him to conclude a peace with the Fantees. It urged him to set the four innocent white prisoners free at once, and thus give the Dutch governor a proof of his friendship. It stated that Akjampong was already released, and it was hoped that the king would act on the same prompt plan towards his prisoners that all might see how warmly his heart beat for his "friends." K. translated this letter for the palace. On the envelope was written, in prince Ansa's hand, " I am coming."

Meanwhile the feast took place. On the 16th, the chiefs and warriors streamed into the town more noisily than usual, and the king's wives, decked with gold, their bodies besmeared with yellow green powder, passed through the streets, without the men withdrawing. The gigantic prince of Mampong, sworn enemy of all formality, shook hands with us heartily, while the "brafo" and "adumfo" (executioners), coloured red, danced with long chains of jawbones round their necks, which rattled like castinettes, drank something which looked like blood, and ate their feast together out of a monstrous dish, in the middle of the reception place. On the next day all laws were abrogated, and every one drinking freely was permitted to do that which seemed good in his own eyes. Even funerals were celebrated for those who had suffered capital punishment.

The great day was, of course, consecrated by a festival

offering, and any stray person at the palace door might be suddenly attacked, slaughtered, and divided between the "brafos" and "adumfos." One took a finger, another an arm or foot, and whoever obtained the head, danced in crazy ecstacy, painted its forehead red and white, kissed it on the mouth, laughing or with mocking words of pity, and finally hung it round his neck, or seized it with his teeth. Another took out the heart and roasted it, carried it in one hand, and a loaf of maize bread in the other, and walked about as if he were eating his breakfast.

The king (in common with his people) had disfigured his face with red stripes, and wore a black helmet, on which were engraved many gold crowns. The pomp and display on this occasion, gave me a deeper impression of the riches of Ashantee, than I had ever before received.

In the evening, they brought the skulls of their most important enemies from the mausoleum at Bantama, and placed them in the stillness of night in front of the Fetish, solemnly enquiring after the state of their spirits. Amongst them was the skull of Sir Charles Macarthy, who was killed in the battle of Esamako in 1824, and since kept in a brass basin, covered with a white cloth. We did not see this, but we met some forty men, each bearing a skull in his hand, round the forehead of which, a red rag was thrown, leaping, cursing and jumping, in the wildest confusion. The whole affair was the more distressing to us, as it happened on a Sunday, and we thought of the change which might come over this land; if Christendom took the misery of such people more to heart.

On the last great day of the festival (December 22nd) the king, before eating the new yams, washed himself in fetish water, brought in bottles from distant springs, sacred to the fetish. It was poured into basins in which the chiefs performed frequent ablutions during the day, and also sprinkled their chairs. On that occasion the king's wives may be seen, so my wife went with our baby to one of the Dampans, when all crowded round us to look at the little one, calling her "Amma Coomassie;"* "'tis a miracle—they are children of the gods," we heard them exclaiming, and often the enquiry, "which is the wife?" was made especially by the women, who could not take their eyes off the little Rosa.

The queen mother was passing as we arrived, with the glass and silver ornaments, followed by the eunuchs with the women. It appeared that the prohibition to look at them was again in force, for the men retired, and only a few mohammedans were allowed to remain beside us.

The ladies appeared in groups, with a highly decorated leader at their head, which gave one the idea that the female part of the court was well organised. The favourites were dressed in silks, velvets, and gold ornaments, while others followed in more simple or even mean attire. Between each group came eunuchs with little boys and girls, who carried small boxes of play things. The women had a long chewing stick in their hands, so that they could rub their teeth when they pleased. The most richly ornamented was evidently the first wife who, in virtue of her dignity, did not remove her stick from her mouth. Every age was represented, from young girls to grey-headed mothers. Some of them had been the wives of four or five kings.

As we could scarcely distinguish the court ladies from the king's wives, we cannot give their number, but it seemed as if those who went past with bowed heads were the real wives, and I counted from two hundred and fifty to two hundred and sixty of these, so that with invalids

---

* "The Saturday daughter of Coomassie," all girls being called after the day of the week on which they are born. See note at the close of the chapter.

and others necessarily absent, the total number cannot be less than three hundred ladies. That however is not known to any Ashantee. These are kept in such good order by the eunuchs that I only saw one cast a stolen glance at our little Rosa, though, doubtless, they all wished to see the white baby.

The king's eye beamed with joy when he looked at her, as he turned to his people on both sides of his sedan, and pointed laughing to the babe on its mother's lap. This was a sign for hundreds of black heads to show us—shouting, laughing, and singing—their white teeth. His majesty may well be proud, for none of his predecessors have ever been able to boast such white property, which will ever be spoken and sung of with great exultation throughout Ashantee, and he evidently thought much of the honour. His looking-glass, which is always carried with him, was on this occasion so large that two men could hardly stand upright under it. About seventy bearers of sheep followed, hundreds of which were slaughtered.

Very simple, in comparison, was our yam festival, *i.e.*, Christmas-day. We had given Bosommuru due notice but the king only sent us a sheep and a load of yams—salt was wanting, and nothing had arrived from the Coast. We had to relinquish the idea of an intended feast for our people, our purse being very low, and could only give them an extra fufu. Indeed, our means had become so limited, that we seriously thought of making a change in our household. Joseph had been entrusted with it hitherto, but too many people were supported at our expense, and our own folks were fed sparingly, while our stores vanished unaccountably. The kitchen was always open, and it was perfectly impossible to exercise any control. We determined therefore, that in future we would provide for ourselves only, leaving prince Ansa's people to care for themselves, so we divided with them our Adae money, and tried the experiment.

Note.—"The Saturday daughter of Coomassie." The girls' names are according to the days of the week:—

1. Akosua, (Akwasibwa).
2. Adjowa.
3. Abena.
4. Akuwa.
5. Yawa (also Aba, Ayaba).
6. Ya (Afiwa, Afwa).
7. Amma (or Amemenewa).

CHAPTER XX.

PRINCE ANSA'S TRANSACTIONS ABOUT THE RANSOM MONEY.

THE close of the year 1871, found us in no small commotion, for though it was Sunday, yet Cæsar, who had hitherto remained in Fomana, brought a letter from the prince, which informed us that he was already near—only three miles from the capital, where an extraordinarily grand Adae was to be celebrated, at which we must be present.

One of the king's proclamations gave us real pleasure, for it seemed indicative of peace; the sounding of a gong announced that the ruined Dampans were to be restored. We took courage from the fact that the king appeared to have discovered how the marks of decay were becoming apparent in the town; we supposed that if it were to be again restored, we should have peace.

We spent the evening with Palm, Joseph, and Robert, drinking coffee without milk or sugar, and eating our maize bread, and a little marmalade, the remains of former prosperity. We drew lots from our text books, and talked of the past, and of the future, until the year 1872 opened upon us.

On the evening of this New Year's day, we found ourselves in the reception place of Mogyawee, and by torchlight saw prince Ansa in uniform, with gold epaulets, his sword by his side, just as he was being joyfully welcomed by the king and the court. Our hearts did indeed beat, as we pressed the hand of our friend, and his face beamed as we returned the pressure. Then at our simple supper, he rejoiced us with letters, a photograph of our lost darling, returned to us from Switzerland, and the news of ten boxes, which he had brought for us from the coast, thus putting a temporary end to our poverty. No sugar had come, and only six ounces of money, but there was that which we valued far more, the whole Tschi bible in one volume. What grace had God given to our dear Christaller, in permitting him to complete this work! The prince too rejoiced greatly, for he could now read the word of God in his mother-tongue.

But our return seemed as far off as ever, though the governor urged it, and hinted at unpleasant consequences in case of a refusal. The way to the Coast being already blocked, the king manifests little concern, or he would surely not have left such an important matter in the hands of his councillors. He did not perceive that he was exposing his weak point to the English Government, and that he might live to regret it. But there was no time for reflection just then, for we had to finish the celebration of the festivity of the protecting deity of the dynasty. Bosommuru addressed the people throughout an entire day; when the whole aristocracy sprinkled themselves with fetish water, and danced in white in honour of the god, who is represented by a pretty little chest about one and a quarter feet square, with rich silver clasps, and a lid of leather in the form of bellows. The feast lasted three weeks, and closed on Friday, January 13th, which was specially kept as a day of purification in honour of the "king's souls," he having been born on a a Friday, hence his name (Kofi; Friday*).

Whoever wished to honour him appeared on that day

---

* The names of boys were according to the days of the week, as follows :—1 Kwasi, 2 Quadwo (or Kwadjo), 3 Kwabena, 4 Kwaku, 5 Yaw (Kwaw), 6 Kofi, 7 Kwame.

in white garments, and painted white on the breast, shoulders, and forehead. We saw hundreds of these "servants" of the "king's souls," who enjoyed the prerogative of not being beaten or insulted by anyone. What the "king's souls" exactly were, remained a mystery. One must just suppose it a "protecting god," personified by a silver urn filled with gold.

The prince accompanied us to the festival, where we, with many others, saw the "king's souls" carried past. Our baby was with us, and greatly delighted both the king and his mother, whose astonishment found no expression. One of the bystanders directly named it, "a thing of the gods."

The next day we distributed our presents, To the king we gave a piece of violet velvet, and four of foulard silk; to the queen mother, two looking-glasses, some soap, hair-oil, and Eau de Cologne; to the king's brother, Mensa, and to Bosommuru, such things as we thought would please. The latter afterwards gave his Eau de Cologne to the king.

In private conversation with Ansa, the king appeared kindly disposed towards us, and owned that the campaign against which the prince had warned him was a mistake. But anxious as he was for peace, and a flourishing trade with the Coast (for he is very desirous to possess manufactured goods); wishful also as he was to see his chief, Akjampong liberated, he showed no disposition to let us go: though he allowed us to send for sugar and money, and was ready to do us any little service, Ansa did not think he was aiming at a ransom. Remembering how in 1826, after the battle of Dudowa, the English had sent back the king's own grandmother, and other princesses, without any recompense, although they were actually prisoners of war—" It would be such a disgrace," he said, "to *sell* the missionaries!" But money was an important thing in the eyes of the chiefs; even Adu Bofo had been seriously accused of having plundered our station to enrich himself, and on this occasion we were almost brought forward as witnesses.

In the midst of all these disturbing questions, our friend Smith, the mulatto, was called away by death. He had welcomed our visits, and liked us to pray with him, and we trust had really given himself to the Lord, who casteth out none that come to Him. I buried him on Sunday, January 21st, and spoke from the words, "If any man keep my sayings, he shall never see death." No one from the town was present, but the king afterwards sent us four dollars and a half to defray the funeral costs. The following Sunday, we united with the prince and Joseph in taking the Lord's Supper, and in the afternoon we preached in the street; many gathered round to listen, and the king's favourite, Sabeng, enquired the time of service, and a week later, attended with his followers, to hear us tell of God's love to poor sinners.

The barricading of the boundary greatly enraged the king. On January 22nd, a man returned, his mission unaccomplished, with the message that, "The English will not have anything to do with Ashantee, until the king had let the Europeans go." The Fantees had scornfully added, "Only buy powder and shot, and we will fight you."

In vain did the prince try to soften matters; urged on by the company around, the king exclaimed excitedly, "Are not the white men my property? Can I not set them at liberty when I like?"

On the night of the 29th, Kotiko first gave his report of his mission to the coast in the preceding year, and in a few well chosen words, did full justice to the prince's entreaties for peace. The prince then read the governor's letter, the main point of which was, that he must return to the Coast, bringing the white prisoners, if public intercourse was to be reopened. After several questions, the king exclaimed, "Well, I will try and let you go back soon."

The prince's own brother then spoke so bitterly about the way being closed, that Ansa declared it had been mainly *his* own doing, giving his reason. While living in Cape Coast, he had been repeatedly solicited to intercede for the Ashantee traders, when they got into difficulties with Fantees. Now that he was away, there would be no one who understood English, and had, at the same time, the good of the Ashantees at heart. He therefore, conjointly with Kotiko and Afirifa, the representatives of Ashantee, thought it best for communication to cease, so that during his absence, no inextricable complications might occur. The monarch, and nearly all the council, agreed with the rules which had been adopted, but they were opposed by Ansa's brother, and the queen mother. We are evidently held in such high value, that it will be hard to secure our release; indeed I was gravely asked by one person, whether we were not relatives of Queen Victoria.

When prince Ansa was privately sounded as to his opinion with regard to a demand for ransom, he replied: "If this question is seriously mooted, I beg to be spared the disgrace of carrying any message on the subject to the Coast; you must send another person."

The matter was left in abeyance during the celebration of a festival in honour of the king's guardian spirits, which was accompanied by the sacrifice of numberless animals, and dancing on the part of his majesty. At length, on February 17th, all of us were summoned to appear in the royal presence. We found the king and his mother seated on an elevated throne, and the counsel of chiefs gathered round them; but we had scarcely taken our places when an alarm of fire in the town caused the whole assembly to decamp in a hurry, and half an hour elapsed before the royal personages reappeared, and we were once more permitted to stand before them in the blazing heat of noonday sunshine.

The king commenced proceedings by informing his chiefs that his friend the governor desired our liberation; he readily granted the advisability of complying with the request, but would be glad to hear whether Adu Bofo agreed in his views. I had been accompanied to this interview by my wife and our child, for I really had ventured to think something might come of it; but on hearing this my fair vision of hope suddenly collapsed, and I despatched her homewards with little Rosie, who was growing tired and fretful.

Adu Bofo simulated surprise, and pretended to confer for some moments with his friends. Very soon however he began to explain that Asen, Akem, Akra, and Aknapem, which all formerly belonged to Ashantee, had been drawn over to serve the white men, who on their part had subsequently broken their treaty of peace with Ashantee by refusing to give up a runaway chief. The king here remarked that these were matters of the past, which need not be stirred up afresh. "At all events," replied Adu Bofo, "the right thing would be to regain our authority over these tribes. I have been to war!" he shouted; "I have gained victories, used much powder, and lost more than a thousand men, and now am I to give up all that has been gained? No!" he roared, with furious glances in our direction, "never, never will I let these prisoners go free! never, I say!"

When asked to reconsider his sentence, he again appeared to reflect, and then began: "The wish of his heart," said he, in a deprecating manner, "was never to give up the white men; but to please the king, his

THE RANSOM MONEY. 159

father, he would agree to their release, but not without a ransom. " We will sell them," he added, " or I will never consent to let them go." Several others were then asked their opinion; that of the town chiefs agreed with Adu's, so did the representatives from Dwaben, Nsuta, and Bekwae, and the king's speakers, Opoku and Nantschi, took the same view. One Coomassie chief however, backed by the princes of Mampong and Adanse, spoke thus: " If his majesty deem it advisable to set the white men free, it seems better to us to let them go without any ransom. If that cannot be done, we are for war."

Then followed a general grumbling, scoffing and confusion, on which the opponents repeated in decided tones, " This is our firm and well-weighed conclusion," and retired. Prince Ansa was then requested to withdraw with Kotiko, and reflect upon an answer to the decision of the council. He drew us aside for conference, not however without opposition, which the king silenced. Kühne and I were of opinion that mission money ought not to be taken for such a purpose, and M. Bonnat said that he had lost all his property in Ho, and that instead of paying an impossible sum, he would rather stay in Coomassie.

The brothers Afirifas (who were still held in Cape Coast), wished the prince to ascertain the exact sum desired, that he might inform the governor. The king told Adu Bofo to express his wishes; he replied, " The king may demand a thousand peredwane; I, as his slave eight hundred " (£6,480). The prince was then asked his opinion, which he declined to give, saying he had not come to make bargains, but simply to bring the king's answer to the governor. " Would he himself then go to Cape Coast?" they asked. " Yes," he replied, whereupon the meeting broke up.

This comedy was not so well played, but that we could see through the whole plan, still it was our impression that the propelling power was not Adu Bofo individually, but the so-called "Kotoko;" the assembly of speakers, old miserly fellows, to whom the good of their country was a mere trifle, compared with the filling of their own coffers. We returned home deeply distressed. There seemed no hope of a peaceful solution of our difficulties. We felt that Ashantee would have to be humbled, for thousands of murdered victims were crying to heaven, while we who so gladly would have brought peace, must be the means of bringing misfortune upon this blinded land! Oh, how much we wished and hoped that after we were set free a mission might be established in Ashantee! Yea, that we might even work in it ourselves! But what insurmountable barriers seemed still in the way!

In a private conversation with the king, prince Ansa represented to him the disgrace and shame he was bringing upon his country; but he said he could not act "against his people, so few were on our side."

The next day was Sunday, and the sad thought came within me, "Shall I continue to preach to a people who seem so unworthy?" but overcoming the temptation, I went forth, and found not only more listeners, but a readier tongue, a greater joy. How could the poor people help having such leaders?

After further discussion, which was altogether fruitless, the royal answer was despatched to the Coast on February 20th. It ran thus, "Tell the governor that I and my great men have decided that the treaty of peace shall be entered upon as soon as the ransom is paid to Adu Bofo, and not before." This was signed for the king by his linguists, each with his signet, witnessed by three European prisoners.

We announced at the same time to the government our views of the state of things, and hinted that nothing but a continued barricading of the borders would bring the Ashantees to their senses. We also called the governor's attention to the fact that this time the court had not condescended to give any return presents to the ambassador of the colonial government, whereas to the former deputies they had been lavishly dealt out. Neither had anything been given for his maintenance, four and a half dollars on each Adae being all he had received from the king, so that he found himself in no small pecuniary embarrassment.

While thus standing as it were on a volcano, the king continued to delay Ansa's departure, professing that he must first pay for the goods he had brought him from the Coast, and also settle another account. Ashantee had taken goods from Asen to the value of seventeen peredwane, during the last two or three years, a debt which Kari-Kari acknowledged. The governor had therefore advanced it to the prince of Asen, to prevent further quarrels. Ansa was ashamed to return without this money, but this annoyance was not spared him, for on March the 17th the chamberlains announced that it had been decided to delay payment until the ransom could be obtained—a most revolting proceeding.

The prince preached in the streets the same evening on the words, "The wages of sin is death." How humbled I felt, and how I longed to be able to speak as clearly and fluently as he did.

An important decision arose out of Ansa's delayed departure, on a subject I had been pondering unknown to my wife, till she one day said she would almost rather stay where we were, than agree to an exorbitant sum being paid for our ransom. We duly weighed the matter, and then proposed that should our committee approve, we were ready to remain, believing that if we were once away, others would scarcely have the courage to start a mission in Ashantee.

Of course many things had to be considered, such as

M

what was to be done if a war broke out, shutting us up entirely from all communication with the Coast, or in case of severe illness. We felt, however, we could leave the future. Mr Kühne was perplexed for a time, partly because he had come on mercantile business, partly because he could not get on well with the language, but he finally agreed, and the prince departed with our varied communications, leaving us once more alone.

Just before Ansa's departure, one of his servants, a Fanti, had taken a leaf of a particular tree to clean his "calabash." The tree was a sacred one, which the Fanti did not know. He was however observed and led away, his master was but too well aware of the danger, for he had seen a youth beheaded under the same tree for a similar offence; but the king was induced to commute his punishment, and command that a sheep provided by the prince should be sacrificed instead of the boy. Unpleasant as it was for him to be thus involved in the superstitions of his country, he sent four dollars and a half to Bosommuru to buy the sheep and carry out the king's command, but eventually the king sustituted a sheep of his own, feeling apparently ashamed at his shabby treatment of Ansa.

CHAPTER XXI.

PROLONGED WAITING DURING A REVOLUTION IN THE COLONIAL POLITICS.

ONE night a light-coloured youth from Aja, a mountain in Krepe, a district assigned by the king to the chief Kwasi Domfe (with whom J. Smith and Palm had lived), rushed trembling into our kitchen. The chief's mother having died, several men were appointed to be slain, one of whom was missed at the last moment. The lad happened to be near when this was announced to Kwasi, who angrily rejoined, "Then take this boy quickly and kill him instead." The intended victim cleared the court with one bound, hid in a bush till night, and then escaped unperceived to the white men. We took him in, promising if possible to save his life, but failing to find Bosommuru the next morning in his house, had to follow him to the palace, and had not made our errand clear to him before he was summoned to the king sitting in court, whither we were soon ordered to follow.

We entered amid more noise than we usually encountered in the market-place, for a plaintiff was screaming to make himself heard above his surroundings. While trying with Joseph's help to explain my business, the king, to my great astonishment, bid me speak for myself. A complete silence ensued while I endeavonred to tell my story, and when I ceased, his majesty, in company with all the assembly, united in a hearty laugh, for my foreign accent and my ignorance of the terms used in court amused them greatly; I gained my object however, and was assured the youth had nothing further to fear. We kept this lad (Kwaku by name) with us, and he was only too glad to remain and work in our service.

The old mission house was becoming increasingly decrepit. Not only was the roof unsound, but our dwelling-room required new flooring, if in the approaching rainy season we were to have one dry place for our little Rose. With Kwaku's help we took these matters in hand as far as our scanty means permitted, but the king was building two new villages by our old Ebenezer, so that wages were especially high just then.

Prince Ansa, who had commenced a plantation about a mile out of Coomassie, had obtained the royal consent to leave it in our charge, and M. Bonnat set to work diligently to uproot the bush and plant the ground. We also cultivated a small piece of land which had been given me by a chief in return for a little present. The twenty minutes' walk to this garden would have been a pleasant one, but for the fact that our way lay through a morass caused by the overflow of the river Suben. Whether we should ever reap the fruit of our labours was problematical, but M. Bonnat built himself a hut where he and Palm might sleep during the summer months in order to guard the ripening harvest. The plan promised a twofold advantage, it would show the king we were not the grand people he supposed, and also that we were perhaps making arrangements for remaining.

An incident of this period excited afresh our deepest sympathy. Vultures being regarded as sacred birds belonging to the royal family, fly over Coomassie by hundreds, all untouched. They pounce upon meat or fish carried in the hand, and still more on that conveyed in larger quantities. A poor woman on her way to market with a basket of provisions on her head, was visited by one of these voracious birds, which fastening its claws tightly in the straw work, could not extricate itself. This was a strong temptation to the people around to possess themselves of its feathers, valuable for many purposes, and several ran forward, seized the larger ones, and disappeared in a moment with their prize. When the bird had freed itself, it was unable to fly, and a general lamentation ensued. The poor woman was carried off and put in irons, and would we knew be sacrificed.

On Easter Sunday (March 31st), we were much in spirit with our dear ones at home. These seasons cause us to realize how entirely we are sundered from every christian association, so that I set out with a heavy heart to my usual service in the streets. Yet, as often before on similar occasions, I returned strengthened and encouraged, and could rejoice in Him who is " the Resurrection and the Life."

The king had left the previous week, overladen with presents, to spend his yearly vacation at Amanghyia. He dealt out his gifts lavishly on all sides, but forgot us, to whom a piece of fresh meat would have been so welcome. He however surprised the capital by a sudden resolution to hold the Bantama feast on the 1st April (Easter Monday). A painful contrast to the glorious christian festival we had quietly celebrated!

Numbers of poor victims were now slain in our immediate vicinity, and we were helpless! How the whole land groaned under its oppressors! Almost every Ashantee felt how little such sacrifices were pleasing to God, yet not one dared to express his conviction, though had the king announced that very day that none but murderers should become victims, a universal cry of joy would have burst forth from multitudes of voices. But Kari-Kari was persuaded that his whole strength lay in his power to take life at any moment. One of his highest chiefs was said to have lost his head for daring to suggest that he spent too much money on his wives. It was quite evident that unless *compelled*, he would never alter so convenient and time-honoured a custom.

A joyful message from prince Ansa, who was still in Fomana, gave us an opportunity of seeing the magnificent Amanghyia. He advised us of the dispatch of eleven boxes, which obliged us to apply to Bosommuru to have them at once conveyed to us. We did not see the king, who was sleeping, but admired the tasteful and durable building he had erected, in lieu of the poor temporary huts which had served his followers in former years. The whole was in keeping with his own beautifully situated villa.

In advance of the expected boxes came Robert Kwansa, with not only letters from home, but what we then needed almost more, twenty ounces of gold dust. How thankful we were to the kind brethren for thus hastening to supply our wants, before Elmina was ceded to England, and a rupture occurred with Ashantee. The prince, as we have said, was detained on the road, and not until the completion of the celebrations, when the king returned with his court, and we had to be present at the reception, was the royal messenger despatched to accompany him to the coast.

Our boxes were similarly treated, promises were made and broken, though finally one after another was sent, the last not reaching us until the 3rd of May. Then after all the presents we gave to the king and his chamberlain, they were dissatisfied. The king said he must "buy" from us further. We declined, for we were really in need of the materials for our own clothes, but he so persisted that at last we gave him another piece, thus realizing how entirely we were prisoners.

On April the 15th, we were awoke by the rocking of our beds, from a sharp shock of earthquake. Some years before, on a like occurrence, human sacrifices had been immediately offered to appease the spirits, but prince Ansa had explained to the king the causes of such events, so that this was happily discontinued, but field work was forbidden on a Thursday, because of an earthquake which had once happened on that day.

Our darling child was growing strong and healthy, and though only seven months old could stand by a chair, and we needed a girl to take care of her, the nurse being occupied with her own child. When seated before her toys, and the little thing began to prattle, we felt what a treasure we had to cheer us in our continued solitude. We requested Bosommuru to supply us with a servant; he hesitated, perhaps he felt it was the king's duty to do this unsolicited, but finally a girl of thirteen, for whom we had to pay twenty-four dollars, was given us, and proved a great help.

Letters from Administrator Ussher and from Mr. Forson, which were brought to us to translate, gave us some insight into the state of affairs. Mr. Ussher expected that prince Ansa's mission would restore peace, and that since Adu Bofo had returned, we should be set free. After taking possession of Elmina, the English Government would take care that the king should still receive the yearly sum which had been paid by Holland, not as tribute, but as a friendly offering.

In reference to the slaves who had fled from Ashantee to Cape Coast, the British authorities could not according to their laws send them back, but the king was advised to place a guard at the Prah to prevent his subjects leaving Ashantee. Nothing was said about Akjampong, but the authorities seemed willing to send him back from Cape Coast (whither he had been transported), though we should find it more desirable for him to be kept at the Coast till we were set free. Mr. Forson begged the king to let his people (sent eight months before with presents to his majesty), leave Coomassie and return to him. The surrendering of Elmina occasioned much vexation in the palace, nor was this the only one. Ashantee had quarrelled with Asen about some debt, and the latter had struck a kra ("king's soul"), which was considered a deadly insult.

We too were not without our grievances. I had worked very hard at our plantation, and more than eighty yam roots had been put in the ground, when one morning I discovered that thirty-five had been dug out again. We were prepared for robberies at harvest time, and had arranged to sleep out of doors, but we had not dreamt of such insolence as this. And how to guard against it we did not know. It would have been easy to get the king to announce with the gong that no one was to approach our plantation, but what if it occurred after all? The king regarded the mangoes growing in the court of the mission-house as his property, and desired that they should be better watched; but we could not even protect them from night robberies, and if a thief chose to run the risk, how could we give him up to be beheaded?

We had bought a steady man (Kwaku), belonging to a village near Ahudome, for twenty-two dollars: he could not speak Ashantee, and was beside himself with joy on entering our service. Poor fellow, how I longed to be able to take him back to his own country, though he was very useful to us. The other Kwaku was by the king's order compelled to leave us to his own and our sorrow, and though we had put ourselves to all sorts of inconvenience out of pure regard for him, hoping to be able to give his master what he considered his value. How could thieving and lying decrease in a country where human goods were so revoltingly disposed of.

The chief of Wusutra was ordered to have all his young men ready to fetch something for the king, and four hundred were sent northward, under an Ashantee colonel, whither and for what purpose no one knew. A few days later, the single women of the same village were summoned, the king promising to give them work, but as we believed to be sold, though they had given themselves up voluntarily, and had been assured they should be sent back to their own land. Truly it was difficult to entertain a warm affection for such a nation, and yet I painfully felt that my poor words would be powerless unless they proceeded from a loving heart.

When the Adae fell on a Sunday, we could scarcely attempt street preaching, on account of the drinking and general excitement. At other times we were greatly encouraged, as on one occasion, where two of the king's sons were among the audience, on another when we had more than four hundred attentive listeners, and yet again, when a chief visited me with his two sons who had expressed a desire to know me; still our hope of making any lasting impression was continually checked.

On May 30th, the wife of one of the king's brothers died, and he to express his sympathy, sent more than a dozen victims for sacrifice, accompanied by the wild music of the horns. At such times the question would arise, what were we that we should attempt to do battle against this mighty bulwark of Satan? It almost seemed as if we heard his scornful laugh! but we sowed on in faith and hope, looking to God to preserve and fructify the seed.

A letter from the prince on June 4th occasioned us much concern. It accompanied a box with a variety of things we had ordered, and told us of the arrival of the governor-in-chief at Elmina, the taking of which place caused all other affairs to be put on one side, so that the king's letter remained unanswered. The prince deplored that new comers unacquainted with the country declined to take advice from experienced natives.

His excellency, Mr Hennesy, had already proclaimed that the way to the Coast was open to every Ashantee, without reference to the prince. Akjampong, who was sent by the Dutch to Kwantiabo, was said to be no longer in custody, and might be expected in Coomassie in a month. This we had long dreaded, knowing well how this proud, cruel man would let loose the bridal of his hatred against all Europeans, and turn the heads of the people. The double-tongued Afirifa, too, was expected with his friends from the Prah, the man who above all others urged the king to insist on a ransom. Mr. Plange was likewise on the road with presents from both the Colonial Governments, among which was a gigantic mirror, so difficult to transport that the king was requested to light the path through the forest, that it might not be damaged. We did not anticipate that Mr. Plange would intercede for our release, and could only trust in the Lord for help in His own good time.

It was now exactly three years on June 12th since we had been taken prisoners. How little we should have believed it, had we then been told that we could have sustained a three years' captivity. But the darker the prospect the more earnestly did we desire to do something for the Ashantees, and I arranged a room in the adjoining building for reading and praying, hoping that it would also serve for a school-room.

I had for some time been trying to collect a few poor children on Sundays, showing them pictures, singing to them and telling them of the Saviour's love, and more came than I had ventured to expect—why therefore might I not try to teach them daily? I spoke to them of my wish, and they not only expressed anxiety to learn, but offered to help in the repairs. We opened an entrance from the street that they might come straight into the school-room, and as they entered the scene moved me beyond expression.

It was about this time that the queen mother made over the treasures of the former king to her son. According to Ashantee custom the mother of the heir keeps possession of the treasures on the death of the sovereign, until her son has acquired experience. Kwakoo Dooah had now been dead five years, after a reign of thirty-three without going to war, with the exception of a single campaign on the Prah, which was without conflict. He had therefore collected more money than any of his predecessors. It was weighed in a large scale held by four strong slaves, but it was not till three months later that the elders allowed Kari-Kari to take possession.

CHAPTER XXII.

MR. PLANGE'S SECOND EMBASSY.

The heavy rains of July were almost too much for the old mission-house, with its soaked walls and leaking roof, yet so many new Dampans were being built, that canes needed for repairs were not procurable, and we petitioned the king to allow us to use grass instead. Forty years before this same request had been denied the Wesleyan missionaries, a grass roof being prohibited in Coomassie, but our petition was successful, and the king said, "Begin as soon as you please."

Under an inundation of tropical rain, Mr. Plange and his wife were ceremoniously welcomed on the mpramaso place, after a terrible journey of ten weeks, during which his money was exhausted, and he and his people nearly starved. He brought a number of boxes with him which aroused the cupidity of Opoku, who zealously offered to receive him. Indeed the king had to interfere before the old man yielded the point, and we were allowed to welcome him into the mission-house, and to receive the letters and presents he had brought us from unknown friends in Berne.

Mr. Plange had been sent by both the English and Dutch governments, and gave the king official information of the ceding of Elmina to the British. He was commissioned by the administrator, Mr. Pope Hennesy, to offer not only the usual yearly present, but to double it, that peace might be secured, and he expressed the hope which had been so often expressed before that his majesty would set his innocent white prisoners free. The Dutch governor Ferguson also sent, with the news of the termination of the confederacy, presents to the king, consisting of the costly mirror before alluded to, and a general's helmet and sword.

He described Akjampong as having behaved in so violent a manner that had an Ashantee king been thus treated by a guest, he would certainly have had him beheaded, but out of regard to the old friendship of the two governments he had only had him conveyed to Asim, from whence he would find his own way back to Coomassie, and he begged the king to forgive him as the governor had done.

The sympathy of de Haes, the Dutch commander of the frigate Wassenar lying before Elmina, touched us deeply; he interceded for us in a special letter, sent presents to the king, and begged in his own name for our release. The official answer to the king's letter was entrusted by Mr. Hennesy to the Ashantee messengers, Kotiko and Afirifa. He agreed to a ransom of £1000, but not a farthing more, and if the king permitted us to leave, the money was to be paid at the Prah. Mr. Plange hoped the king would be so satisfied with his yearly present being doubled, that he would not desire any additional ransom. But our hope was not bright, we had ceased to look for anything from men. Our trust was in the Lord, in the crisis which we felt was now at hand. (See Appendix V.)

One day we were suddenly summoned to the palace with Mrs. Plange, that the king might show us his wives, and little Rosie was especially invited. After long waiting we were led into the inner court, where sat the monarch surrounded by little boys; opposite to him, and the central figure in a group of thirty others, was the first wife, weighed down with golden ornaments. The entire party seemed much pleased to have so good an opportunity of inspecting us, but the little one was the chief attraction. "Could she run," asked the king. Kokoo put her down, just holding her under the arms, when she ran straight up to him, to his and every one's great delight. He held out his hands, drew her between his knees and played with her. Rosie, all unconscious that she was a prisoner, could not take her eyes off his sandals. What pleased me least was that the king insisted on being saluted by each of the women, and made my wife take her hat off to look at both sides of her hair, comparing her with a white albino. But we were prisoners, and we had to submit.

We were also obliged to show ourselves at the reception of Kotiko and Afirifa. Opoku, that nephew of Adu Bofo, who had been sent by him in July, 1869, to the Kroboes as a guarantee of our speedy release, was also present, together with forty soldiers, part of the troop which had accompanied Akjampong to Elmina. From the opposite side there approached a procession bearing presents of rum, sheep, and oxen from Yœw Boakje, a son of the late king, who wished to express his thanks to the reigning sovereign for having offered numerous sacrifices to celebrate the death of his mother and brother, which had taken place some years before!

But this was not all we were compelled to witness. Boakje followed the present with a party of warriors painted red, who stood firing before the king for a full quarter of an hour, then came their wives, who also returned thanks, after which the king gave his presents, consisting of gold, various ornaments, clothing, &c., carried in three divisions. At the head of each marched a royal messenger, loudly proclaiming to all the chiefs what the king gave for the funeral celebration, in money, jewels, dresses, sheep, and finally in human sacrifices, and hardly had the presents been produced when a number of odumfo (executioners) appeared, followed by a bloodthirsty multitude, who rushed into the next street. Three chosen victims were led forth, who had been already lying between life and death for some weeks, with their feet and hands in irons, understanding too well the cause of the firing.

Presently, one of the party who had gone off returned in a state of high excitement, displaying a knife. One of the intended victims had somehow procured this weapon, and with it had wounded the odumfo, who sprang upon him. Another of these wretches speedily ran him through the cheek, and he was brought here bound.

The multitude hearing the death drum hurried in the direction whence the sound proceeded, the fatal signal was soon heard, and a [muffled sound announced that the execution was over, the band returned playing and uttering cries of joy, and sat down by his majesty. We afterwards came accidentally upon the blood-stained ground, where lay the headless trunks, their hands bound on their backs, and a warrior standing by, deliberately smearing his fetish with the blood of the last victim.

We had already seen a great deal of Coomassie, and our eyes and hearts were in some degree accustomed to its horrors, but this was overwhelming. The Ashantees stood around laughing and joking, whilst I attempted to hurry home to sigh and cry for this poor nation. But no! we were forced to stay to see the king pass. He came, surrounded by torches, in his sedan chair, which is bordered by a dozen swords covered with gold. He saw and saluted us with a smile, but looked confused as if he were struggling with serious thoughts. Oh, when will christianity help these poor deluded people?

Weeks passed by, and Mr. Plange was not invited to

appear, or remembered with any presents. It was said that Kotiko the privy counsellor had reproached the king with spending too much money on strangers; people here however seem fond of surprises, for on July 29th he was suddenly summoned to the palace, and we were to go with him. In the outer yard we met Afirifa and Kotiko with others, which led us to suppose that they wished to acquit themselves of their embassy. When therefore Mr. Plange was ordered to read his letters, he stated that he had arrived at the capital before Afirifa, and could not allow his affairs to be mixed up with his (Afirifa's), whereupon the latter was sent into the outer court. Mr. Plange commenced reading, but the remarks of the Dutch governor upon Akjampong's unjustifiable conduct were so severe that we were sent to the other side of the court.

When the words were read, "King William III. transfers Elmina with all rights and possessions on the Gold Coast to her majesty the queen of Great Britain, etc," the interpreter Nantschi explained, "The king of Holland is queen Victoria's husband; how is it that he sells his possessions to his wife?" Mr. Plange did not attend to this interpretation, but went on reading and explaining in the Fantee dialect.

The king enquired if the chiefs of the various races in and around Elmina had given their consent to this transfer. He was told that the king of Elmina had mounted the British flag and fired seven times to express his joy at the English present of rum, etc. The announcement of a yearly present of forty-eight oz. of gold instead of the usual twenty-four, was received with universal approbation, but the king broke up the interview with the unmeaning phrase, that he "wished to live in peace with the white people, and hoped to dismiss their messengers with good reports of him."

In the meantime he seemed to wish to raise his own

position by elevating that of his friends. Men who till now had only been his chamberlains, and whose office it was to carry his sedan chair and large umbrella, were made chiefs.

On August 5th, these men dressed in a style denoting the highest rank, thanked the king publicly in a large assembly in the Elmina street. Each of them aimed at showing himself off to the best advantage by boasting of his greatness and power, and displaying his jewellery and riches, whilst his followers danced furiously, and endeavoured to outdo each other in screaming and firing off guns.

These proceedings struck us as of a very warlike nature, and there were other movements amongst the important persons present which were somewhat inexplicable. For instance the prince of Kokofu was honoured by a reception in the evening, on which occasion the king presented him with seventy-six powder boxes. The prince of Bekwæ also arrived, and these gentlemen will not be allowed to leave the town until after the feast of yams has been celebrated, which is to be unusually early this year.

On August 5th, Mr. Plange's present arrived. It was poor in the extreme, consisting of two lean sheep, fifteen small bananas, and thirty-six dollars, with nine more for his wife. This parsimony might result from a wise precaution on the part of the monarch, who knew he must make a much greater effort when he dismisses the ambassador, especially if he send us with him. He had privately informed prince Ansa that this time he would really let us go, but we did not rely on his word.

Mr. Plange tried in a later assembly, which was attended by the whole council, to show the king things in their true light, plainly telling him that if we were not released, the barricading would certainly be enforced, and repeating that £1000 would be the very highest sum which would be paid for our ransom. The conversation at length took a confidential tone, when the king remarked that he would beg the governor to send more missionaries, "who would pray to God, and repair the mission-house." He might have thought that besides the ornament to the town of a stately building, a certain blessing would be connected with it, proceeding from the Christian's God. His superstitious mind probably fancied some earthly good would come to him in a mysterious way, if he so far protected and assisted missionaries.

Amidst so much that was painful, we had great satisfaction and comfort in our little school—from ten to thirteen boys came regularly one hour a day, and though they had difficulty in learning the letters, they enjoyed singing, and were able to manage the two songs we taught them, "Great Emmanuel," and "Oh how joyful," pretty well. They were wild little fellows, and accustomed to idle about in the market-place, and often quarrelled, when one or another would stay away; their singing too was in the onset dreadful howling—calling for much forbearance and patience, but we felt it such a mercy to be able to set to work even in this simple way, that we were not easily discouraged. When Joseph, on his return from the Coast, brought amongst other things some slates and pencils, our scholars were very much delighted.*

---

* In a letter of the same date Mr. K. wrote, "I must add some words to brother R.'s note, for he speaks too humbly of our work in Coomassie. We have an irregular congregation, which has seldom numbered less than three hundred individuals, mostly men and youths. Our school contains from fourteen to fifteen boys, sons of respectable Ashantees, who, although they must often be summoned when they idle about the streets, yet always come. I can hear them from my room just now, singing really well to the tune of 'God save the Queen.' We have also contrived a little chapel from the ruins of a house, where we hold our school and services; and better than all, the Ashantees know us and begin to trust us, so that we have already a footing here."

We were so far encouraged as seriously to contemplate establishing a permanent mission in Coomassie, and I looked forward in the event of our gaining our liberty, to joining David Asanti in this work. I soon found an opportunity of stating my wishes to the king. He had seemed so well disposed towards us in all his dealings with Afirifa, that I placed before him the question of our committee on the subject.

He replied, "That is just what I want, missionaries ought to be here, and I will send my own sons to the school." On my continuing—that I had now lived among them for three years, loved them, hated no one, and was prepared to return if my elders would send me,—"Yes," he replied, "now you speak sweet words, but when you are once at the Coast you will forget everything."

I immediately approached nearer and answered, "I am a missionary and do not tell lies. To return is my firm determination. If my elders will not send me, I must refrain. If they send me I will come with joy." To which he again replied, "Very good, if you come or your brother, I will confide to you my son to train, and will visit your mission-house from time to time." Several of the chiefs joined in at this, saying, "We too will send our sons to school." Still the day of our release remained undecided.

The Yam festival that year was less numerously attended than usual, but the Sunday was spoiled, and we were obliged to omit street preaching. The human sacrifice on this occasion was a Fetish priest, whose severed head the wretched old Odumfo exhibited before us. The king danced with a small silk handkerchief in his hand instead of his sword and gun, a change which we understood to signify his peaceful intentions. Much drinking followed, but he was not intoxicated as usual, and parted from us with a warm pressure of the hand.

The first day of sprinkling and purification fell on

Friday, August 30th, and I was again forced to witness headless bodies dragged by a rope to the horrible receptacle which already contained thousands. On the second day of purification, September 17th, we withdrew from the ceremony held in honour of the protecting Fetish Bosommuru, and went to our plantation, for in the meantime our horizon had again darkened; indeed, the storm was already begun.

On September 2nd, the high council met, at which were the Princes Dwaben, Mampong, and Bekwae, while Adu Bofo, who was seriously ill, was represented by his son, and a subordinate officer, Nantschi. The subject of the ransom being first discussed, Nantschi expressed his astonishment at the governor naming £1000 as the *highest* sum, when their demand had been £4860 at the *very lowest*. To this the king replied, " Süsse will come again and found a school, but with such demands we should make this return impossible," he then suggested the sum should be lowered to £2000, to which, after a long palaver, they all agreed.

Mr. Plange was then called upon to give his opinion. Utterly unable to conceal his annoyance, he said abruptly that the governor would not pay a farthing more than £1000, and if he returned to the Coast without us, the way would be blocked immediately.

Fatal words! The chiefs first laughed, then a general tone of dissatisfaction was apparent, and the storm broke out in curses, oaths, and threats. "A few days ago," said the king, " I thought you were joking, if you are in earnest you may come. We are ready! Your governor cannot leave his fort without an umbrella, so afraid is he of sun and rain. Let him try to come to us. For a long time the Ashantees have been going up to Fantee, and then the white men hid themselves in their forts, it would be something new if the Fantees were to come here!" This was spoken amid thundering applause. The Bantama prince then shook his fist in Plange's face, and in the most offensive and insulting language, threatened war. The queen mother said, "I am only a woman, but would fight the governor with my left hand." "I am but a small chief, said another, yet shall the governor pale before me;" while many voices cried, "whoever sells fixes the price. We had trouble enough to get these goods here; if the governor will not buy them, he may leave them." At last there was a frantic and united cry of "We will not give them up. Let him fetch them with fire and sword, we will kill them;" while the king turned angrily to Plange, adding, "if you wish, I can show you my supply of powder."

One man alone remained quiet in the uproar—the gigantic prince of Mampong, who had before voted for our freedom without a ransom. To him Plange turned with the request that he would try to soften down the high council, while the king exclaimed, "that is a good word, we will now break up." It was evident all wished that things should take a milder turn, as the interpreters remarked that Mr Plange need not repeat to the governor what he had just heard.

That after their recent heavy losses of money, men and first-rate leaders, the chiefs should again wish for war, we could scarcely believe, though if it were declared, they would doubtless march into the field with spirit. But far worse to me was the thought that in that case the idea of a mission in Ashantee must be given up, and I greatly doubted whether the king would set us free, even if £2000 were offered for our ransom, though at the same time I did not believe there would be war on our account, neither did the committee expect it.

For some weeks Kühne had been suffering from his old complaint, cough and hemorrhage; the continued disappointment told upon him and depressed his spirits, so that I much desired speedy freedom for him, whilst we, having better health, might remain yet. Our Rosie was a year old and strong for her age; our delight in her greatly softened our affliction, especially when she took her first step alone.

Mr. Plange remained with us, while a royal messenger was despatched to the Coast with a determined answer to his demands, which had been fully discussed in council. Kühne too wrote to the governor, telling him that the chiefs here had the upper hand, and would gladly draw the king into another war; M. Bonnat and I added a few lines begging that if possible K.'s liberty might be brought about.

The king privately represented to Plange how unwisely he had behaved. He professed himself in favour of peace, but said the overbearing chiefs insisted on a ransom in gold. He also dared to boast how well he provided for us (nine dollars for five persons for three weeks!) without our working for it. He had of course observed K.'s delicate health, and would have given him a wife if he had only asked him, to which the ambassador replied that missionaries were not so easily satisfied in the choice of a wife, and the best thing was to send the sick man to the Coast at once.

The king was however not to be persuaded, though he hinted that he might eventually take £1500, and finished by making a request that the governor should send him five casks of chalk, and all sorts of oil colours to restore his stone house; also clocks, bells, waterproof boots, &c. Ansa's nephew, Owusu Kokoo, a man whom we could trust, whom the king regarded as his grandson, and made the only channel for confidential communication with the Coast, was despatched with these requests. How childish would this behaviour appear to the governor.

CHAPTER XXIII.

A CRITICAL TIME.

THE long threatened crisis now seemed imminent. People from Aguogo (belonging to Ashantee Akem) had sent word to their relatives in Akem to be on their guard, as the king thought of making war with them, and when this came to his ears, it was immediately brought before the high council. The chiefs of Ashantee Akem pleaded not guilty, and had to drink the odum water, after which six of them were condemned to death. Our acquaintance, the chief Asamoa, escaped, and was afterwards pardoned on paying a heavy fine, but the friendly Mampong was kept in irons. When this became known, many of the inhabitants of Aguogo and Sokore hastily concealed themselves.

A chief in the vassal state of Serem had been amusing himself with making an image of gold to display his riches. The king sent messengers to demand this image, whom the chief dismissed, saying, if the king wished for an image, he could make one for himself, upon which other messengers were despatched, and the way was ordered to be barricaded until their return.

To the north of Asini, and west of Fantee, a day's march further into the interior, was the commercial town of Kinshabo, numbering about four thousand inhabitants. Its Prince Amatifu, an ally of Ashantee, had delivered a large number of powder-boxes on credit to the king, for which he offered in payment the hundreds of Wusutra youths who had been sent away from their homes (*see* page 169). The chief refused to take them, and sent word that if the king did not pay in gold, he would wait no longer. From this, and from the fact that, on account of the expense he declined to visit the abode of his Fetish during the yam festival, it appeared that Kari-Kari was really suffering from want of money. Kwakoo Dooah's treasure (*see* page 171) was regarded as crown property, that might be used for national but not for personal expenses.

An Ashantee one day tauntingly exclaimed to a Fantee, " Only wait a while, and the king will march against you and drag you all here." In a private interview with Mr. Plange, the king declared in angry tones his love of peace, and commissioned the ambassador to write to the governor that very night, stating that if it was a case of necessity, £1000 would be sufficient as ransom, but it must be paid immediately. The letter was to be dated October 1st, but the messenger, Owusu Kokoo, was not to deliver it until the governor had really refused the demanded £2000. Mr. Plange conceded so far as to draw up the letter, but privately communicated its contents to the governor, through a bearer. To us it seemed as if the Ashantees would be satisfied with *any* sum that might enable them at once to declare war.*

* This letter may serve as characteristic of the style of the Ashantee courts :—

" It is the pressing wish of my great chiefs that I should communicate to your excellency, that with regard to the ransom for the white men who are here, which has been valued in my letter sent by my chief Owusu Kokoo Kuma at £2000, my views have now undergone a change, viz., that your excellency has now only £1000 to pay, which is promised to me and my chiefs, for, considering the now firmly established peace, it seems unnecessary to me to enlighten your excellency further upon it. I have done all that I could in this matter, also your excellency's messenger, Mr. Plange, has exerted himself extraordinarily with my chiefs, and I have endeavoured to foster good feeling towards your ex-

A CRITICAL TIME.

The next day the man who had threatened the Fantee was charged and found guilty. Plange begged for the poor fellow's life, but the king would not listen. "You shall see how I chastise such deceivers," was his angry reply. A further petition to the queen mother was successful so far, that the cruel monarch consented to sleep over it. Meanwhile the offender was placed in the block and unmercifully thrashed, amid scornful cries of contempt.

We were just then gladdened by letters from home, brought us by two Fantees on September 30th. Friends, relations, and fellow-workers, overwhelmed us with love and tender sympathy. They also unconsciously aided me in a profitable transaction.

For a long time the mohammedans had been trying to persuade me to part with my clock for a slave, but I did not like to give it up, and promised to send for another. A beautiful watch sent from Mr. Michaud in Neuchâtel gave me the opportunity of gratifying them. I hesitated to accept the thirty dollars they offered, as it was only worth about three, but willingly took a little girl of eight years old, who had been stolen from her country and kept in slavery. The buyers had seen a similar watch in Timbuctoo, and were especially astonished at its striking the hours, and went off quite proud of their treasure.

Other things had been sent, but the king's prohibition

cellency. Therefore I beg your excellency, in order that this affair may be quickly concluded, to pay me the sum, partly in goods, partly in gold dust or coin, through my messenger; so that I may be enabled to send the white men to the coast, and to announce peace to all my land. I hope your excellency will send back the messenger twenty days after sight, and expect that your excellency will allow no delay to take place in the matter, but complete it according to our mutual wishes."

KOFI KARI-KARI.
(COFFEE CALCALLI.)

made it difficult for us to get them. For upwards of two months five boxes had been lying in Akrofrum, only three days journey from the capital, but our repeated entreaties to be allowed to have them were answered with promises only, and when I sent messengers they were turned back, until at length after continued applications, Bosommuru sent a sword-bearer to accompany my people, and they finally brought them on October 19th.

My school was causing me some anxiety. We gave a fortnight's holiday to allow the boys to attend the yam festival, and when I heard (Oct. 3rd) that some had returned, I called them, and begged them to come again to school. They seemed frightened, for a boy who had only once attended had been complained of to the king and well thrashed. When I doubted the truth of the story, and spoke of mentioning it, they begged me with tears not to do so; it would cost them, as tale bearers and betrayers, their heads. I quieted them with the promise not to tell anything of what I had heard, but took the matter, which seriously troubled me, to God in prayer.

While I was thus free from my daily engagements I went with my wife, who needed a change, to M. Bonnat's cottage in the plantation, where we remained some weeks.

I asked Bosommuru why the children did not appear, and if the king had forbidden it. He professed to know nothing, but would enquire, and a week later gave me the king's permission to gather them together again. Still I felt under restraint. On my way home however, I beckoned one of them who was standing in the market place, but he ran away as if he had seen a ghost. Prince Ansa's relation too, Kwabena, had been taken away from us by his friends, though he had been with us for some time. They said he should come back in five days, but he did not return, and when I saw him he told me that his people did not like him to be with us.

Amid these many discouragements, the welfare of these poor people pressed heavily on my heart. One day, meeting several of my former scholars in the market place, I again invited them, and promised to give them oranges. They came for this, but persisted in saying they were afraid to come to school, although I told them they had the king's permission. Later in the day others arrived, attracted no doubt by the oranges, promising they would come back the following Monday. And they really did so (October 23rd), that is three of them, whom we begged to bring others.

We had soon eight Ashantees, who came with our own boys and sat down again to learn, rejoicing greatly at the Christmas gifts we were preparing. But alas! first one and then another was called away to follow his Adamfo (friend). Most of the free youths being destined to be followers of this or that chief, to make a parade before him at the ceremonies, and when grown up to follow him with a gun.

On (October 22nd), we heard that a high council had been held in Bantama, when the chiefs had sworn they would march against the Coast, to which the king replied, "If you go, I shall go with you." A few days later we were told that Ashantee had promised assistance to the prince of Kwantiabo, who had long sought its help against a neighbouring state.

That something was going on, Mr. Plange had to learn to his bitter cost, the king declaring in an assembly of the council that he "interfered in the politics of the kingdom, and acted as if no one could read." It was evidently known that the ambassador had secretly written to the governor, and unscrupulously compromised the king by communicating the proceedings of the council—

(see page 184). He was somewhat disconcerted, although he was not altogether without means of defence, as he had been censured by the governor for not having acquainted him with the storm of indignation which had burst forth as detailed at pages 180-81. After a painful explanation the ambassador was made to write to the governor in the king's name to ask him to send the rest of the Ashantees to Apollonia.

CHAPTER XXIV.

SEEMING LIBERTY.

"WHEN the Lord turned again the captivity of His people, we were like unto them that dream," so sang the captive Israelites in Babylon, and so were we now inclined to sing in Coomassie. Yet our hopes on former occasions had been so often dashed that they were even now mingled with many misgivings, which subsequent events, alas! justified.

On the 8th, the king, with his assembled chiefs, gave audience to Mr. Plange and ourselves, under one of the spacious galleries, when it was stated by Osee, the attendant, that £1000 was the ultimatum of the sum offered by the governor for our release. Some of the chiefs rose on hearing this, and rudely demanded £2000, declaring that Adu Bofo had expended thus much, whereupon the king affirmed that the outlay had been *his*, and he would accept the £1000; then addressing himself to us, he added, "you will leave to-morrow for Fomana, I will prepare everything to-day; from there," said he to Plange, "you will write to Ansa, and when the money reaches the Prah, you can cross."

The thankful joy with which we heard these words, and the throbbing of our hearts as we thought of reunion with our loved ones, cannot be described. We at once approached, took the jewelled hand of the monarch in ours, and expressed our gratitude, while Plange thanked him on his knees. Our words would have been warmer but for sad remembrances too vivibly impressed on our minds—unjustly captured! sold for £1000! Still we tried to feel hopeful and happy. The general's representative was not satisfied, but the interpreters stood and cried, "as the king has decided, so let it be."

The uproar that followed was awful, and we soon perceived that "to-morrow" was an indefinite future. A severe trial was already in store, for the very next day our treasured little Rose was seized with fever and convulsions, and for many hours struggled for life, so that we almost anticipated the dreadful alternative of having to leave her behind should we ever get free ourselves. The king however seemed to wish to hasten our journey, and to be rid of us and all our belongings, and we expected Sunday the 10th to be our last in Coomassie.

We had before planned a kind of Christmas entertainment for our school boys, but in our excitement and our anxiety for Rosie, we could only arrange a few presents on two small tables covered with a white cloth, and when ready we rang a bell to call our guests. These poor little untamed and noisy fellows came in quite subdued, and listened attentively while I addressed them. They joined us in singing, after which I prayed, and they again sang the pieces they knew.

I then told them of Jesus, the children's friend, who loved them and their country, and would make them holy if they would come to Him and ask Him. I explained that as we might not perhaps remain among them till Christmas, we were fulfiling our promise beforehand, and giving them our Christmas gifts now—to each, material for a dress, a handkerchief from Berne, and some biscuits and oranges. The joy was great; they received these unaccustomed riches with beaming eyes, sang again and left us.

This was the happiest day I had spent in Coomassie, for truly God had permitted me to see great things from a very insignificant beginning. We had been sowing for eternity, and I prayed, "Oh! may this seed take root in the hearts of the little ones." The hymns they have learnt they will often sing, such as, "Where may the soul find her home and her rest," the result I committed in faith to the Lord. Fever prevented me from rising the next day, but I received a visit from Bosommuru and Sabeng, who brought us two peredwane (seventy-two dollars) for our journey, and nothing now remained but to take our formal leave of the king.

I resolved on making an effort to redeem Palm and his wife Kokoo, who otherwise must be left according to our promise, when we had received permission to keep them with us. I begged Bosommuru to intercede with the king, offering a ransom. Their owner, Kwasi Domfe, demanded eight peredwanes, but finally, after much opposition, consented to take six—two hundred and sixteen dollars. This we advanced from the mission funds, for we felt it would be unkind and ungrateful to leave this worthy couple to return into captivity, and be separated for the remainder of their lives. To the woman we were especially attached for her devoted care of our child. Palm promised the repayment of the debt in one year, for which he pledged his two houses in Akra.

Feverish and exhausted by packing, we paid our final visit to his majesty in the evening, and found him in good humour, counting out the money just received for the Palms. "Now," said he, "I shall see if you will keep your word and return; and when you meet the governor, tell him to send Akjampong and his suite back to Coomassie." He expressed a wish that *one* of us would go with his messenger to the Coast, that it might be evident we were released, but we declined, saying, we "preferred to receive our freedom together," and left.

Troubles and annoyances of every description delayed our departure for two days, when with only half our escort of bearers and hammocks, we turned our backs on Coomassie, followed by a crowd of insolent and abusive beggars, who snatched all they could from us to the very end. We saw with great pleasure that our scholars remained true to us, for they followed us to the river, and there took an affectionate farewell.

The next morning we found the river in Dasu so swollen that it was hazardous to cross the crazy bridge, which consisted of the trunk of a tree. I was too ill to venture that night or the next day, but on the 14th we made the perilous attempt, and crept tremblingly over, holding on by a long trailing plant, while a bearer carried my wife on his shoulders, and another took Rosie.

For many days afterwards I was prostrated by fever, and it was only by almost superhuman efforts, urged on by the merciless royal messengers, that we on the evening of the 15th, reached Fomana. How gladly would we have then rested, but this was not permitted. Exhausted though we were, we had to undergo a formal reception by the chief, who however treated us very kindly. Our dear child's state continued so critical that we still despaired of her life, but our prayers were graciously answered, and she was spared to us.

From Fomana the messengers were sent forward to inform the governor at Cape Coast of our arrival thus far, and to receive the £1000, with which we were told they were to make purchases. We at once saw our position, and how problematic it was that we should cross the Prah. Afirifa arrived on the 19th, professedly as our escort to the Coast, there to conclude a formal treaty of peace. Haughty as his usual bearing was, he was now civil and even respectful towards us. Several of Mr. Plange's people, who had remained behind to finish their preparations, soon joined us, and brought news that in Coomassie all were preparing for a campaign. We

SEEMING LIBERTY. 193

observed signs of this in loads of ammunition, rum, and salt, continually passing through Fomana, and we felt sure that the pride of Ashantee had reached such a height that no lasting peace with England could be maintained. Most truly should we have rejoiced could we at that moment have seen the Prah behind us! Thus we thought while still lingering near the river in November, and when our written narrative was resumed on December 17th, our apprehensions proved to be well founded, for we had then been cruelly driven back again to our old prison house.

We had evidently been sent to Fomana to induce the governor to pay the £1000, whilst we were yet in the power of Ashantee, and that we might be kept in ignorance of the preparations for war against the Protectorate, which had been decided on for months, but were only now openly commencing. Until the end of November, we waited in suspense the return of the two messengers, Osei and Owusu Adum, from the coast, wondering much as to the means of paying for the costly war material always in transit, being certain that no credit would be allowed by the governor. We afterwards found that prince Ansa, deceived by the fair promises of Owuso Kokoo, and hoping to hasten our release, had with another friend agreed to stand security for his nephew's (Owusu Kokoo's) purchases.

On December 6th twelve bearers arrived from the governor, bringing a letter from prince Ansa, telling us he hoped to welcome us in a few days at Mr. Blankson's country seat. He regretted Kühne's refusal to accompany the messenger Osei to the Coast, as his arrival there would have given the governor confidence in the payment of the money, and he thought would have hastened our departure. We had declined this, fearing to be caught in a trap; and we soon saw that we were right.

O

The two messengers arrived on the 7th: we could get no intelligence from them, but were told by a Fantee that Mr. Dawson, the governor's interpreter, was on his way, and we hoped that he might be the bearer of our ransom. He arrived the same evening, and handed us an official letter in the presence of the chief, whom he saluted. The £1000 had been weighed out before the Ashantee ambassadors, and was then to be sealed and given into the charge of Mr. F. Grant, a merchant, who would hold it until our arrival at the Coast. We were hardly allowed to speak to Mr. Dawson, but found that he was going on to Coomassie, at the request of the king, and had permission to remain as a hostage for us, lest the king might doubt whether the governor had really sent the money. Owusu Kokoo was also on his way back to Coomassie.

Sunday the 8th was a painful day to us. The two ambassadors paraded the village with ominous looks. Owusu Kokoo saluted us on his arrival in his usual friendly manner, but made no communication. I held a service in the street with great enjoyment, but noticed that the Fomanians kept aloof, and after closing, a christian from Elmina told me that he and his companions feared they would not be allowed to return to the Coast. One of them who had tried to start for the Coast was sent back with an intimation that, as the priests were "making fetish" all along the road that Sunday, all strangers must be forbidden to pass. I tried to comfort him by reminding him how little we could rely on such reports; nevertheless, I could not divest myself of grave fears.

In the evening, whilst bathing in the river, Palm came with the news that messengers from Coomassie were waiting for us, and that they were accompanied by hammock-bearers. I was at once convinced we were to be carried back, and on entering the house of the chief Obeng, I saw these same bearers behind Afirifa and an unknown chief. We were greeted with great gravity by the messenger, who rose and delivered the king's salutations. "His majesty had heard that we were badly treated in Fomana, which aroused his indignation, and must be altered." A sheep was to be immediately caught in the streets and given to us, another to himself, &c. A fresh messenger would to-morrow give us leave to travel further, and provide more bearers.

This sounded assuring, but we had learned in Ashantee to suspect everything; and whilst at breakfast the next morning, we were summoned to the chief Obeng. Not hastening immediately, a second and more pressing call was made. We found the chief's court full of people, amongst them many strange faces. M. Bonnat recognised the man who had murdered his two assistants, which excited our apprehension, especially as many were running to and fro, and whispering together suspiciously, while we wondered what would occur next. The Fantees were summoned together, who were placed in the further corners of the court to listen to merchants and bearers with the king's message.

After long continued suspense, the messenger arose and said, his majesty had, " out of friendship to the governor, exerted himself to free us from Adu Bofo, and send us to the Coast" (in negro language this message occupied much time, and was expressed in endless words); but 'Ata' (Plange) had played false by urging the governor to pay the money *after* our arrival, and until then, to detain Akjampong. Such conduct, at the very time he was treating for peace, he could not understand. He was indignant at the false 'Ata;' and as the business was done through him, and the road was now blocked, he commanded him to restore his property. Before the white people could be set at liberty the royal messengers must return to Coomassie with Akjampong and the £1000."

Scarcely was the speech concluded when a wild rabble rushed upon the Fantees, marshalled them in order, and led them away. Our own servants were torn from us, and Mr. Plange seized by his arms and legs and dragged away, as was Palm also. We too were ordered off, but I refused to move one step without my wife. When they began to maltreat me, I protested against it, and told them I knew the king would not allow it, appealing to Owusu Kokoo and Afirifa who stood by. They gave orders that we were not to be touched; and as I was resolute not to move a step till my wife was fetched, Afirifa himself went and brought her, which was a great relief to me in this perplexing moment.

She had gone through an hour of deep anxiety. Alarmed by a great noise and screaming in the street, she ran to the front of the house, where she saw Kwaku, the lad we had ransomed, lying bound and bleeding on the ground, and the girl who was given us by the king being torn away by an Ashantee. She was then herself seized by the arm and pulled violently. She resisted, and begged to be allowed to take her hat and a covering for Rosie. Unable to shake off her captor she struggled into the room, her child in her arms, but he continued his attempts until the master of the house appeared and freed her from his grasp. She was then led into a court behind, where she was found by Afirifa, who brought her to me. We were conducted to the house of a good-natured subordinate chief, who at first seemed unwilling to receive us, but seeing our unpleasant position, took us into the court, and when it was too hot allowed us to remain in an open room.

We were surrounded by some dozen lawless guards, who as time passed became so civil, that I ventured to ask permission to return to our old house. That however was not to be thought of, for reasons not difficult to perceive and very soon made manifest. We had received many packages from the Coast, and they knowing this supposed we must have hoarded up a great deal of money, they required time therefore to make a thorough search, but assured us all was right and safe. So here we remained still more depressed in spirit than on our first captivity, for the three years and a-half had not passed without leaving traces behind. We had long had difficulty in cherishing any love in our hearts for Ashantee, now the measure of their blindness seemed full, and punishment deserved.

Palm's wife being allowed her liberty on the child's account, told us that "Pisangs" were being dried at the fire, which her former master said were preparing for the campaign to the Coast. The promised sheep was now brought, with the intimation that the king did not wish us to starve, which interpreted meant, "we want it killed that we may have our share." I coolly told them to do as they chose, but we required some soup, so it was soon despatched, and as quickly divided, a leg being given to us.

When asked who could cook for us, I demanded that our own servants should be restored, and after a great search most of them were permitted to return. We then tried to regain possession of some of our property. M. Bonnat, attended by a guard, procured a few things and a Bible, and Kokoo was permitted to fetch the beds, and my watch.

All my attempts to induce Afirifa to let us sleep under our own roof were unavailing, whilst we received the painful tidings from Kokoo, that Palm and Mr. Plange were both lying in the stocks. On the 10th, we met Mr. and Mrs. Plange in the presence of the chief. Their luggage had been searched, Mr. P. beaten and nearly strangled, stripped of all his clothing and placed in the stocks; in which he remained until late in the evening, when the chief, "Obeng," had a few of his clothes restored. Mrs. P. had received no personal injury, but was of course deeply distressed.

We were then commanded to open our boxes, "to ascertain," so they said, "if anything was missing." I told them I understood their manœuvre, they only wanted our money, and if they would treat us gently, I would show it them to the last coin. Some seemed confused, but Yaw Agjie said, "Yes, it is so, we want to see the money." They believed me when I said it was needless to open the provision boxes, for they only contained eatables, though one of these, being very heavy, was questioned. I showed them the money in a little bottle, and the dollars wrapped in rag. They were very much interested; "this must be weighed," said they, "that all may be safely restored to you." I knew the people too well to believe this, and I replied, "that would be quite unnecessary, for the weight was known."

Afirifa caught sight of some candles, and attempted to take them, which we resisted stoutly, threatening to complain of him to the king, when he desisted; but to pacify the covetous creature I gave him six bottles of wine, and thereby succeeded in getting leave to take part of our property back to Coomassie. Six chests were left behind with the keys, which we only relinquished after long resistance.

On the 11th, our return was arranged. I demanded at least for my wife that bearers should be found, and inquired for those who had been sent by the governor from Cape Coast. After much altercation, some men of Akra appeared with ropes round their necks to carry the heavy luggage, and what remained was brought by men of the place. It was with a feeling of relief that we left these unfriendly people, and again set forth, hoping to find rest in our more familiar prison house.

Both to our joy and sorrow, we at the first stage met Mr. Dawson, whose bearers had been placed in the stocks, so that he no longer doubted war was decided on. We were grieved that he on our account had been caught in this trap, which he had not apprehended when he left the Coast. Happily for us and himself he was a true christian, and knew how to conduct himself as such, so that in him we found a calm and wise counsellor and friend. The Ashantees took without leave from the inhabitants two pigs and a sheep, and brought us food in abundance, with which they thought to solace us in our sorrows.

The next day's journey was a very hard one, we only reached Akankaase in the afternoon, and but for Mr. Plange's help poor Kühne could never have reached it at all; his illness had taken a very serious turn, and he could no longer travel out of his hammock. Bearers were demanded in the king's name in every village, untrained men, whose roughness inflicted needless pain on our poor brother.

Tired almost to death, drenched with pouring rain, and smothered with mud from the swamps, we reached Amoaforo, where nothing but fish was to be had, as the troops were announced to arrive the next day, showing us the campaign had already been begun. We commenced our last day's journey on the 14th, a double one, that we might arrive in the evening; whether we were able for it or not they never enquired.

Poor Kühne was committed to the care of the already overburdened Akras. No Ashantee would submit to such a degradation as to carry a burden, so we crept on as well as we could, and at Kaase we were met by a royal messenger, who hurriedly ordered Mr. Dawson off to the palace to a reception. Accompanied by two armed men, we slowly followed, and by eight o'clock crossed the swampy Suben. The capital was unusually quiet, not a drum was heard.

We halted in the open street, and painfully waited the orders for our appointed lodging.

K. was so ill that we longed for home, which was at last reached in the old mission house, where the good Joseph had prepared comfortably for our reception. Bosommuru came after ten o'clock with a few words of pretended comfort. "A disturbance had taken place, without the king having any ill will to the white people or to the Fantees. The war was only against his old slave states, Asen and Denkjera." Empty words! we knew where we were, and begged to be left in peace, and allowed to move to our plantation.

CHAPTER XXV.

THE REASON OF THE WAR.

9th December 1872.

IT became every day more evident that Mr. Plange was but the pretended cause of the war. He was said to have threatened the king, and in his letter to the governor called the Ashantees scoundrels. Yet on the other hand they declared they had no quarrel with the whites, and only waged war against Akem and Denkjera! They further stated that the governor wished to give the fortress of Elmina to a certain prince of Denkjera, which must be prevented by armed interference, but we believed that war had been decided on months before, and had been wished for and planned for years; not by the king, but by his great men whose influence he could not resist, though his predecessor had made short work with any one attempting to dictate to him.

The real reason of the war was that the British had refused for ten years to give up the chief Gjanin, who had escaped to the coast; this had likewise been the cause of the fruitless expedition of 63-64. After Kwakoo Dooah's death, king Kari-Kari had written to prince Ansa at Cape Coast, assuring him that the past was forgotten, but the chiefs were not satisfied. Kwakoo Dooah had once asked them if it was to be submitted to, that a subject, having taken the king's oath, should find protection in another conntry, while they had no power to demand him back.

They all agreed that under such circumstances no kingdom could stand, such an insult could only be avenged by war. Whatever the secret wish of the king might then have been, he had at that time no war material, so they were forced to wait. Owusu Kokoo, the second man in the kingdom (Ansa's brother, and Kwakoo Dooah's uncle), swore the king's oath that he would restore the honour of the kingdom, and that if the people of the Coast were like deeply-rooted palms, he would uproot them, and bring as many prisoners as would avenge the insult. Having thus sworn he set out, and in the summer of 1863 crossed the Prah, without however effecting much.

When he had escaped a trap set for him by the Fantees, he re-crossed the river with forty prisoners, was stationed there for some months, but was finally recalled by the peaceful king. Whilst preparing for a second attempt he met his death (in April 1867). The nobles said he had died of grief because he was unavenged, and when assembled round the corpse, declared he should not be buried until Gjanin's insult was avenged, and the head of the Denkjera prince, Kwakju, brought to his burial. The young king Kofi would not consent to this. It seemed to him a disgrace to leave the dead unburied, but he wished to honour him with elaborate death ceremonies. Gjanin's matter was not to be forgotten however, notwithstanding all mutual assurances, but the right time must be watched for, and when the highest nobility placed Kofi on the throne, he swore "my business shall be war."

An eventful result was that in 1868, when Akra was transferred from the Dutch to the English, the latter made over their territory west of Elmina to the Dutch. This caused great rejoicing in Coomassie, because the people of Denkjera, their slaves, who had escaped to the Coast fourteen years before, had thus gone from the strong protection of Britain to the dependency of the lenient old ally of Ashantee (Holland).

But this treaty of the European powers was more easy to frame than to enforce. The coast towns thus transferred swore they would never adopt the Dutch flag, combined in a general resistance, and called in the help of the Fantees. The Dutch could not extinguish the flame, although they bombarded the towns Sekondi and Commenda, which increased the irritation of the Fantees, who threatened to demolish Elmina, and actually stormed it for several weeks. The English at length succeeded in persuading them to retreat, and quietly await the result. During this bombardment, the chief of Elmina sent a messenger to Ashantee, asking the king's assistance; this man was still living in Coomassie when we were there.

The Akwamers to the east of the Volta had already begged for help from the Ashantees, and as it was thought this help might, with wise management, be given to them without irritating the English, Adu Bofo was sent there, with an army of thirty thousand men. No arrangements were made in regard to Elmina, for it was not doubted that after gaining a great name by subduing the Krepes, the general might successfully make war upon the Protectorate.

Meanwhile Akjampong (the king's uncle) was sent to Elmina with a hundred men, to watch for a favourable opportunity, and to prepare for an attack upon the British power. He went by way of Kwantiabo, and his track was marked by murder and rapine whenever he met with Fantees. It was intended that at the right moment the English territory should be attacked on three sides, by the two generals on its flanks, and by the king himself making a charge on the Prah.

All this planning however proved unsuccessful. It is true, Adu Bofo made many prisoners amongst the inhabitants of neighbouring towns, but the invasion of Dompre, combined with hunger and sickness, so weakened him, that he was forced to return home, and the affairs at Elmina were equally unfavourable, as Akjampong, who had undertaken the command, and who had sworn to defend the town against all attacks, was finally forced to take refuge in Apollonia. To all this was added the transfer of the Dutch possessions to Great Britain, which threatened to put a stop to the Ashantees trading to the Coast.

War was therefore resolved upon by the chiefs at that time, but as the store of ammunition and salt was then very small, it was desirable first to re-open the trade with the Coast, in order to procure a supply of these necessaries. Powder might be had in case of need from the far distant Kwantiabo, but salt could only be got from the Coast, and the plan was to make use of us as a means for opening the way to it.

For this reason, every enquiry of the English government respecting us was answered in a friendly tone; the royal messengers who were constantly hurrying backwards and forwards on our account, always had a suite of twenty men who were at liberty to purchase as much as they pleased, and the people of the boundary also held large markets yearly at which Ashantees could buy salt although at a high price; prisoners too were constantly exchanged in order to lull the governor and the Fantees to sleep, and confidence was so far restored that the Fantees again ventured to go to Coomassie for trade.

At last the governor, in a complaisant manner, proclaimed peace between the Ashantees and the Protectorate, and thus the "great nation" had what it wished for, free liberty to trade in order to prepare for war, which was unceasingly desired, as the surrender of Elmina could not by any means be prevented. A hint

THE REASON OF THE WAR.

from Coomassie was however sent to the Elmina chief to wait quietly, so he hoisted the English flag; but the Ashantees fully believed Elmina belonged to them, though the king wrote (through prince Ansa) that the surrender of the fort was a grief to him, but that he would forget it.

It was also made a cause of complaint that Akjampong had not been followed to Apollonia by the full number of his troops, but in December, after we were brought back from Fomana, he was sent forward to the Prah with the desired escort.

Meanwhile the desire to prepare for war was so ardent that it was not easy to deceive the Fantees who were in Coomassie, so, after every conceivable report had been spread as to the object of the campaign, such as expeditions to the interior, &c., the mask was thrown off. On December 9th, the day we were seized in Fomana, all the chiefs marched from the residence, and every town and village united in one cry, " War, war, against the Coast!"

To measure themselves for once with the white men was the secret desire of every Ashantee chief. That the critical hour had arrived they all acknowledged, when the news came of the surrender of Elmina. They could not allow the kingdom to be broken up bit by bit, as they considered. Not that all were agreed in opinion: many an Ashantee owned that the grounds for war were that we were unjustly kept prisoners, that the governor had shown himself well disposed by sending the quarrelsome Akjampong back to Coomassie, &c.; but all this did not alter the resolution to make war to the knife.

Every one knew that this campagin was very different from that against Krepe. It was to decide once for all whether the Fantees were to be subject to the Ashantees, or the Ashantees to them. For myself I had not the slightest doubt that Ashantee was running blindfold to its doom, but this seemed absolutely necessary before this poor country could be taught the source of healing and unchanging strength. Some time or other it will have to acknowledge that Kari-Kari is not God (as Afirifa and others declare), and that it is nothing, and can do nothing; then the message of salvation may be acceptable.

The campaign at length opened. Two divisions marched in advance, the right against Denkjera, the left against Akem. But the main army consisted but of few troops, for many a chief who formerly commanded twenty or thirty men, was only followed by three with two guns. Both divisions were ordered to make their way to Fomana, and the plantations were quickly plundered, for the supply of food to the troops was quite insufficient, and they feared they were going to die of starvation; there was also a report that small-pox had broken out in the camp, and that one of the chiefs had died of it. We could only look up to the Lord who would doubtless glorify Himself in Ashantee.

CHAPTER XXVI.

IN COOMASSIE AMID THE FLUCTUATIONS OF WAR.

We remained in the plantation (till January 10th), the cold not allowing us to stay longer. We also preferred the mission-house, for in those disturbed times no native was secure from being sold into slavery, and little Rose, not being free from fever, we felt more comfortable in Coomassie. Several christians were there, Mose Ajesu, the former teacher, Richard Kwabin, and Theophil, the cobbler's boy, who were found in Ashantee-Akem, and brought in bound, but at once set free.

The British Administrator released Akjampong, the king's uncle, in December 1872, and when the Asens wanted, on his journey through their country, to detain him a prisoner, he ordered them to leave him alone, hoping thereby to give an assurance to the Ashantees of the good will of the English towards them. When he and his suite were to receive their welcome, it was proposed that we should attend. Kühne and M. Bonnat were prevented by indisposition, but I was invited with the two ambassadors, Plange and Dawson, to be present.

The procession was headed by an official, three hundred of Akjampong's warriors followed, then three Fetish priests painted white, with their Fetish on their heads. Some of these gentlemen saluted, others insulted me, and still more Messrs. Dawson and Plange. Akjampong himself behaved very badly, although he must have known that he was greatly indebted to the kindness of the governor. But judgments were already becoming apparent.

Afirifa, who had said in Fomana that the king was God, was accused by Akjampong of surrendering Elmina to the English, and of being the cause of his (Akjampong's) imprisonment in the fort, and now his God allowed him to be beaten, his hands and feet to be put in the stocks, and his wives and property to be taken from him. Truly his falsehood and wickedness deserved punishment, though of these special crimes he was not guilty. If he *had* sworn the king's oath that Akjampong had gone to Elmina against the king's order, he had been commanded to do it.

He was doubtless treated with enmity because he had returned home a wealthy man, and though afraid to offer his goods for sale in Coomassie, he made his headquarters for business in a little village. Nothing could be kept a secret in Ashantee, where the most faithful follower of the king was not secure from the machinations of jealousy, envy, and ambition.

For some time we had been obliged to content ourselves on Sundays with few but attentive listeners, but on January 25th I had again the happiness of proclaiming to large numbers the Word of Life. It was difficult, however, to regain the feelings of former days when faith and hope were bright. The state of our dear child also depressed me. I prayed for help to testify, under all circumstances, of God's unchanging grace and love both in season and out of season, and he gave us ere long cause to bless Him for the restoration of the little one's health.

Great excitement prevailed around us from the varied reports. The Akems were said to have attacked the camp by night, and carried off prisoners with powder and provisions. A huge gathering assembled in the market place, and the king summoned his Fetishes to prophecy for six hours as to the result of the war. Some fifty priests foretold that the army would conquer the

Akem, Asen, Fantee, and Denkjera tribes, and that many Akems would take refuge in Ashantee. The great Fetish declared "if the white man interfered he would kill him, and put another in his place." Other priests professed to drive away the evil spirits by throwing small packets of gold dust and crushed food into the air, and guns were loaded with papaw leaves, and fired aloft amid tremendous shouting. Large promises of at least a thousand slaves were made to the Fetishes, if they would give the victory. A live sheep was pinned to the earth with wooden skewers, and the priests were lavishly rewarded for their efforts. The king, who spent his nights in dancing and drinking, gave them ten peredwane (£81), twenty loads of salt, twenty goats, twenty sheep, and seventy bottles of rum, together with fifty slaves (from the betrayed Wusutra). See page 169.

On January 29th, dark clouds appeared in the horizon, sounds of distant firing were heard, and it was evident that the Ashantees were fighting. The women ran through the streets singing, and the king not only played and danced to drive away the evil spirits, but offered many sacrifices, and at day break visited his ancestors at Bantama,—all signs of bad news from the south.

Twenty or thirty men were said to have been drowned in the Prah, others to have been carried off by the enemy, while Amankwa, the proud chief of Bantama, and head commander, was reported among the slain. This we disbelieved, and soon heard that it was an under chief of Bantama who was drowned, and that the Asens, after firing a few shots at those who first crossed, had retreated to Fusuwei, thus causing great confusion.

Mr. Dawson's depression now increased, for he feared the king regarded him as a prisoner. Obtaining an interview with him after many efforts, he was speedily dismissed, the king smilingly remarking that "the roads

P

were too uncertain for travelling, and it would be highly improper to allow an ambassador to go through a crowd of excited people. Mr. Plange's threats had brought on the war, while the king had only to do with Asen, and not with Fantee or the governor, but if these latter interfered, his majesty would himself go to the field." Mr. Dawson replied that "the governor would hardly understand the crossing of the Prah in that sense, but if Fanteeland were really unconcerned in the war, why were so many Fantees lying in chains?" His majesty was dumb. He then added, that if he had to remain longer in Coomassie, he and his people could not subsist on the nine dollars which the king gave him at the Adae. Kari-Kari quieted him on this point, seeming himself full of care, and gave him thirty-six dollars, with nine more for his bearers, and nine for the servants.

On the little Adae, February 5th, Mr. Dawson was asked to stay away, as he did not wish to give him anything again so soon. We received our nine dollars, Mr. Plange only half the usual sum. As the purse became lighter, confidence also decreased. Of the Krepe people who were serving in the camp, some deserted to the enemy daily, as was to be expected, and Asamoa Kwanta, the real commander, was said to have told the king that they would never conquer unless he sent all the prisoners to the Coast.

Monday, February 10th (Kidjo), was counted one of the luckiest days of the year, so the king commanded a victory! but it transpired later that there was no fighting on that day, though the women made a dreadful noise, running about with guns, or sticks as a substitute, and some with green papaw fruit run through with knives, in imitation of Fantees' heads, thus seeking to insure a victory for their husbands. The king having sent to a mohammedan in the interior to consult an oracle, received as answer, "this war will not end to your advantage as long as you keep the white men, who are constantly crying to God,—prisoners; let them go, and you will conquer." It was in consequence reported that we were to be given over to the ambassador of Akwamu, who was in Coomassie, and to return through his land.

As the people believed that we were the cause of their troubles, we discontinued street preaching, and only held our service at home, where our friend Mr. Dawson and some Fantee and Elmina christians joined us, and several boys came in the afternoon.

It was not until some time afterwards that we heard how on Kidjo Monday, both the ambassadors were summoned to the palace for examination before Akjampong and his followers. By the king's desire the chief stood up and explained that Dawson was a most dangerous man, inasmuch as he constantly travelled about bribing the Coast tribes to submit to Queen Victoria; and had even gone to Apollonia, there to alienate the people of Ashantee, and to extol the protectorate of the English.*
"Thus," continued he, "this mulatto landed one day with a European in Apollonia, and informed me that by the command of the governor he had brought me my men from Elmina. Whilst I was rejoicing at the news, they suddenly informed me that I must accompany them, and even refused to allow me to bathe and eat before starting. Some soldiers seized and bound me and my servants,

---

* Mr. Joseph Dawson, formerly in the employ of the Wesleyan Missionary Society, came into public notice in 1872, by taking up the idea of self-government. This was repeatedly brought before the people of the Gold Coast by the British government, and Mr. D. endeavoured to form a confederation of all the Fantee chiefs. The minor princes were to unite in protecting and guarding the country. Thirty-one of them signed the agreement on November 24th, but the government withheld its approval. Mr. Dawson nevertheless succeeded in persuading the chiefs of Wasa to promise that in their land human sacrifices should cease.

roughly dragging us on board the boat which was to take us to Cape Coast. They stole all my jewellery except my bracelets, and sixteen peredwane in gold. I wonder what I shall get from these mulattos in return." Mr. Plange was next held up for disapproval. "A bad man that! He told them at Elmina they must adopt the English flag, for he was sure from what he had heard at Coomassie that the power of the Ashantees was declining. Although he had brought a mirror, he had obtained charge of it by subtlety. It was given to *my* care, but having no place for it, I asked the governor to take care of it, upon which Plange persuaded him to let *him* bring it here."

Dawson then rose, saying, "I thank God that I see people before me who have ears." (The interpreter Apea interposed, pointedly, "We, too, thank God that we have ears"). "All accusations made by Akjampong are lies, or misrepresentations of facts." (The king, "nothing of the kind; how about the sixteen peredwanas)? Apea, you are a bad man, hold your tongue." "I am in the king's power," said Dawson, "who may behead me if he likes, but I will refute lies."

Thereupon a diabolical noise ensued, and though both Dawson and Plange were invited to speak and defend their rights, not a word could be heard. All kinds of threats were uttered, and the king dismissed them, saying, "My people go to war against the Coast, and you are in my hands; when they return, you will see;" while the others added scornfully, "we will not eat any more with you." (An ironical phrase used towards those who are condemned to death.)

Akjampong then swore that he would hasten to the help of Elmina, and the Elminians were ordered forward to state their political opinions. Those who had refused to adopt the British flag were ordered to the war, the rest detained in Coomassie. Amongst the former (there were but seven), was a christian and his wife. He was ordered to join the troops, while she was to remain. After begging permission to take her, and failing to obtain it, this man declared he would stay in Coomassie. She was his wife, with whom he had come there, and he would not leave her. Half angry, half astonished, the king acquiesced.

Akjampong then set out to collect forces in Safwi, and Kwantiabo to free Elmina from the British yoke, though it was next to impossible to be assured of this, for almost everything proposed had a hidden meaning. For instance, when Mr. Dawson had an interview with the two Bosommurus and Mensa, and told them how wrong it was to hear one side of a subject, they only laughed and said, "you must think nothing of these things, the king and we *know* that Akjampong has reason to thank the governor for bringing him back to his country, but we were obliged to act thus."

Mr D. then ventured to plead for the Fantee and Akra prisoners, who were still in the stocks. "When the king has time, he will release them," said they. The fears of these poor men were not without reason, for it was already rumoured that Akem had been sacrificed for the Fetish. As the nine bearers the governor had sent for us were still languishing in irons, we urged Mr. D. to beg for their release. He represented the case to the king, who gave an assurance to their safety. Want of provisions and heavy rain still prevented the forces from marching, and the king was now threatening, now scorning the entreaties from his chiefs to send for more men.

We turned our thoughts to more happy and peaceful occupations, and set to work to extend our plantation, and improve M. Bonnat's cottage. Mose and the other christians dug and planted some land likewise, though the uncertainty of everything around prevented the interest they might otherwise have had in the work. We waited in vain for the chests from Fomana, much as we and little Rosie needed clothing. She was recovering her health, and enjoying herself in playing with our two lambs.

On February 23rd, at the Adae, it was reported that the chiefs in the field (strengthened by the young Barentwa, who had crossed the Prah with some hundreds of men), were greatly dissatisfied with their commander, Amankwa Tiawa, who was constantly drunk, and refused to obey him. His habits were well known in Coomassie, but he appeared determined to redeem his oath, and to conquer the enemy, and had reached Mansu, when he had obtained a quantity of tobacco and salt without the slightest resistance. The king looked grave, but seemed to have been drinking, and though he came near, did not salute us, but ordered the sedan chair to halt, made a few dancing movements with the upper part of his body, and held his sword to his temples for some time. We feared this might have an unfriendly meaning. However, he sent an ox to Mr. D., perhaps to appease him, and with it came from Bosommuru the unusual advice to smoke the meat, and save it that it might last a long time.

On March 6th, Mrs. Plange was called to the palace, the royal ladies wishing to see her. The king also wanted to ascertain whether she belonged to Elmina, and inquired why she had discontinued coming to the Adae, telling her she ought to attend, and would receive something for her support.

Whatever might be the reason, the king was evidently out of temper, spent many nights with the Kete music, and made Fetish continually. On the day the three Akems were sacrificed, a young girl going to draw water was also seized and slain. Oh, the power of the "murderer from the beginning!"

On the 8th, the king marched in state to Amanghyia, to give audience to a messenger from Cape Coast, who bore a joint remonstrance from prince Ansa and the British governor, warning the monarch against making an attack which would risk the loss of his whole army. The people had threatened to behead this poor man on his journey, but he courageously declined to deliver his message to any but the king.

On the 12th, we were rejoiced by the release of our nine bearers, who were sent to work in the plantations for Asare. At the little Adae on the 19th, we heard in the palace that a sharp encounter had taken place, and that the Ashantees had retired to cover their retreat. As a matter of course the king danced the Kete all night. We were aroused in our first sleep by two young officers who entered the yard with torches, crying "Quick, quick, the king calls." K. and I hastily dressed—M. B. was in the plantation; the king did not want Plange, which caused him great apprehension.

We hurried through the empty town, and to our surprise met Dawson furnished with pen and ink, which reassured us. We went through six courts to the golden gates, viz., two small doors inlaid like a chess-board, with gold and silver. Here under the decorated pillars of the verandah sat the king with a few councillors and interpreters. Seven sword-bearers crouched on the left, and on a sign from the king we were seated.

Instantly a man got up, his hands in a block and a rope round his throat, so that we feared there was to be an execution. He was a Fantee prisoner or actor who understood his profession, and was to tell what he knew of the war. He said " I am a native of Anamabo, a relative of Mr. Blankson. It had long been known that Europeans had been captured in Ashantee, and that the heads of different governments had applied on their behalf to the

Queen of England, and even wanted to come themselves and see what could be done, but she had undertaken to obtain their liberty.

The subject of a ransom was under consideration when the news came that Ashantee was at war with the Coast, but this the governor did not heed. They then informed him that the Ashantee army had arrived at the Prah, and that the white men as well as the governor's messengers were killed, one only having been spared, whose head was shaved, nose and ears cut off, and himself made to carry the king's drum, all which the governor disbelieved. They then told him they would leave their towns and villages, and seek for security in Akem and Denkjera. Soon after, the governor finding that the Ashantees were really approaching, ordered the people of Cape Coast and Abora to march against them, and gave orders that whoever was not at his post on a certain day should be shot. The Fantees then flocked together and rushed upon the Ashantees, but were unable to resist them and soon fled. I hid myself in the bush," continued the poor man, "but was soon discovered and taken, and because I spoke more readily than others in the camp, I was chosen to announce the news to the king. Thus I have the honour of now standing before him."*

Mr D. enquired where the battle had been fought, and was told in Nyankomase, which was not far from Cape Coast. The king then turned abruptly to us, and said, "I sent for you to write to the governor, against whom my army has not marched, but you are not to do as Mr. Plange did, and write an underhand letter. The words were then dictated thus—

"The king greets the governor, prince Ansa, and Mr. Blankson. He is grandson to Osee Tutu, who conquered

---

* This prisoner really spoke the facts of the case, as was afterwards ascertained.

Denkjera, and Elmina was under his protection. He heard the governor was going to march against his troops. Would his Excellency understand that the campaign was not directed against him or the Fantees. The king had already heard, through Mr. Plange, that the British intended taking Elmina with the fort in less than four months, and giving it to Kwakjei of Denkjera, and also wanted to humble the king of Ashantee. This has so roused the anger of his chiefs that they had sworn to go to war with Denkjera, for the fort must not be given up to them. If the governor wish to recall his troops, he must send back the Denkjeras, the Asens, and the Akems, as they all belong to Ashantee, but if he refuse to do this, his majesty will himself lead his army to the field. It is reported further that he has killed the white men and the ambassadors. In order that his Excellency may see that these are in good keeping, his majesty allows them to sign this letter."

At Mr. Dawson's intercession, we were permitted to enclose a few lines to our friends. One of his people was to carry the letter to the Coast, accompanied by the imprisoned Fantee. As he was leaving, I mentioned the boxes waiting in Fomana. Kari-Kari seemed angry, but promised to have them sent. Before midnight we were again at home, filled with anxiety as to what might be the object of the letter, but took comfort in the words from which Mr. Dawson preached on Sunday, March 23rd, " All things work together for good to them that love God."

I felt much cause for humiliation and self-abasement in my daily life at this time, for though I wrote my journal, continued the study of the language, and by daily visits to the market, managed to supply the wants of our small household, and to work at the plantation, what did it all amount to ? The time seemed rapidly passing; we had already been three years and a half in Ashantee. Alas! how little was accomplished. Again I renewed my vows, and earnestly sought to do more than before in my Master's cause.

On April the 3d, we received a packet of letters through Mr. Dawson, which had arrived months before. In them the governor inquired what the king's real intention was. Why had his army taken a hundred and twenty Akems prisoners? If he wished for peace, why did he not keep the peace? If for war, why not say so?

"I have sent Akjampong," said he, "in spite of the resistance of the Asens, to show that I keep my word." We were sorry that Mr. D. was not allowed to translate this letter literally. Prince Ansa wrote, "pray father, send the Europeans." A letter from Mr. Buhl, of November the 7th, spoke of boxes waiting for us at Cape Coast; meanwhile we were thankful to receive the two from Fomana, after four months' delay.

April 6th, Palm Sunday, at the great Adac the king danced in the wildest manner, stretching out his hands towards us, as if he would say, "I will get you all yet." Mr. Dawson preached in the afternoon in Fantee. I was discouraged by finding how little I could follow him; and though on the 11th (Good Friday) I hoped the Fantees, to whom I attempted to speak on Isaiah 53d, understood much; yet I was painfully conscious how cramped I still was in the language.

News of a second battle a day's journey from Cape Coast now arrived, and the Ashantees were reported defeated. Another night of wild dancing and music followed, though they appeared to have gained some advantage, as prisoners began to arrive. On the evening of Saturday, the 13th, the king took his seat in the market place to receive the greatest trophy of the fight, Amanaman, a chief of Wasa, who, after having sworn the king's oath, had withdrawn from his government, and was captured unawares by Adu Bofu. Against our will we were forced to be present, and were surprised to see so many people still left in Coomassie, and rushing to get a sight at these poor unhappy creatures, who were dragged forward amid hideous cries that sounded far above the wild music.

Most of them were nearly naked, with only a cloth round the waist, and their hands fixed in the block which they carried on their heads, and bound together in companies of ten or fifteen, by cords around their necks. They formed a sad spectacle as they passed, looking dreadfully frightened. The women, old and young, followed, some with infants on their backs, others leading bigger children by the hand, who crouched in terror at their mother's side. The cruel spectators not satisfied with threats, struck these little creatures, causing my very blood to boil. There is a time to be scornful, and a time to be scorned; a lesson Ashantee was soon to learn.

The king's son, who conducted the prisoners from Adu Bofu to his father, was profusely complimented. Following these poor miserable creatures, and with a rope round his neck, came old Amanaman, who was received with a shout of execration. How we longed to give them a word of comfort, as these wretched beings turned their large eager eyes on us.

For the Momone women it was a day of great rejoicing, after their weeks of painful suspense, when songs of woe and lamentation alone had been heard in the palace. The king at once went to Bantama to attend at a sacrifice of fourteen men from Wasa; we really felt like the disciples of old, who wished that fire would come down from heaven; but the patience of our God was greater than ours.

What a relief was it to us to turn from such a spectacle, to our quiet little service, where on April the 9th, with a few Fantees from the Coast, we enjoyed sitting together at the Lord's table. Two of these people, Peter Asaba and his wife Martha, gave us great joy by their consistent Christian conduct; they lived with us, and often united in prayer. Peter was earnestly striving to learn to read and write.

My wife's health had become a subject of great anxiety to me, and made it necessary to seek rest and change of air at the plantation. I entreated Bosommuru to refrain from suddenly visiting us, as any shock increased the irritability of her over-excited nerves.

Songs of lamentation were now sung every night before the king, and news again came of a battle and heavy loss to the Ashantees, who lay like "corn on the threshing-floor," under the fire of the enemy's guns. The prince of Mampong was reported among the wounded; and the rumours spread, although the Ashantees allowed "no one to speak of this war on pain of death."

The king's conduct grew more and more strange. On the 29th of April he summoned the Fantees from the surrounding villages to sing and dance before him, and when they came sent them back, but a day or two after recalled them, when about thirty-five performed. He rewarded them by some rum and eighteen dollars, told them of his good-will to their nation, and that he would soon restore them to their country. He also presented our three native christians with some old military dresses, in which of course they looked ridiculous. These too he assured of a speedy restoration, as he had nothing against the Akwapems, and but one thing against Denkjera. He invited my wife and Mrs. Plange with Rosie, but the former was too ill to go, so Mrs. Plange took Rosie with her nurse, returning in an hour and a half.

The king and his aunt, for whom the visit was chiefly intended, were much pleased. The little thing played with a cat, and amused herself by adorning her foot with the white painted earth made for the Fetish. Kari-Kari seemed really to love this child, and said, "when she goes to the Coast they will say, 'at least something good grows in Ashantee.'" Before leaving, Mr. Plange took the opportunity to prefer a request for salt, which one of the attendants said we also needed. A load was sent to Mrs. P., with nine dollars, and the like sum was sent to Rosie, but no salt, though we had so often begged for it.

During the night a poor old man, one of the Akra prisoners, died after undergoing great sufferings. He had been in the block with insufficient food four months, and was never allowed to wash the whole time; how sad that for no crime or wrong he should have been thus tortured. He had often brought our boxes for us by the king's order, and we had pleaded in vain for his and his companions' release.

Before our pretended journey to the Coast, we had, as being more economical, kept separate tables, and now returned to the same plan. M. Bonnat was most anxious to spare expense to the mission; not regarding himself as one of its agents, he therefore restricted his personal expenses to two dollars and a quarter for the three weeks intervening between the great and little Adae, when the usual supplies were given us. This sum was really insufficient, and his health suffered in consequence, but he most thankfully managed with it and a little supply from the plantation.

The 5th of May proved a day of mourning, and songs of lamentation were sung throughout the night, while early in the morning the king, with his face and arms painted red, went to Bantama. The chiefs were besmeared with the same colour. He had previously visited this and other places three times in one day, hoping thus to avert the impending evil by offering many human sacrifices, and amongst them the poor old chief Amanaman. The cause of all their excitement was that a great chief had fallen, that two others had gone over to the Fantees, and a person of great consequence had been killed by accident.

So urgent had our need of salt become, that I wrote to the king about it, and also told him of our serious loss of gold dust and dollars, which had been abstracted from our boxes in Fomuna. Mr. Dawson translated the letter, and Bosommuru Dwira affected great surprise, and pretended to enquire if Ashantees had stolen the money, which we knew was the case." "The king must be told of that," he said, but "the salt was a mere trifle, and could be had at any time." Happily, it did arrive very soon, with strict injunctions to be careful of it; and we felt it too great a treasure to waste, for the price had become exorbitant.

We heard that the Ashantees were at Dunkwa, six miles from Cape Coast, but did not know what to believe, for even the king himself knew little that was reliable, though he left no stone unturned to obtain correct intelligence. A man from Akra, who had escaped from the block, told the king he had been sent from Ata the king of Akem, to the governor, who questioned him about the war, on which occasion his excellency had called the king of Ashantee a false man. The governor sent him back to Kjebi, from whence he escaped.

When asked if the Fantees, Asens, Denkjeras, &c., and their families had really fled to the fort, he replied, "I will tell the truth, even if it costs me my life. All is quiet in Cape Coast, only Asens and Denkjeras have fought with the Ashantees, but no Fantees." The king was very angry at having been misled by false reports, neither could he understand why his messengers were detained so long at the Coast.

His conduct before the next Adae, when as usual he was drinking publicly, was increasingly strange; he

danced wildly, and appeared incensed against us. Dawson with difficulty escaped from the violence of the people. On our seeking an explanation, he assured us he meant nothing, but was obliged as on former occasions to affect displeasure, and even hostility, to satisfy his nobles.*
In accordance with this statement, he behaved in a friendly manner at the Adae itself (May 18th), danced with a rusty old sabre (probably to a Fetish), but with all due honour.

When I returned to the city (May 23rd), I found Kühne in an alarming state. He coughed day and night, and was distressed by constant sickness and sleeplessness, accompanied by so much nervous prostration that I feared we must leave the plantation and come in to the town to nurse him. I applied to Owusu Kokoo to ask for the delayed boxes, as one of them contained a medicine chest. I wrote to the king also, and finally got them on June 23rd!

* What the king really said was, "I am the grandson of Osee Tutu (who delivered Ashantee from the yoke of Denkjera), and this "Ata" (Mr. Plange), comes here to tell me that in four months my power will come to an end ! Who, who will come against me? Who dares to approach my throne? I will kill him (with a gesture of beheading), Fantee, Asen, Denkjera, Akra, Aknapem, Akem, are *all* united against me, but who dares to enter into a contest with me? I will kill them." This is the style of a Coomassie proclamation.

CHAPTER XXVII.

WE BUILD FOR THE KING.

THE king had suddenly been seized with the idea that as prisoners it was right we should work for him, and ambassadors, missionaries, and christian Fantees, were all required to unite in building him a European house. On Sunday morning (May 25th) Mr. Dawson entered, and with a very grave face told us that the king intended to call us Coast people together, to accompany him to Amanghyia, and there to erect for him a house. Although struck with this strange caprice, which reminded us of Israel in Egypt—D. begged his majesty to allow us to spend our Sunday in peace.

On his way to us he had encountered some natives painted red, acting a tragedy (Sokada) and dancing, as if possessed, to the mournful music of the horn; they approached him in a threatning attitude, crying, as he tried to avoid them, "He who fights is he who dies." "I am Kari-Kari's slave and fear none." These words sounded alarming, but there seemed no reason to fear danger to our lives, while so many Ashantees were in the hands of the English.

Whether we should be allowed to remain in Coomassie to witness the return of the army and its humiliation appeared, however, doubtful. The king, it had been said, was preparing the house in Amanghyia, to be inhabited by Europeans, and we therefore thought it probable our little dwelling would be stripped, and we have to return to our former life of privation.

Anxious for my wife and child, who still remained at the plantation, I united with my brethren in childlike, simple prayer, and then went to tell Rosa of our new experience. She took the news very calmly, assisted me to pack up at once, and bade farewell to our harbour of refuge, to which we had really become attached.

When I got to Coomassie, I set out with D. to find our friend Bosommuru, who had been asked in vain to visit us; he saw we were uneasy, but made light of it, and said the king had been building a new village, and wished the Fantees to help him; he was ready to swear the oath of the king's father, that there was nothing more in it; I thanked him, and said he had removed a heavy burden from our hearts, still we preferred knowing the truth, bitter as it might be, to undergoing a second edition of our Fomana experiences; to be treated with a sheep one day and put in irons the next, did not suit us; he laughed and said there was nothing of the kind to fear.

On Monday (May 26th) we set forth after a long delay in waiting for Bosommuru. Dawson, Plange, M. Bonnat and I went first, and were followed by the Fantees, forming a procession, which seemed to surprise the Ashantees. We halted at the cross road to Duro, a few steps from our old Ebenezer. The king appeared in a sedan chair, saluted us kindly without stopping, and as he turned into the bush, said, "I will send for you directly." Acordingly a messenger came, who led us by a foot path to a small plantation, behind which we found a good sized piece of land, recently cleared of grass and reeds.

The king began, "I like this place, therefore I want to build here. How I wish that you would build a little for me; something handsome, a European house, in order that I may be reminded of you when you are gone to the Coast. You 'Mmorowa' (D. Pl. B. and I.) will come when you can to see after and direct the work." The king's request was so modestly made that we felt pleasure in agreeing to it; with one accord we all, including the Fantees, declared that we should be glad to do his majesty a service. Then a bullock, two loads of salt, two sheep, and a peredwane (thirty-six dollars) of gold were given to us four "Mmorowa;" and one load of salt, one sheep, and eighteen dollars to the "Mmofra" (Fantees). Thus the work was undertaken with real energy, though we thought sadly of the many thousands obliged to live without salt, unable to pay the nine dollars which was the price of a load!

After the king had left, we returned home laden with our riches, slew the ox, and divided it as well as the money. From this time we devoted ourselves to the king's building, for although it had been said, "Come when you please to inspect," it was carefully noticed who came and who was absent. Owusu Kokoo and two other princes were always on the building ground, but not much progress was made. When we urged that the foundation should be laid, we were told that the king must come first and perform a ceremony, and he could not go out for a week before the Adae, which falls on June 11th.

On the 13th, this ceremony took place, much to our distress. A sheep was slain, and the blood sprinkled on certain places, while numerous prayers were offered to the Fetish. One prayer or wish ran thus—" The old ones have done their work, now Kari-Kari sits on the throne, he has taken a few Fantees prisoners through whom he wishes to build something. The chiefs are all gone to war against the tribes at the Coast, so help us here, and bring Fantees, Asens, Denkjeras, Akems, Akwapems, Akras, and all here. Crushed bananas, mixed with palm oil, were also thrown about, and the slain sheep was torn to pieces in a moment by the people.

The kind of house we were to build remained undecided. I drew a plan of one fifty-three feet long, without stories and galleries on one side. The king wished to have them all round; but it was difficult to get the beams for their support. There were only two sawyers, the others were but learners; as until the Fantees had seen sawing at the mission house, they had no idea of it. Counting Joseph our servant, we had but three carpenters, to whom the king gave a set of tools.

Whilst waiting for wood we proceeded with the preparation of sun-burnt bricks for the walls, covering them with banana leaves, which were not water-tight, yet answered the purpose, as but little rain fell at that time. Necessary materials were always freely promised, and as certainly never ready when wanted. The 16th was fixed for the laying of the foundation stone, and we wished to write a short account of the circumstance as a memorial of the building; but they were so fearful of our witchcraft that they jealously watched our every movement.

When the king understood that the ceremony which Mr. D. described as done in Europe could be performed in the evening, he expressed a wish to be present, and enquired by Owusu Kokoo if we required a sheep, which we declined, although we were always thankful for any gift. We were ready at two o'clock and waited for him, till heavy rain came down, from which we had no protection but the workmen's sheds, so we turned our steps homewards. On the way we met the princes with a sheep and some gold, who ordered our return, and commanded the business to proceed notwithstanding the king's absence, delivering the sheep to us, with thirty-six dollars, and nine for the six Ashantees. Mr. D. took some of the money, laid it in the hole, and prayed that God would give the king wisdom, he then adjusted the stone, and covered it with earth. The people wanted to slay the sheep on the stone, which we peremptorily forbade, for we could not allow their fetish practices to be in any way mixed up with our religious observances and prayers, they "might kill the animal where they liked," we said; which they at last did, and connected the act with the expression of their own wishes to their god. Thus, after all, the affair did not conclude very satisfactorily.

This impression was strengthened when we found that Owusu Kokoo, from a sense of gratitude on account of the princely hospitality he had experienced at the Coast, had actually brought this sheep from Mr. D.'s stock, because he thought he wished to hold a Fetish ! ! Supposing the animal to be a present, we had rejoiced in the hope of being able to give a full meal to the poorly fed workmen, but now our own supplies were thus diminished. From this time forward the king appeared nearly every day on the building ground.

The 7th of July was the fifth birthday which my poor wife had spent in captivity, yet in the review of the dark shadows of those years, how blessed we had been by more than gleams of sunshine; many things we should have delighted to possess had been denied, yet what mercies had been granted, even more than we had asked for in our prayers. Our little daughter was a blessing indeed, and our experience with her helped us to cast the burden of the future on our gracious God.

By the end of the month, notwithstanding the unfavourable weather, the house had made some progress, the walls had reached the height of the windows, though the constant rain prevented the brick-work from drying—and we prepared to lay the beams for the first floor, but as a very small part of the wood required was ready, and could not be for some time, we decided to take a few weeks' holiday.

During the discussions about building, the idea of an erec-

WE BUILD FOR THE KING. 229

tion for a vane was incidentally mentioned; the king caught at it, and gave M. Bonnat no peace until he promised to construct one similar to that he had described, viz., a rotunda supported by twelve pillars with four arrow-heads in the centre of the roof to denote the direction of the wind. When his majesty saw M. B. climb the roof to adjust these, he was excessively amused, and child-like expected the mango stones which Kühne had sown as a future ornament for the walls, to come up as rapidly as Jack's bean stalk.

There were reports that cannon was heard thundering on the Prah, and the king enquired of D. what was meant by firing seven times, he said it might mean a salute, upon which Bosommuru answered, "that is right." We only hope the king will not, as in 1864, only encamp by the Prah for months, but fight the matter out at once. Whether it might be deemed necessary to humble Ashantee by pushing forward to Comassie, we could not guess, although without wishing for such an event, we were inclined to believe it would be so. We felt that if such were God's will, He would protect us, and it might prove the very means of our deliverance; indeed, if the troops came to Fomana only, Ashantee would be in terror and might hastily release us, but they might also take us away into the interior. We trusted to be kept in the exercise of faith and love, and ultimately to be allowed to work, and not cast aside as useless tools.

At the ceremony consequent on the death of two princesses on the 16th, several unhappy people were sacrificed, women amongst them. Alas! what blood had been uselessly shed since our detention.

We noticed increased depression, and heard many enquiries around us as to how matters would end. Food became so scarce that the people were selling their goods and furniture to procure it, and bitterly complained of their losses. Even in the palace they seemed anxious and almost parsimonious. Mrs. Plange, Palm, and the mace bearer of Dawson received but one and a half dollars each at the Adae, instead of three, as formerly; we still had nine for three weeks, for which we felt most thankful, as all our stores were rapidly diminishing. The king's behaviour was enigmatical. He often danced "Kete" the whole night, and in the morning appeared on the building ground in high spirits, seeming to have no cause for an anxious thought.

We suggested to him the propriety, or even necessity, of having but one storey to his new house, not only on account of the scarcity of material, but from the fear that the walls being damp, would not sustain the weight of a second. The caution was useless, "No," he said, "if the rain hinders, you can suspend work for a month." This decision dashed the sanguine hope of the Fantees, who expected when the house was finished, to be sent home. For ourselves, we concluded the delay would make little difference, and neither hasten or postpone our freedom. If we asked for meat or money to provide for our people, the king at once complied, but it was always a very long time before any supply came.

On August 8th the first floor was finished, and then came a pause of two months, for we could get no saws. It seemed also cruel to urge men to work who were suffering from hunger, and we could provide no food—the folly of beginning to build under such circumstances struck us very forcibly. The king doubtless cursed the hour when he had allowed his chiefs to draw him into war, by promises which were never fulfilled, of supplying him with treasure from the Coast. Meanwhile the Momone women continued dancing and singing bravely. On the great Adae (August 10th) the king appeared serious and subdued, and when passing the Dampan, on which Dawson sat, and the sword was offered him by the sword-bearer that he might dance, he refused it, which implied disaster.

In the evening we overheard a woman crying aloud, "mother, what am I to do now?" leading us to fear she was being placed in the block; most of our neighbours being Asumankwas (doctors), who are often entrusted with the care of prisoners. When Mr. Plange drew nearer he heard an Ashantee who had returned from Serem, and had given his message to the king, talking excitedly. It appeared he had been sent with an Asumankwa with powder, to purchase a very strong medicine (aduru) which would destroy the people at the Coast. The mohammedans in Angwa, about four or five days' journey from Salaga—the great market-place—took the powder, but refused to give him the medicine. High words ensued; the messengers swore a great oath, the moslems seized sword and dagger, and in the wild skirmish which followed several on both sides were killed, and the Ashantees returned home.

Soon after the moslems sent, requesting their return to settle the affair, promising them goods; they went, and thereby fell into a trap similar to those with which they had often decoyed others. They were conducted to a place where powder was laid, which was fired and exploded, killing some on the spot, and mortally wounding others, while a few escaped. This occurred forty days before the barricading of the road, and they found it difficult to make their way back.

Among those who fell was Amoaku, and it was his wife we had heard crying so bitterly. From other houses similar sounds of distress soon proceeded. It was thus evident that the central tribes had thrown off the yoke of Ashantee, of which they had long been weary, and the course which events were taking at the Coast became clearer. To our surprise, however, a mohammedan hung himself in the town, and the affair at Serem was represented as a dispute between the Ashantee chiefs.

Owusu Adum, a brother of Owusu Kokoo, was sent to Kwantiabo, but could not proceed because the road was blocked. The Ashantees had not of late gone to that town, but had traded with the people on our side the Tano river. They were therefore now placed in a difficult position, for it was said that a messenger from Kwantiabo had warned the king to let the white men and Fantees go without delay, otherwise the English would be at Coomassie by Christmas. It was further said and quickly believed that communication was cut off between the two divisions of the army.

Every effort to gain the ear of the king was now in vain, and when at length Dawson met him, he enquired four times if we might proceed with the house before obtaining an answer. He was told how unreasonable it was to require men to work without food, and that it made us heart sick and indignant to think how well the captive Ashantees were treated at the Coast, while the poor Fantee prisoners were required to work on empty promises, without the necesssaries of life.

On the 20th, the king appeared on the building ground earlier than myself, and blamed Dawson severely, complaining of the delay in progress. The want of food was again urged, and again more supplies promised. At length only half the men would work.

On the few previous Sundays, especially on the 24th, we rejoiced to see more Ashantee listeners, who came uninvited. We had also many temporal mercies. Both my wife and child were well, spite of their many privations. Bread, sugar, coffee or tea were unknown luxuries, yet little Rosa ran merrily about all day with her foster brother Kwame, the nurse's child. This fact had however its dark side, for we knew not how or where to procure more shoes. She talked nicely, and her feverish attacks yielded readily to treatment. We daily prayed that she might be kept from the evil influences around us. On her birthday, September 2nd, M. Bonnat surprised us by a pretty little chair of odum wood, with back and seat of plaited straw.

Poor Kühne's depression increased, and his distress was great when at the Kete dance the king had an Ashantee killed, and four more accused of desertion given over to the hangman. An attack of hemorrhage came on, and though a sweet sleep and a cheering dream followed, his settled conviction was that he should find his grave in Ashantee, ardently as he longed for his native land, and to see his parents' graves once more.

We were increasingly destitute of food for the workmen, and Dawson at last begged the king to lend him money to buy it, but in vain. The chief who was appointed to protect the wall neglected his duty, and D.'s patience at length gave way. He came into the town and declared to the prince Owuso Kokoo that he would not go again to the building until help was provided. Former assertions were repeated. The king had begged us to hasten the work, and we delayed it; he had therefore "turned away his eyes from us." We felt this to be very unjust, for we could neither help the rain, or create workmen or tools, but as we wished to ensure the goodwill of the king, we put the matter before the men, and entreated them to work on rainy as well as on fine days.

The masons now played us a trick. Professing to have heard there was no dry brick they ceased to come, and Dawson felt it needful to keep them in punishment until the prince saw them. They begged for six lashes and to be set free; but as false reports and spiteful assertions were constantly carried to the king, who professed to make full investigation, but ended by upholding them, we would not yield. After much discussion and misrepresentation, this vexatious affair was ended by a conciliatory message from his majesty, and we as usual tried to think the best. The prince however believed these Fantees to be ill-disposed, and capable of very bad actions, Akjere Mensa had said many things against us all, but especially against Dawson, as untrustworthy. The king gave us no opportunity to explain, so we resolutely refused to employ him. He went to the palace to complain, and returned with a message that we were to allow the men to work, and that his majesty would come himself and see us; thus the backbiter remained, but no work was given him.

Our small affairs were now forgotten, for a sudden death plunged the palace and the town into great grief. On our Rosa's birthday the 2nd crown prince Mensa Kuma died, at sixteen years of age. This was publicly announced at four o'clock, but before that hour royal servants occupied all the streets to catch the fugitives. Kwabena, the captive son of the chief of Peki, who had often been our informant, brought us the news, warning us to let none leave the house lest he should fall into the hands of the odumfo, who were searching everywhere for victims.

His master Kwantiabo had been sitting in council half an hour before in the palace with the other chiefs, surrounded by their followers. A messenger suddenly appeared and whispered to the king, who stooping down, rubbed the tips of his fingers with red earth, and painted his forehead. On this all the servants rushed from the palace, and on a sign from his master our young informant did the same, without really knowing why, for this was his first experience of this savage custom. Soon after came Dawson in a state of alarm, to enquire the reason of the awful tumult. The people outside were frantic, seizing poultry and sheep, killing them and throwing them away, and men were eveywhere falling victims to the odumfo's knife.

From one of Bosommuru's followers we afterwards heard that the king's brother had died, and that nearly a hundred and fifty men would be sacrificed at his funeral. In the evening of the same day we saw men carrying numbers of long fresh cut branches, which were to serve for binding the sacrifices. Owusu Kokoo at length appeared greeting us from the king, who sent us word that his youngest brother had died, and as his friends he must inform us, and we must tell the Fantees of the event, but we need fear nothing, although the customary sacrifices were not pleasant. Indeed they were not! This was an attention which induced us to suppose he had heard of our anxiety and excitement about passing events.

The deceased youth was to be followed to the grave by slaves only, some of his own, and others who had long been languishing in irons. It was expected that every great chief would offer a gift of human life, and many men who were going about free, fell beneath the knife of the odumfo. Up to midday the king and his followers had been sitting at the north side of the market-place under the tree where we used to preach. Around him were crowds playing the wildest music, who all fasted, but drank the more. These offerings from the chiefs were presented—dresses, silk cushions, gold, ornaments, sheep and MEN! In the afternoon he resumed his seat in the market-place, and all who had guns fired them; at this signal some victims fell.

M. Bonnat and Kühne, who were in the street for a few moments, saw three odumfos rush upon a man standing among the crowd, pierce his cheeks with a knife and order him to stand up; they then drove him before them with his hands bound behind like a sheep to the slaughter.

The deceased prince had besides several wives of royal blood, three of low birth, who when they heard of his death ran away and hid themselves. The king supplied their places by other girls, who, painted white, and hung with gold ornaments, sat around the coffin to drive away the flies—and were strangled at the funeral. The same fate befel six pages, who, similarly ornamented and painted, crouched around the coffin, which was carried out at midnight. For three days previously the poor lads had known they were doomed to go with the unhappy women to the grave.

On Friday, the day of the "king's soul" (he was born on Friday), no blood must be shed, and all the bodies of the slain were dragged away early in the morning to the entrance of Apetesini. The Fantees were filled with horror at the sight; they had witnessed the murder of twenty human sacrifices, some of them lads of ten years, others old men. We wondered how the people could sit down to eat after the appointed three days' fast. The town was quieter, and the king divided sheep among his chiefs. The funeral ceremonies were continued on Saturday the 6th, by every one having their heads shaved.

The dancing women attended at the palace to comfort the king, for which they received presents of gold. On this occasion, a princess quarrelled, and allowed herself to utter insulting words. The king ordered her to be taken out on the spot, and not only did *she* lose her head, but a prince and other Ashantee nobles fell on the same day. It was really a reign of terror, and none could understand whether it was an outburst of ungoverned passion, or an intimation of absolute power. On Monday, a week after the death, a fast was again observed, and we knew too well the sad accompaniment. We could only sigh and cry to the Lord of Hosts, and we knew that He would hear us, although we were taunted by the question, "Where is thy God?"

From the 1st to the 10th of September, the slaughter

continued. The king himself actually killed some members of the royal house, many slain corpses lay exposed, and in forty days the same dreadful doings were to be repeated!

We now heard that Amakje, king of Apollonia, had just eaten fetish (joined himself) with the Ashantees. His people refused to follow him, so he was induced to go almost alone to Adu Bofo's camp, where he was seized and laid in irons. He is accused of having given up Akjampong to the English without fighting, and subsequently of giving up his throne to them. The proceedings of these negro chieftains are very mysterious. They know how the Ashantees deceived the princes of Wusutra and Tongo, in the last war with Krepe, and after enticing them here with their subjects, sold or slew the latter, leaving the chiefs alone and destitute, yet they prefer the yoke of Ashantee to the mild British protectorate; they like to be without restraint, and to behead or hold death wakes at pleasure till they fall at a sign from the majesty to which they have looked up for protection.

On the little Adae (September 3rd), we received orders to stay away on account of the great slaughter demanded by the general mourning. This involved the loss of a couple of dollars, which were worth much to us just then. M. B.'s allowance was only two dollars and a half, and Mr. D. had come to his last farthing, yet we were expected to go on building the king's house. We ordered our two servants to earn their living by trading in palm wine; for ourselves we felt confident that our Lord would not forsake us, and that He would enable us to forgive the people who had taken our money from us in Fomana (£60), and whom we were now obliged to serve. Some candles and a small box of butter remained of our provision; these were carefully saved for Rosa. We took much pains to manufacture sugar, and with M. B.'s help we succeeded in making six pounds of syrup or molasses, but could not crystalize it.

September 10th, the king at length opened his purse and sent us seventy-two dollars; of these the carpenters received eighteen, and the thirty labourers the same sum, but the sawyers were forgotten; we had our share, and tried to procure something extra for the sawyers who had the hardest work, and were treated most inconsiderately. Ten days ago they brought eight beautiful planks as a present for his majesty, but when boards were wanted for the prince's coffin, six of these were taken without ceremony. Sometimes the king comes to the building ground, gives the men brandy, and orders them to dance and sing before him till they are very merry; this is intended to make up for every disappointment.

September 20th, the king came to see the verandah, at which we had worked very closely. Instead of thanks, he only remarked that we did nothing. He took no account of the rainy days, but thought the house ought to have been finished long before. We were told that he very much wished to show the finished house to his chiefs to make them ashamed, because they had sworn to bring the governor's castle bodily to Ashantee. *He* had gained a house from the Fantees without war! Building in West Africa is certainly no child's play, and in this case our patience was put to a very severe test.

At last, September 5th, after great exertion, the front verandah was erected. His majesty rejoiced like a child, and gave an ox to Mr. D., and eighteen dollars to the dancing Fantees, but instead of rewarding the poor sawyers as he had promised, he complained that they had sold several planks to his cousin, a man who was within a hair's breadth of becoming king in his stead, and whom he regarded with great jealousy. In his anger he explained " that should not happen again; he would buy the planks." Besides this, he discoursed upon politics, "I have done nothing to the governor, and yet he has taken up arms against me. If I had wished to fight against the white men, I should have gone to the war myself. You, too (addressing D.), I have learned to know, and have proved what your real spirit is." This was meant as a hint that we were ungrateful, and ought to esteem ourselves happy to build for so great a king.

We happened to hear from an Akwamer who had come to Comassie with an ambassador, that the white man in Odumase had presented his majesty with a large umbrella, and had interceded for us. We supposed that our brethren were trying in this way to influence the king, but we had little hope that they would succeed. Messengers from the camp also came, who reported that Adu Bofo had actually captured a whole tribe by means of the old trick—that he wanted to eat fetish with them; these poor people belonged to Apollonia, and had formerly sought help from the king.

Adu Bofo continually begged for men and money, and a proclamation was issued, ordering all soldiers who were in the plantations to hasten to the camp on pain of death for delay; at the same time the army sent a petition to be recalled; to this the king replied, "you wished for war and you have it. You swore you would not return till you could bring me the walls of Cape Coast, and now you want we to recall you because many chiefs have fallen, and you are suffering. When I danced on the market-place in times past, you said, 'he wishes for war.' It was not I, it was you who wished it. What can I do? I am drunk to-day and must play Kete with my wives. In due time I will send you an answer."

On October 13th, the forty days since the death of the king's brother expired, and the sacrifices began afresh. Amongst others, the king laid hold on a Fantee, which grieved us much. He had emigrated ten years before, and had gained his living by trading, but as he earned more than the Ashantees he was avoided by them, and at last resolved to escape. On the road to Akem he was seized near Dwaben, and brought back a prisoner. He professed to be going to reclaim a debt, but as he had taken all his goods with him he was pronounced guilty, and delivered to Kwantabisa, the chief of the wood-bearers, to be watched over.

Kwantabisa did all he could to save his life; he removed him to a neighbouring house, and six times dismissed the hangman who was sent to fetch him, declaring he did not know what had become of him. He hoped that the king would repent of the step he had taken, for he did not always know who had been led to the block. But when the odumfos came the seventh time, and said that if this man were not forthcoming another would be taken in his stead, Kwantabisa was obliged to give him up. This execution naturally enraged the Fantees, although they hoped that on reflection the king would acknowledge that he had committed a rash act.

In October we set to work vigorously on the second floor of the house, which wonderfully pleased the king. Still our entreaty for salt was neglected. Happily, my wife continued well, though occasionally rather nervous and excited by trifles. Poor Kühne was no better, and his cough was very trying, though he sometimes managed to visit the building carried in a hammock.

The chief of Aguogo was now accused to the king as not having sufficiently guarded the border against Akem, and was sentenced to lose his head. He however escaped to Boakje Tenteng, who succeeded in effecting a mitigation of the capital sentence to the payment of a heavy fine (ninety peredwanes). We pitied this man, who was a simple-hearted friendly fellow, with but few Ashantee characteristics. We heard at that time that the Ashantees had suffered a defeat, and lost several

WE BUILD FOR THE KING.

chiefs, and we learned the particulars from the Krepe, Kwabena, who always accompanied his master to the council. The king asked his councillors what was now to be done? He had heard from Akwamu that many European soldiers had landed at the Coast, and the governor wishing to finish the war during the dry season, had joined with the Coast tribes, and was hastening on to Coomassie. The Fantees and the white men in the centre, on one side an army from Kwau-Kodiabe, and on the other a mixed host from Akra, Akwapem, and Akem. Amankwa had thrown coals on an ant hill, and now the insects were spreading themselves in all directions.

It was truly no joke this time. From Ada to Cape Coast the land swarmed with troops, especially Hausas from Lagos, and numbers of white men. As usual great weakness was manifested. Guards were dispatched in every direction to prevent the possibility of flight, and to press in all capable of bearing arms, while the king grumbled and accused Amankwa Tia.

There were indeed signs of evil omen, but we knew on whom to cast our care, and were assured that many prayers were ascending on our behalf. The king sent a messenger to the interior to a renowned moslem, begging for medicine to the value of a hundred peredwanes, for the destruction of his enemies, and then gave orders for his army to return over the Prah, promising to have branches thrown across to help them. After these preparations he danced all night, and in the morning (October 20th) proceeded to Bantama to perform fetish, and offer two human sacrifices. He saluted us, and I went to work, glad to be freed from the deafening noise of his followers.

Discouraging reports were increasing. The Akems had taken three hundred Ashantees, and Amankwa Tia had experienced another defeat; thus our last remaining chance of obtaining the much needed salt was gone, as the governor had sent to Kwantiabo and arrested the chief. Nothing was so likely to convince the Ashantees of their real position as the impossibility of procuring this indispensable necessary.

But we had to sustain a new misfortune. On Sunday morning, October 26th, we heard that the house, which had reached the second floor, had fallen down in the night, in consequence of the incessant rain. When I beheld the ruin I could not help weeping. The king was very sorry, but was willing to admit the real cause, and seemed well pleased that we were ready to begin again as soon as dry weather should set in. When the Harmattan commenced we determined to rebuild, but before doing anything else we resolved to erect a shed in which to store the dry bricks. The Fantees had cleared the greater part of the rubbish by the 31st, and exerted themselves so much as to elicit praise from the Ashantees; but they were still kept without payment from the king. We afterwards heard that six houses in the palace court had fallen on that same Sunday, and the stone building had suffered considerable damage.

The king was so struck by this, that he called for a Fetish priestess, and demanded an explanation. "It is on account of the foreigners," replied she; "if the king let the Fantees and the white men go all will succeed, otherwise nothing." For this declaration she was placed in irons. Still the rain would not leave off, but recommenced every evening, to the amazement of the Ashantees.

CHAPTER XXVIII.

JUDGMENT APPROACHES.

LATE in October it was apparent to us that the Momome women were arranging a procession which betokened something unusual. We heard that a great council had been held on the 27th in Amanghyia, when the chiefs had begged the king to recall the army. But he had not been willing, unless his great men would repay him for the outlay, which he estimated at six thousand peredwanes (216,000 dollars), and they had bound themselves to do so. It was a fact that the Akems were pushing on, they had evidently cleared a way through the forest as far as Dadease, which was on our side of the boarder. The Wasas were said to have deceived Adu Bofo's army and beaten them.

The ambassador of Akwamu was dispatched with the answer, which follows:—" The king thanks you for your news, and the hints you gave. I too have a warning to give you. Do not be enticed to Akra or you will be imprisoned. I am young it is true, but I would not bring misfortune upon my country. My forefathers were all benefactors of their kingdom, I would be the same, and I will see what is to be done. I cannot possibly send the white men to you yet, they are making something that is to be finished in two months, till then one must have patience."

It was reported that the army would return to the

neighbourhood of Coomassie, and if positively necessary, the white men and the Fantees would be set free.

We made a last attempt to secure the release of our poor invalid, Kühne, by sending his own written statement of his increasing illness to the king, and pleading for his prompt removal to a dry mountain air, which he had formerly found restorative, and where he would have suitable nursing and nourishment. We hinted that thus the king might at once open communications with the Coast without in any way compromising his dignity. But we received in reply only this message (Oct. 20th), " Cool your heart, I will see what can be done, and send you word in a short time;" which time never arrived! Thus our last hope, that this application might give an opportunity for D. to speak to the king, was cruelly disappointed.

The poor king still clung to the belief, that as water never went up the mountains, so the British could never come to Ashantee. But if this should happen, his heart would certainly fail him, he was much too weak to hold out against the united Coast tribes, especially with the added assistance of the governor, and in the event of their success, nothing but the influence of the governor could restrain them from wreaking their vengence upon Ashantee until he and his people would have to sue for mercy. The governor however would make no treaty until we were set free; thus we felt assured no violence would be offered by the king for fear of retaliation upon himself, and this led us to believe he would yield.

Meanwhile his wives sang the old national songs to him every night, praising the deeds of his forefathers, in wild plaintive tones which moved him greatly. Many a one did he send to these same forefathers through the cruel hands of the executioners during those hours, and in the morning visit his building with a smiling face, striving to hide by a great effort, the uneasy state of his mind.

After long consideration, I resolved to recommence my street preaching, but very few Ashantees came, and I did not ultimately pursue it, feeling uncertain if the king approved; if he did, I thought he would soon let me know. I prayed that I might have a heart to testify warmly of a Saviour's love to the lost, and a ready tongue to proclaim it faithfully, and that the bread cast upon the waters might be found after many days.

Four messengers having arrived from Akwamu, the chiefs were hurriedly summoned to the palace (November 18th), and later in the evening Mr. D. was called. The dialogue began thus:—

"You were sent here respecting the ransom."

"No," answered D.

"Have you brought the money with you?"

"Certainly not: How could I have kept it here a whole year?"

"Has the money been handed over to Owusu Kokoo."

"It was weighed before my eyes, and given to a mulatto (Mr. Grant) in charge, but as I left before Owusu Kokoo, I cannot know what occurred in Cape Coast afterwards."

To the king's last question as to whether the money would be paid out in Cape Coast if we were all sent back, Dawson could only repeat, "I do not know."

On the evening of the 20th he was again summoned to the palace to read two letters from the governor to the king, of October 3rd and November 1st. The first contained the only direct news we had heard from the Coast for a year. The second referred to another which must have miscarried, Amankwa Tia being closely surrounded by the enemy. The governor sent a copy of the missing letter by an Ashantee captive, and required an answer to three points contained in it in twenty days (while twenty-two had already elapsed). The king had broken the peace by invading the protectorate, burning villages, and killing their inhabitants. Yet the governor had pushed back the Ashantees with a handful of troops. Now he was commissioned from Europe to chastise the king himself; and the troops were daily arriving at the Coast. His Queen however was enduring, and was willing to believe that misunderstanding had led Kari-Kari to enter on the war. She would therefore make the terms as easy as possible. If the king wished for peace, he must, before any treaty could be entered into,—

I. Recall all his troops who were stationed in the Protectorate.

II. Restore all innocent prisoners, men, women, and children, with their belongings, and send them to the Coast.

III. Engage to make good all damages done to the said prisoners.

It was not to be supposed that the king could resist the British army, when the native troops had already pushed back the Ashantees.

The letter was heard in profound silence, its very truth made it the more painful, and all became serious. We could only beseech the Lord to open the eyes of the king.

We had heard much of the proceedings at the Coast from our friend, Kwabena. The English were, he affirmed, determined to push on to Coomassie, and were even then advancing. The king had therefore better not listen to those who would flatter him with the assurance that "no one had dared to attack Ashantee from time immemorial." Things had changed, and it was now high time to wake to the impending danger. Great preparations for the campaign were being made at the Coast.

After the letter was finished, the queen mother arose and addressed the great men. "I am old now, I lived before Kwakoo Dooah, and I have now placed my son on the Ashantee throne. Three or four years ago, Akwamu begged for help against Krepe, the Ashantees obeyed the call, and brought some white men here and much booty. The chiefs have now marched against the Coast, the war is going against us, the enemy threatens. The chief of Akwamu entreats incessantly for the white men, for until they are set free he will have no peace, and perhaps be taken to the Coast. What is to be done ? I do not wish for our successors to say my son was the cause of the disturbance of the sixty nkurow" (towns, *i.e.*, the whole land).

"From olden times it has been seen that God fights for Ashantee if the war is a just one. This one is unjust. The Europeans begged for the imprisoned white men. They were told to wait until Adu Bofo returned. Adu Bofo came back; then they said they wanted money. The money was offered, and even weighed. How then can this war be justified ? The building of the house cannot be given as a hindrance, for if peace were once declared, the governor would gladly send builders. Taking all into consideration, I strongly advise that the white men should be sent back at once, and God can help us."

The chiefs adjourned. Hard as it appeared to them they knew that their reduced half-starved army could not stand against fresh troops, so we thought they would try to soften the enemy by setting us free, while they still had a choice.

On the 21st we were filled with gratitude at the birth of a little son, whom we felt constrained to name Immanuel, in memory of God's faithful guidance throughout our captivity. It was noticeable that this boy spent his first months in almost entire obscurity, the Ashantees regarding it as an ill omen when a son is born to an enemy on their territory; his existence was therefore as perfectly ignored, as was that of his little sister noticed, wondered at, and rejoiced over.

On the same day Mose was summoned to translate the governor's letter, in company with the other two Akwapems.

On the 24th we had to attend to write an answer, unaccompanied by Mr. Plange, who was set aside. It was modelled in Ashantee fashion, one point made prominent, the other not noticed. We were seated when the king hastily cried, " Dawson, write to my good friend and tell him that I have received his letter. Before it came I had sent to recall Amankwa Tia; now I will send a fresh messenger to call all back. I have no quarrel with the white men, they are my dear friends, only when I heard from Plange that the Elmina Fort was given to Kwakje Fram, my chiefs grew angry and marched out to bring him here ; but now that I hear he is dead, I am content. The fear that my soldiers might go too far, and make things unpleasant for my good friends, has caused me to recall my army! As regards the white people, I have detained you on their account; as soon as I get the £1000 I will send them away with you." Of course he wished to have his army near him, if only to defy the governor anew.

On the 25th the king's answer was signed, and Mr. Dawson read the heads of a letter to his Excellency, in which he asked if the £1000 could not be sent to Coomassie. Whilst I was silently considering this proposal, the king suggested that I should write to the same effect in order to be set at liberty. I replied that we had never interfered in money matters, and should still less like to do so now. Several chiefs exclaimed, " It is so !" Apea alone remarked ironically, " If you don't care to be set free, do as you like." Nevertheless, by the king's permission, I did write to several friends, and the Fantee, Asiedu, was sent to the Coast with the letters, accompanied by a messenger of the governor.

JUDGMENT APPROACHES. 249

In one of our interviews with the king, M. Bonnat and I again begged him to send K. at once to the Coast on account of his health. His majesty answered, " K. swore formerly that he would not go alone." When D. remarked, "the white men are not in the habit of swearing," Owusu Kokoo rejoined in a stern tone, " the king does not tell lies."

Having laid the foundation of the new building with stones, it was agreed that if I were obliged to be absent on account of my wife, D. should keep watch over the workmen. We had a narrow escape of taking all this labour in vain, for it entered the king's head to fancy that he would rather have the house built in Twere-. boanda, in the neighbourhood of our old Ebenezer, because this place was supposed to be the special haunt of evil spirits. Some Fetish priests enquired into this matter, and decided it was not so. The position was therefore not to be altered, and the basement was happily completed.

On the 29th the king came to inspect our work, and told Mr. D., with a face beaming with joy, that his army was on the way back, and had already reached Fusuwei (a day's journey from the Prah). We gathered however from other sources that though the army had broken through, it had been thoroughly beaten, many captured, and numbers scattered. Owusu Kokoo's brother Osei told (December 5th) his people when the Akwapems were supposed to be asleep, that such a battle as that at Fusuwei had never been fought by the Ashantees, all fled, Amankwa lost twenty peredwanes of gold-dust, Kwasi Domfe the whole of his jewellery, and Akjampong was taken prisoner. Almost every night Kete was danced at the palace, and the excitement was excedingly painful.

Kotiko and Kwado, Ashantee messengers, who had been more than a year at Cape Coast, were now said to be advancing, as the governor had sent them to Amankwa's camp, accompanied by numerous soldiers. They were ceremoniously received (December 6th) on the Bogyawee place, when the king and all his chiefs danced about the streets, painted white, to express their joy; glorious news having been brought to the king. "Kwakje Fram the Denkjera prince had fallen, together with his nephew, seven Fantee officers, and one European! Amankwa Tia had killed many Fantees and chased the rest into the sea, besides punishing the other Coast tribes, and because a fellow on the Akem side had annoyed the king, this glorious captain had returned to punish him." Then came grand bursts of hurrahs! It seemed incredible that the king could so misrepresent matters to his people; but such was the fact.

This message was delivered in the open air, so that it was immediately made public. Whether the king thought that his subjects were so completely in subjection as to believe those statements, we could not decide; but we were pretty sure every one knew how matters really stood. Perhaps he thought it right to avoid all outward signs of despair and mourning that he might give new life and courage.

In a more restricted circle he testified his sympathy with the army in another way. He had sworn the great oath before his chiefs, that whoever dared to make game of a soldier, or even to hint that the army had achieved nothing, should be put to death. Besides this he sent the troops forty small casks of powder, and gave the mohammedans ten peredwances for using sorcery to hinder the white men from rising. He even took one of our porters, who had said he was a Fetish priest (no doubt by way of obtaining food) into his service, and gave him a new house; but the poor fellow always went about guarded, thus paying dearly for his folly.

On December the 7th, the king with his followers again danced through the streets, but ceased long before daylight.

The messengers entered merrily into the king's ideas, and Kotiko related how many Ashantees had been put to death by the cruel governor. "My wife," said he, "was about to lose her head, when just in time to save her came the king's letter, assuring the governor that the white men and the Fantees were still alive, causing him to regret that he had been so rash." A true Ashantee messenger.

When these gentlemen visited us, a royal guard was present, so that we could not ask many questions; but when I inquired after Ansa's health, Kwado answered with some hesitation, "he is well." We afterwards discovered that Kotiko had told a Fantee of his acquaintances, "these were three Ashantees who fell victims to the rage of the people, who on hearing of the murder of the prisoners, attacked Prince Ansa's house, destroyed everything, and killed three of his servants, The governor sympathized with the prince, and promised him a full compensation." This report sounded credible; it was further said that the prince had been taken to Sierra Leone with the prince of Elmina.

New reports were continually circulated; one was that an Akwamu in a European dress was on his way to Coomassie; then it was prince Ansa who was coming, and certainly if he could help his country, this was the time to do it. Again we heard that the English were making a bridge over the Prah.

The entry of the jaws, and a week later the triumphant return of the army, was next spoken of. There being no jaw-bones of the enemy, all those from the beheaded were to be sent to meet the army, for they could not return home without a trophy!

The king had (December 12th) proclaimed in the villages that there was nothing to fear; that he had conquered and slain all the inhabitants of the Coast. Meanwhile in spite of the royal commands, soldiers came continually into the town, some of whom said plainly, "Even if the king send us forward again, we will not go unless he accompany; we are sick of it. The white men have guns which hit five Ashantees at once. Many great men and princes have fallen. Amankwa wandered for days in the forest, and only escaped by the help of two porters, and with the loss of his great umbrella and chair." The king on hearing this sent him at once an umbrella and three chairs to Fomana. From Akem came the news that on the 14th a village of Kwau Kodiabe had been attacked, and its inhabitants carried into captivity.

In the meantime we were concerned to hear that the king's letter with our own had only reached Akrofrum, from whence it had been sent back with the trophy. This was told to D. by the friendly Asiedu, that he might write other letters instead of those and deliver them to him, in case anything injurious might have been contained in the first. But we had long refrained from writing on politics, even in our French and German correspondence. D. had however sent through the Fantee letters in English writing, both to the governor and the editor of the African Times, containing political discussions upon the cause of the war, Ashantee weakness, etc. These every runaway schoolboy could read. When the Akwamu in European dress arrived, we feared the letters would be given him to translate, still we felt sure that all would be for the best.

On the morning of December the 15th, the king sat to welcome the chief Barentwa with the jaw bones and the prisoners, trophies of the campaign, and with him appeared Asiedu, the letter carrier, from whom all writings were taken before dawn, whereupon he returned to his old quarters at Mr. Dawson's. Through him we heard that the danger for the Coast had been greater than we had supposed. The Ashantees had really pressed on to Dunkwa, within six miles of Cape Coast, and had burned every village. This was incomprehensible, and very dishonourable to the Fantees. After the Ashantees had taken the residence of the Denkjera prince, Kwakje Fram, they marched against Elmina. Half the town took the side of the British, but the upper town, where the prince lived, not only refused to fight the Ashantees, but supplied them with provisions and ammunition. It was therefore bombarded and burnt down.

In the villages around were Fantees, who would be delivered up to the Ashantees without mercy, and who would be the only prisoners made by them. When Tschama was bombarded, many of the inhabitants were ready to emigrate to Coomassie. Deceived in their expectations of the willingness of the Elminas to join them, the Ashantees retreated to a camp which was by degrees surrounded, so that the army was almost destroyed by privations. Two bananas or a handful of palm nuts, cost three pence, and numbers were starved to death. In this dilemma they corresponded with the governor, who humanely advised Amankwa to hasten back, but not by way of Abakrampa, unless he wished to deliver up his army to slaughter.

The prince of Mampong and most of the commanders followed this advice, but Amankwa took a route round Cape Coast, which brought him face to face with the enemy in Fusuwei, and caused heavy losses of both men and baggage, together with five hundred prisoners, who had been brought thus far. Mampong, on the contrary, crossed the Prah unhurt. The Ashantees had agreed that Amankwa caused their defeat, and that the governor's advice had saved those who accepted it. The king had not recalled the army, but the army, contrary to his orders, gave up the unsatisfactory campaign.

Asiedu asserted that Kotiko had brought back false reports, which the king punished by arresting him. He, although a Fantee, declared he had never abused any of the soldiers. Mose and his followers affirm that the jaw bones with which twenty men were laden are very old. Behind some prisoners came the bones, and then followed the Tschama people and other volunteer emigrants, amongst them a mulatto boy of eight years in European dress, and accompanied by his mother. Volunteers and prisoners together numbered eighty persons! And this was the result of a war which had cost Ashantee thousands of lives; from Akrofrum to Kaase alone, Asiedu saw innumerable bodies either dead or left to die of their wounds. Twenty Fantees are said to have been seen wearing the great chain which showed they were to be sacrificed. At this time Amankwa demanded that all the Fantees should be killed, others foretell a general slaughter, "when the army returns plundered."

December 17th, the king was much rejoiced in visiting us, to see that we had begun the second floor, and much to our surprise gave us eighteen tins of preserved meat, taken no doubt from one of the Coast towns. This was the first gift since the downfall! A man from Elmina told Mr. Plange how shamfully he and his countrymen had been treated when they fled with their property to the Ashantee camp; nearly all of them had returned to British teritory, and encouraged by the governor, were rebuilding their town. He was obliged to go on to Coomassie because his wife and child were in the Ashantee camp, but was rejoicing in the hope of returning to the Coast. The Elmina women who had gone with them belong chiefly to Akjampong's train.

On the morning of December 18th I stayed with Rosa while D. and M. B. went to the building. All was quiet till towards noon, when the king seated himself in the

Bogyawee place, and there advanced towards him, as if by chance, a deputation from Amankwa Tia, to announce to him the number of those who had fallen, and the names of the important chiefs.

Suddenly a cry of distress arose which rolled like a wave through the whole town, and people ran into the street painted red, crying and howling till I was cut to the heart. The sacrifices were then freed from their chains, and after being pierced through the cheek, beheaded amid the beating of drums. Almost despairing, I cried out, "O God! how long shall these things be?" We saw fourteen of the prisoners dragged by a long chain to the hangman's quarters; while howling and crying continued through the night.

Dumb and depressed the king returned home; and the queen mother is said to have mourned in the street with her court ladies, her hands folded over her head; for the loss is dreadful. Bekwae, a small country, is said to miss a thousand of its men. Officers who went with twenty, returned alone with their baggage on their heads! Sabeng was really dead; either carried off by small pox or attacked by Akemers and beheaded.

On Monday, December 22nd, the town was filled from far and near with the triumphant entry of the army. We asked the king if we should go to work, as the Fantees had gone accompanied by M. B., and the Ashantees could not wish for our presence at this ceremony. Had we been there we should have been more surprised than at Adu Bofo's entry; whole rows of boxes were carried past wrapped in precious materials, followed by their (supposed) mourning wives, and their attendants painted red. Two hundred and seventy nine persons had perished by sacrifice, and more would follow. Very few could be seen in the crowd who were painted white; the majority of the people were wailing in the red ornaments of mourning.

Though living at some distance from the market place, we were driven almost frantic by the incessant beating of drums, accompanied by screams and occasional firing. From eight in the morning till seven in the evening the army passed in file; and the streets which opened on the market-place were so crowded with soldiers that nothing could be seen but a black mass swaying to and fro, whilst over it the many coloured umbrellas waved conspicuously. We had often been told that the whole Ashantee army had gone to the war, which was no doubt true, and on that day all Ashantee appeared to be in Coomassie. M. B. who made his way unhindered through the crowds, reckoned the number of those present at about one hundred thousand.

The losses of the campaign were undoubtedly great. Still, about half the army survived, and some of the chiefs who had been reported dead returned in safety. Not only Sabeng, but another prince, Karapa, was mourned for as dead. The Abesui chief had been crushed, with all his servants, by the trunk of a tree falling on his tent at the opening of the campaign. Altogether two hundred and eighty chiefs had fallen. The loss of soldiers was announced in the following way. Every chief who passed before the king threw into a vase as many grains of corn as he had lost people. It was said that sixteen battles had been fought, and the army had been attacked four times in retreat, and suffered each time terrible loss.

On Christmas day, after an address from Mr. D., I baptized our little son, Louis Immanuel. For this purpose we all assembled under the mango tree in the mission court-yard, and the day was to us as another oasis in the desert. We could only offer to our God glory and praise for His faithful care over us, although we were deprived of all European comforts. With one of our lambs a feast was prepared, to which we invited the three Akwapem Christians, and on the same day I sold the other for five dollars and a half, showing how dear provisions then were in Ashantee. The king sent Mr. D. and ourselves an ox as a Christmas present. He also sent greetings to the army, but as no presents to the commanders accompanied them, they were not much valued. Just as we had finished our meal, and were comfortably seated together in the yard, D. was summoned to the palace.

He found the king surrounded by a few confidential friends, and he was accosted thus; " I have already warned you several times not to write any deceitful letters like Ata (Mr. Pl.), for I wish to be able to depend entirely upon you. How comes it then that you have written instructions to the Coast? You announce to the governor that I wished him to send the keys of Elmina, Cape Coast, Anomabu, etc., to Coomassie!" D. expressed surprise. "Is it credible," said he, "that I should set fire to the roof of the house in which I am living? All that I wish is that a lasting peace should exist between Ashantee and the Coast."

The king then said more politely, "I know that you will be able to secure a good treaty. I only wish you could be a second Bedae" (Governor Maclean), who had sent back many servants to the king.

Dawson replied, "I will certainly do all I can to promote peace, and I should like to know who has reported so falsely;" then turning to Kwado and Kotiko, he entreated them to weigh the consequences of the course they were pursuing. The latter said somewhat confusedly, they had only repeated what they had been told, upon which the king again became angry, and complained that the governor had not answered his questions concerning Asen and Denkjera, which would doubtless have pleased him. "For," said he, "the governor is my good friend, and what he says I will always hear. But now the Ashantees are being killed at the Coast whilst you are going about free: Is that right?" Kwado declared that they had been robbed, and five Ashantees slain at Cape Coast; and that if the king's letter had not arrived which announced that the white men were alive, the Ashantees would all have been killed. Upon this D. advised him to take care, as all he then affirmed would be written to the governor and he would have to be the bearer of the letter.

Finally, D. received instructions to write a letter which showed plainly that the Ashantees were afraid, and would gladly make peace if they knew how. The king complained that the governor had attacked his retreating army, and had taken away their wounded and prisoners—that Ashantees had been slain at the Coast, and his messengers plundered and locked up. These things proved how desirable was peace and friendship! D. was entreated to write forcibly, and merit the name of a Bedae.

Asiedu was to have carried this letter, and I had hastily written a few enclosures, but when the interpreters and Bosommuru had signed their names, it was suddenly observed that Asiedu was far too mature, it would be better to choose as messenger a Fantee boy, who could not say much. Asiedu, it was feared, had received verbal instructions from Mr. D., and saw too plainly the real state of things. D.'s boy, Robert, a lad of sixteen, was therefore chosen in his stead, and hurriedly dismissed, under the escort of a herald, without having an opportunity of speaking a confidential word with his master.

So far had matters progressed, when on December 31st, we were able thankfully to record how graciously we had been brought through this trying year, and to beseech our faithful Lord to give us steadfastness, and to continue to preserve us throughout all our dangers and troubles.

The 1st of January, 1874 (a day of delightful enjoyment at our missionary stations, where all were uniting in fresh songs of praise) was a season of awful festivity in Coomassie, for innocent blood was flowing in almost every street. The distressing cries of the poor widows and other relatives, with bodies painted red and long branches waving in their hands, were ascending continually. In all the principal streets the doomed sacrifices stood beside the corpses of the slain, awaiting the merciful stroke which would end their torture. One poor man was led to his wife's dead body, and tauntingly told to "look at her who had gone before to prepare his supper." We could count nearly sixty victims, chiefly Ashantees and Krepes, slaves and servants of the dead, and many more followed them during that night. *

On the next day, being Friday, no corpse was allowed to remain exposed in Coomassie, but I saw on my way to the building, three bodies which had not been removed. Alas! one gradually became almost accustomed to such heart-rending scenes, and to cease even to shudder. Between Coomassie and Amanghyia, six corpses which Kühne had seen lying in the road, were so mutilated and destroyed by the vultures as to be perfectly indescribable.

* Amongst the Fantees who had been swept away were a girl and boy whom the king sent to a Mohammedan in Duro, when our Fantees had intercourse with them from time to time. The boy described how the Europeans were building a broad street on the Prah, and how Mr. Blankson had been caught buying powder (which he had sent to the Ashantees in bottles), and had been attacked by the mob, but was saved by the governor and sent to Sierra Leone. Twenty or thirty Ashantees were daily taken to Cape Coast, so that the number of prisoners had become a burden, and they were being sent away in ships.

The English report of the war is as follows :—

On the 11th and 14th of April, 1873, the troops of the protectorate fought two sharp battles with the Ashantees between Dunkwa and Nyan Coomassie; on the 15th the Fantees retreated. Their chiefs endeavoured to excuse this step by accusing a member of the council, Mr. G. Blankson, of treachery. They would have killed him if Mr. Rowe had not arrested him in order to save his life; for in the same proportion as the Fantees were cowardly in the battle-field, was their enmity bitter

On the 6th, Epiphany, we united in spirit with all Christendom in prayer for the heathen, especially for that part of the earth so saturated with blood, and that Ashantee might be saved, however deep the darkness in which it was now sunk, and we pleaded for a living, active faith. Doubtless, we had failed in much, and were still very powerless to effect good. We could not continue the street preaching, owing to the bitterness of the poor deceived people, yet we knew the Lord could make even our residence amongst them a blessing.

The chiefs were now ordered to repay to the king the cost of the campaign, and to replace the ammunition which had been used in vain. Of some was demanded sixty, of others forty or fifty peredwanes. They were terribly excited, and appealed to the council at the palace for a mitigation of these enormous demands, with little success. Similar sums were demanded from some of the chief people, one of whom had to sell not only his slaves, but his wife, to furnish the five peredwanes; he sold his son too for nine dollars, and the poor boy cried bitterly. There were many upright, quiet men who had wished for peace and free trade, who lost half their families by the war, and were afterwards obliged to sell the other half to pay for it. But whether the real promoters of the strife would remain unpunished, remained to be seen. An under chief entreated Dawson to speak plainly to the king, who he thought could not continue to be deceived. This man asserted that Akjampong was dead.

The king now seemed to care but little about his new house; Owusu Kokoo also passed it with indifference; we were waiting for wood to finish the windows; could we

against every one who had friendly dealings with Ashantee." It was a true report which we had heard of the dreadful doings of a Fantee mob at Cape Coast; they had actually attacked and killed five peaceful Ashantees in Prince Ansa's house, and then stormed and plundered it.

JUDGMENT APPROACHES. 261

have procured that, the roof might soon have been placed on it.

We were told of a chief who had wished to go over to the enemy with his followers; at the last moment the intended flight was discovered, but it was made light of in the camp, and a promise was given that the affair should not be reported to the king. On the march back, however, the whole party were put in irons and afterwards massacred; others were threatened with the same fate. Adu Bofo was also reported to be hemmed in between the enemy and a river, without the power to extricate himself.

On Wednesday, January 7th, we had returned from the Adae at three o'clock, when D. entered and announced that the English army was at Asiaman (a day's journey from the Prah), that Obeng had been sent from Fomana an hour before to the south, with the Adanse chiefs, and that the king had ordered every man to Coomassie, in order to head them himself. Our position had thus become very critical. Whether we should be placed in irons or killed seemed doubtful, but in any case we knew that God cared for us and would guard us.

Few people in the town slept that night, but were constantly playing Sokoda. In the morning of January the 8th, a sword-bearer came to assure himself that we were all there. In the afternoon we heard that Robert had returned, and had been taken to Owusu Kokoo's house. The chiefs were assembled in the palace, and we felt assured that the Lord would speak a word there too. We called to remembrance how on that day eight years before, we had been married in Christianburg, and we earnestly prayed that our faith might be strengthened! We saw nothing of Robert, but Mose was summoned late in the evening, and two letters were given him to translate, the chiefs were however so impatient, that he only finished one. It was from an officer on the Prah, who announced that one of the two Ashantee messengers had shot himself.

This officer had shown both prisoners the bridge he had built over the Prah with casks, &c., had made them observe the cannon and arms, and had added that when this bridge was ready an officer would be sent to the king with an ultimatum. One of them replied that the king would certainly kill such an ambassador, after which he became alarmed at the idea of having spoken injudiciously, and fearing he might be sent back to Coomassie, shot himself. When the king heard this, he remarked, "It would not occur to me to kill such a fellow." He then put off further business till the next day.

On the 9th we visited Bosommuru, and enquired if we were to be put in irons. He appeared astonished, and asked from whom we had heard this, adding that he would speak to the king about it. We begged him in any case to come and tell us himself, as we were accustomed to him. On the previous evening, the old Asare had ordered two Elminians to be bound, but they had been again set free, their landlord declaring that the king had given no such order. Everything was fluctuating and uncertain, and we clung yet more closely to our Rock of defence to save us.

CHAPTER XXIX.

BROTHER KÜHNE SET AT LIBERTY.

On the 9th of January, the day of deliverance appeared at hand, and we thanked God for it.

At two p.m., we were summoned to read the letters in the presence of the king, his mother, and the council. We seated ourselves near the celebrated General Amankwa Tia, and Mr. D. took the unopened letter and read it aloud; while we wondered the hearers did not storm at its stern, sharp words; but they felt their power was already broken, and he was permitted to read it through, word for word, without interruption.

"Sir Garnet Wolseley, knight of the order of St. Michael, etc., reproached the king with having introduced many irrelevant subjects, instead of simply replying to the three questions he had asked. The king knew well that his predecessors had totally resigned all right over Asen, Denkjera, etc.; notwithstanding which he spoke of those tribes as if they were his slaves. He had caused white men to be taken prisoners without the shadow of a reason, and when their friends offered a ransom he had suddenly broken off the treaty, attacked the protectorate in great force, and attempted to take possession of a fort belonging to queen Victoria.

Perhaps the king did not know the actual facts concerning the war. Although he had declared he would keep at peace with the white men, Amankwa had attacked the English troops at Abakrampa, whereupon fifty white soldiers had put to flight the whole Ashantee army. It had been beaten again in Fusuwei by untrained black troops, and finally driven over the Prah. Thousands of Ashantees were now in British hands, besides chairs, umbrellas, and other trophies. The British vanguard was already at Praso; but the real powerful army was following from the Coast; and from other points troops were advancing upon Coomassie. His majesty must therefore acknowledge that the duration of his dynasty was at stake, for he (the general) was determined, if necessary, to crush Ashantee. But peace could be obtained if the king would in the first place set all the prisoners at liberty; secondly, pay fifty thousand ounces of gold for the expenses of the war; and thirdly, appoint hostages for the signature of the treaty in Coomassie."

All this was quietly heard. If an exclamation escaped any of the chiefs, the king immediately commanded attention. The other letter required no second translation. As soon as the king had assured himself that Mose had read it correctly, we were allowed to go.

At home all was in great perplexity. Several Fantees, amongst them our Kwaku, had been placed in chains, and my wife had collected the most necessary articles for our children, lest a similar fate should befall ourselves. Whilst we were still speaking of its probability, a sword-bearer came running with the order, "*Ohene se bra*" (the king calls). We followed him with beating hearts, but had to pass an hour of suspense in the palace, till again conducted to the court we had left two hours before, where we saluted humbly.

The king began, "Dawson, I wish you to write to my good friend, the general, and tell him that I accept the conditions of peace. I will not fight against the white men. I did not command Amankwa to attack their fort.

Nay, my good friend, keep quiet, and only send an officer here with full powers to conclude a treaty of peace. When that affair is settled, I will let you go."

We could hardly believe our ears at these words. Yet it had not escaped us that the general was determined in any case to march to Coomassie, which the king wished to prevent by an expression of ready compliance. We therefore urged him to show that he meant what he had said by immediately setting the invalid K. at liberty. Beyond all our expectation, he at once replied, "Go, go; I will send you to the governor, but you must leave Coomassie to-night!" It sounded almost like Pharaoh's last command to the Israelites; and thus the way was found to bring out the prisoners from the prison (Is. xlii. 7). Encouraged by this concession, we further begged that the Fantees might be released from their irons, which was conceded on the spot.

How greatly we all rejoiced on again reaching home, where everyone was trembling, while Mrs. Plange and the servants stood round my Rosa ready for an attack similar to that at Fomana. We felt as if going ourselves with our dear invalid; to know that he was free, seemed so clearly to point to our own deliverance.

About eight o'clock a chief brought K., from the king, a beautifully woven dress such as was worn only by the royal family, and thirty-six dollars in gold dust. He was to be summoned to take leave of his majesty at nine o'clock, and was then to appear in the presented dress, which was so heavy that he begged to be allowed to defer putting it on till he reached the palace. Accompanied by M. Bonnat he once more crawled through the courts where the guards were posted, who started up on seeing the torches, but were quieted by a movement of the leader's hand. In the smallest court, by the stone house, sat the king, stroking a cat which lay in his lap, while six or seven others purred around him, and let themselves be petted by those sitting next him.

K. thanked him for his handsome present.

"Do you really think it handsome?" he said; "only Ashantee kings can make such presents." He then continued, "Aburoni Tenteng (tall white man), you are now going to Amrado (the governor); tell him that I am his good friend. My predecessors never fought with the white men, but all the blacks belong to me; I do not fear them, for I am the man for them (with a fierce glance of the eyes). Tell Amrado, even if he did come to my market place I would not fire a shot at his white men; he must send a white ambassador, I will arrange all with him."

K. replied, "Nana (grandfather), I will tell him all."

"But you must speak softly; you will forget all when you see the white men."

"God's messengers never tell lies; I will tell Amrado that you have been kind to us, and show him this dress."

"That is right, Nana, I will pray to God to give you much wisdom and many blessings."

M. B. then added a few words assuring the king that he would obtain much more honour by making peace than by fighting.

His majesty declared anew that he did not wish to go against the white men, simply against the black. After he had (according to the mohammedan custom) bowed, touching his brow and his breast he said again, "I thank you; now go!" K. then offered him his hand, and returned home through the empty streets.

The king had allowed him to take four of the captive Fantees as porters; torch-bearers too were to accompany him to the next village. After a most painful farewell, our dear brother, the sharer of all our joys, and of all our sorrows, for nearly five years, departed. Two torch-bearers marched before and two behind his hammock;

then two boys who had been presented to him by the king followed, carrying his few possessions. Thus they left us, and entered the dark primeval forest; K. cheering himself by repeating in his heart the cxxiv. psalm. *

The whole of January the 10th I spent at the building without Owusu Kokoo, who had gone to the south in anxiety, after having made fetish. We were in good spirits as we asked ourselves whether we should be able to place the roof and thus crown our work. It would be impossible to do this in less than ten days, and we hoped we should not have so long to wait for our freedom.

But in the evening we heard that everything was being prepared for war; the men were making bullets of lead and iron, drying corn and cassada, and packing up various provisions. The king would not yet humble himself to sue for pardon. Ashantee must show itself valiant! On Tuesday, January the 6th, the holy tree in the market-place had fallen down; this was a bad sign; a wake had to be held, and among other of the devoted victims, a Fantee prisoner whom the king had assured us should not be killed, was beheaded.

In the course of Sunday, January the 11th, it could no longer be doubted that the Ashantees, either the chiefs or the king, were determined to measure their strength with the white intruders. It was universally believed that Owusu Kokoo and Kühne had been sent to prepare for an invasion, and that the army was to leave Kyidwo the following day, though its departure might not take place for another week. A short respite this for troops so completely demoralised, and great numbers of whom had deserted and fled the country. Surely a month would

---

* Stanley relates :—"January 14th. Yesterday the appearance of a pale prisoner, the wasted shadow of a man, put the whole camp in a state of excitement. It was the missionary Kühne who came to us in Asiaman."

hardly have sufficed to prepare for a fresh encounter. Their plans were however all uncertain, the king alone knew what he was going to do.

But most assuredly on Thursday and Friday affairs with us looked very threatening, for both in Coomassie and the neighbouring villages an order was given that all Fantees should be put in the stocks, and it was said that we were to share their fate. At this critical juncture came a letter, directing the king's thoughts into another channel, and instead of our usual preaching, we had an hour of prayer that we might be resigned to God's will. We were all much impressed by the seriousness of the position, and by God's help our courage was sustained throughout that trying day. We felt that we ought to be thankful if our captivity should serve in any degree to bring about a new era for Ashantee, and we did not doubt that the year 1874 would mark the dawning of a brighter day for this unhappy country.

Mr. D. paid a visit to the chiefs of Mampong and Asamoa Kwanta, to beg these influential men to refrain from giving dangerous advice to the king, at the same time representing to them the serious nature of the present crisis. Both seemed glad to listen to him, and both made the same enquiry as to what effect the last royal letter would probably have on the English general. Of course the same answer was returned to each by D., viz., that he did not know.

On the 12th and 13th of January, reports were constantly circulated as to the progress of the war. The brother of Owusu Kokoo had sold many slaves for the king, and was on that day sent to Kwantiabo to buy powder. The continual excitement was very injurious to my poor wife, for though the town itself was perfectly quiet, troops were constantly starting to guard the road from Daso. We now felt quite sure that the dismissal of

BROTHER KÜHNE SET AT LIBERTY. 269

K. was intended to prevent the English general from advancing. We had another hour of prayer, for we felt the necessity of earnest, united, and continuous supplication.

By the 14th of January, the enemy had advanced so far forward on the side of Akem that the inhabitants of a village belonging to Nsuta had fled to Dwaben, and two Ashantees who arrived from the south told dreadful tales of what was going on there. Yet whatever had happened must have been known to Owusu Kokoo, for he had returned on the 10th, without having spoken to the general himself.

We were now summoned again to read the answer to the letter which Mr. D. translated before the council, no servant being present. It was as follows:—

"Sir Garent Wolseley has received the king's letter conveyed by Mr. Kühne, and rejoices at the peaceful spirit which it breathes. But he considers it necessary to prove its sincerity, that the white men should be released within the next few days, also the Akras, Akwapems, Elminians, and all the Fantees. The king may retain Mr. D. as interpreter. It will not be the work of a moment to stop the progress of the four divisions of the army; as the king must be aware. Queen Victoria wishes that there may be a lasting peace between Great Britain and Ashantee, which he (Sir Garnet), will do his best to bring about. But his majesty must understand that it is as impossible to stop the progress of the white men as to hinder the rising of the sun."

A letter was enclosed for me from brother K., telling me he had sent me six ounces of gold dust, and expressing the hope that the God who had saved him would also deliver us. All listened with great attention to the reading of the general's letter, after which my own little packet was handed to me.

The king then asked whether Mr. D. had brought the £1000, or if it had been paid to Owusu Kokoo. The two ambassadors began a discussion, and a hot debate ensued between the interpreters and the chiefs, of which it was difficult to perceive the purport. Some chiefs appeared to think that the money was in the hands of the Ashantees, because Owusu Kokoo had been speculating and making large purchases. The chief of Mampong rose up and sharply accused the interpreter Nantschi of twisting matters.

Once more at home, we united in our daily prayer, "Open their eyes and soften their hearts, direct them, and incline them to hear Thy voice."

The chief of Mampong summoned Mr. Dawson on January the 16th, to consult with him on the most advisable steps to take. D. declined to say much, for he had been warned not to go to the chiefs, "perhaps," rejoined the chief on hearing this, " he who warned you has prompted me to speak to you." D. then mentioned what he thought requisite, though cautiously, for fear of the king; but afterwards conversed more freely with Bosommuru, who complained that the governor would not receive the king's nephew, Owusu Kokoo, as a negotiator; and that he proposed peace, whilst at the same time he was advancing with cannon, and was going to cross the Monse mountain.

If it were so, he continued, they must oppose the cannon with their small arms, and fight to the last man.

We were much depressed in view of the Ashantees sense of honour, so misguided and ungovernable; they looked upon it as the greatest disgrace to be moved by threats to set us at liberty. The continual excitement of those few days completely prostrated us, and but for special help from the Lord, we should have broken down.

We again sought an interview with Bosommuru, and D., who felt this very important, conducted us to him on the morning of the 17th. We begged the chief to summon Bosommuru Dwira and Mensa Kukua, when Dawson explained the state of affairs, and set all before them in a clear light. Showing them how the patience of the English government was exhausted by four years and a half of waiting, and hope being held out which was never realized. One course only could avert Ashantee's fall, the immediate setting at liberty of *all* the prisoners. " Do not believe," said he, " that it is possible to push back the English. If you destroy those who are on this side the Prah, you will only have defended yourselves from the vanguard, but not from the real army. The English will not rest until they have succeeded in obtaining compensation, even if they have to fight ten years for it."

The three gentlemen listened attentively, assured themselves that *we* were of the same opinion, and perfectly understood that Dawson was remaining as a surety for the carrying out of the governor's word. We, on our part, made it clear to them that the governor was not coming from any desire to conquer, and that if they agreed to his three demands, they would have as much liberty left them as they had previously enjoyed.

To the question why the governor would not even see Owusu Kokoo, we replied by referring them to the part he had played only a short time before in Cape Coast. But strangely enough it now dawned upon us that they had anticipated so much from Owusu Kokoo's mission, because he was armed with a wonderful mohammedan charm, which with a mere shake of the hand was to have the effect of causing the governor to go back. The king's nephew was only considered so far as he was entrusted with a most holy secret.

We parted, yet not without hope that we had made some impression, for the trio pledged themselves to confer at once with the king and his mother, and afterwards to summon a high council which we should attend, that we might have an opportunity of speaking. We waited, however, in vain for a summons, and the contrary of what we hoped for occurred. The chiefs indeed assembled, *but to swear that they would unite in marching against the white men in the field.* Some started at once, others followed the same night. No one was allowed to sleep in the town.

News came at the same time that the white men were at the foot of the Kwisa mountain, and it was declared to us by one of our Coast negroes, a fetish man from Krepe, who was often in the palace, that the king thought of delivering us on Monday the 19th. This man had the day before been performing fetish, on which occasion he had been tying a block of wood with a rope, to be pulled very tight, while our names and those of the Fantees were called out. In the midst of the operation the rope broke, and the exorcist fell full length on the ground. It was then acknowledged the affair was too much for the Ashantees, and they had better let us go. *

On Sunday the 18th Mr. D. came to us somewhat depressed; having heard that the Ashantees in the neighbourhood of Lake Bosomotsche had encountered the Akems, hunted them like sheep, and either killed or taken them prisoners. When he visited Bosommuru, and enquired the results of the council, he was answered abruptly by the words, "it is too late." He again urged peace, only saying not a moment was to be lost, upon which the minister sulkily rejoined, "the governor will not let anything prevent him now, he is having cannon tied to the trees," &c., and concluded by adding, "I have heard it." So ended the interview. We then tried to gain access

---

* That the Ashan'ees have great faith in omens, this incident readily proves; but we never heard anything in Coomassie itself about the anecdote, which was handed round in the English papers, that the king let a white goat fight with a black one in order to see which would win.

to Boakje Tenteng, the husband of the queen mother, but did not find him at home.

The whole of Monday (19th) we spent at the building, hoping to finish one gallery before we left, and I instructed Joseph how to proceed without us. Whilst thus employed, a messenger came from Boakje Tenteng to call us. We went, but failed to find him; and heard from good authority that he and Kwantabisa would be the two last to consent to our being set at liberty. Owusu Kokoo then told Mr. D. that two days before it had been fully arranged that he was to accompany all the Europeans and Fantees to the Coast. The council had agreed with all deliberation, when suddenly the boundary guard, Obeng, sent a message to say—*he* would fire upon the enemy—that if the people in Coomassie had no powder, he at least had some. This stroke wounded their pride to such a degree, that they started, and swore as we have related above.

The next day (20th) another messenger from Obeng announced that the white men were in Fomana, and Kokofu was already cleared of its inhabitants, for the enemy had appeared in the distance. We felt this would touch the king deeply, for Kokofu was the cradle of his dynasty, and regarded as a holy town by the whole nation. Boakje Tenteng danced all the night and morning in the streets, which signified that he was going to the field.

The heavy storm that had been gathering over the devoted land was now about to burst in its fury, and our doubts were great as to whether it would be a crushing storm or a quickening rain, for us as well as for Ashantee. The people in Coomassie itself were getting almost furious. One came into our yard and said to Mrs. Plange, "she need not be at all anxious, but quietly resign herself to her fate! Ashantee would never crawl to the cross, nor give up the prisoners, but rather fight and die with them."

T

Many seemed to think the same. The sight of my dear wife and children was almost overpowering; but I remembered the Lord was our Shepherd, and we should not want.

CHAPTER XXX.

THE RELEASE OF THE REST.

CAPE COAST, February 3rd.

It is a dream no longer! It is a glad reality! We are free! Hallelujah! Yes, our faithful God can still work miracles; our whole career throughout these years had been one succession of miracles. We are in Cape Coast. The place we have often longed for in our best dreams; before us the wide ocean, the sounding of whose tide seems, day and night, to echo in our ears the words of that sweet music which fills our hearts, "free, free, and once again free." Yesterday morning at 10 o'clock, was the hour so long wished for when we were permitted once more to walk through the streets of Cape Coast! As we saw the fall of Ashantee approaching with gigantic strides, we had often asked ourselves, "will the Lord allow *us* to perish with it, or will He save us at the last moment?"

On Wednesday, January the 21st, Mr. Dawson wrote us that he had decided to "eat nothing" until he had seen the queen mother and her husband, which signified that he would force Boakje to listen to him, for the Ashantees know a man is in earnest if he refuse to eat. This resolution took effect, and he soon came to relate to us the result of his conversation with this personage, who had received him kindly, and wished us to place our petition unitedly before himself and his wife; he even whispered to D. that we should start that same evening—an assurance which had so often been made that we could scarcely believe it now.

After eight o'clock, Boakje sent for Dawson and ourselves; we found him in a secluded court, and beside him an old lady, whom he introduced as the sister of the queen mother, who was sent to represent her, she being unable to come out. When every attendant had retired, Mr. Dawson thus began:

"Before everything else we entreat the favour of the queen mother, and beg her to listen to the serious words which we are about to speak, and to make intercession to the king for us."

It is one of the redeeming features of Ashantee custom, that when anyone seeks for protection, or intercession from a high chief, the latter is bound to use all his influence for the petitioner.

Mr. D. continued:—"as we appear before you to-day, to plead for the welfare of Ashantee, we are not moved to make our requests from fear, but because, as missionaries, we wish, as far as lies in our power, to prevent the shedding of blood. We love Ashantee, and therefore wish to impress on her her present position. There is yet a moment left to try to save her, but if she will not listen, she must soon face her ruin. One step is necessary to prove her sincerity to the governor—*all* the prisoners must be set at liberty. Perhaps the king does not believe the governor, but we can assure him that the white men do not lie, and that if he yield, and send away the captives, we will make intercession with the governor for the king. If the king obey, the general will keep his word."

Dawson further declared that "vexation and mistrust on the part of the colonial government was justifiable; it had entreated long, and waited patiently for, the release of the prisoners, till it finally saw the Protectorate suddenly invaded.

"Ashantee should reflect on her situation; not alone

from the Prah would the enemy approach, she would be attacked on all sides. We are now before you for the last time," concluded D., "and beg the queen mother to intercede with the king, that he may let us and the other prisoners leave. We, on our part, solemnly engage to do our best to avert further calamities."

Boakje and his sister-in-law promised to prefer our request at once, and at nine o'clock we were called into the palace, but had to wait until eleven o'clock. Summoned at length to enter, we found the king, looking very depressed, in the fourth court, on a broad verandah surrounded by fifteen chiefs, and his mother beside him.

Mr. D. had to repeat what had been already said, which he did, though with some degree of nervousness. The king at once exclaimed: "Yes, but where are the £1000 ransom?" For such a question we were not prepared, and knew not at the moment how to answer it. Mr. Dawson begged him to consider our words; nothing having been said in the governor's letter about the £1000. I then ventured to add: "The great concern now is that peace be secured; if this is done money matters will be satisfactorily settled." "£1000 has been promised me," rejoined he, "before this is paid I cannot let you go." Hereupon we repeated *why* we had begged for our freedom, not in the first instance on our own account, but because the thought of Ashantee's ruin was so painful to us, and we longed to save further bloodshed. "We promise, and if you wish, we will *swear* that the governor will keep his word if you will send us *all:* that is what he asks from you."

Dark and depressed the king turned to his councillors, spoke half aloud to his mother, and then called out, "Who will go? Whom shall I send to the governor?" Then (receiving no answer), as though he would act the man and hide his fear, he continued, turning to me, "You

Susse, you go." I shuddered at the thought—"Leave my wife and children here?" I asked. "Yes, you go and come back." This was like cold water on our hopes; we all protested "nothing would be gained by this, as the governor intended to have *all* the prisoners;" in short I said at last, "*I will not go alone.*" Dawson then added that "he would remain in Coomassie with his people as a hostage." M. Bonnat advanced, and offered, in case the king felt any mistrust, "to come back himself, so assured was he that the general would keep his word." The king was silent, gazed vacantly before him, then suddenly turned and said, "Go, go, and tell my good friend the governor that I did not march against him. Amankwa Tia attacked the fort contrary to my commands, I have nothing against the white men, go and speak a good word with the governor."

Hardly believing our ears, we advanced and thanked the king and his council, as those whose lives had been given them. Still we were afraid to trust, for although the king ordered two men to accompany us, they were quite common persons; if the order were meant in earnest, why should not Owusu Kokoo, or at least some under chief attend us? "Besides," we asked, "whom did the king include in the command 'go.'" Probably only the white men, so D. again protested that the governor wanted *all* the prisoners, Fantees, Akwapems, Akras; and alluded at the same time to the remaining condition of peace—the payment of 50,000 ounces of gold. This provoked the king. "What," he angrily exclaimed, "Is it not enough if I send *you*, am I to give up the Fantees too?" His mother was also greatly excited, but we could not understand her, for the tumult grew prodigious, and as soon as the king began to storm, everyone else sprang up swearing and shouting in the wildest confusion.

The interpreters accused D. of wishing to deceive the

king, and abused him violently. He vainly tried to justify himself. The king continued, in a rage, " No one shall be set free; no, *you shall all stay here.*" His words were echoed on every side, and we were assured that every one of us should be killed. We stood petrified, feeling that words were no of use, the noise was so great.

At last, with some vexation, we sat down quietly in our chairs, to wait until the storm should have abated. How little did we dream that on that very evening we should leave Coomassie! Every hope of liberty seemed to have vanished, for the nation rushed on blindly to face its coming judgment, and what might be the result of a defeat the Lord only knew. The king was still unsoftened, but at length when I stepped forward and begged him to compose himself, he gradually became calmer, and said, " Oh, I have nothing against you!" and then gazed firmly before him, as if tortured by a heavy weight, and engaged in a struggle with himself.

Suddenly he broke the silence, " No, you shall go, you white men, and tell my good friend I did not make war against him. I have no quarrel with him. As to the £1000 tell him I will make him a present of it. I do not wish that so small a sum should be the cause of differences between us. Go, speak a good word, I have now done what I can. If the governor will not wait, I must leave the matter with God."

Were these words credible? Was no deception concealed behind them. Thus we anxiously questioned ourselves, and while offering formal thanks to the king, doubts rendered the expression of our gratitude rather cold, and our suspicions were not quelled by observing that two very common messengers (a sword-bearer and a crier) were summoned to accompany us. I repeatedly begged to have Owusu Kokoo (who had accompanied Mr. Kühne), but this was refused. We felt that very likely some plan had been formed to carry us from Coomassie to some hiding place in the interior. Certainly we hardly looked like people who had just obtained their sentence of liberty, and yet such was the case.

The messengers now received their instructions. Mr. Dawson was commissioned to go home, and prepare a letter which was to be signed by the interpreter. Then the king asked when we thought of starting. "As soon as possible after you have dismissed us, in fact to-day," was our answer. "Very well," he said, "get ready to start this evening. You shall meet the general at Fomana." We could scarcely believe the words; full many a misgiving cooled our little gleam of hope.

When we told the news on our arrival at home, my wife could not believe the truth of it. Still we began to pack. We had been ready to do so a week before, for we did not know where we might be dragged at any moment, and even now we were left to conjecture whither we might be conveyed. The Fantees, Akras, and Akwapems were much depressed, feeling that they would henceforth be bereft of the slight protection our presence afforded, though of course we promised that if ever we did see the general, we should plead their cause. Hope and fear alternated while the time passed, we packed, planning meanwhile, and weighing the possibilities which lay before us. Our comfort was in the nearness of the Lord. Led by Him, we felt that we could go through anything.

About four o'clock a report reached us that Owusu Kokoo was approaching with the presents, and people entered our yard, bearing the king's parting salutation. For Mr. B. and myself there were valuable native costumes, and thirty dollars. A silk dress for my wife, with eighteen dollars, and nine dollars for Rosie. We not only regarded it a pleasure to receive remembrances from Coomassie, but these tokens also reassured us to the effect that the king really meant to keep his word, and we lifted up our hearts in thankful praise, although we knew that a change of mind might yet occur. Owusu Kokoo told us that his majesty would send for us again before our departure. We begged him to allow us sixteen Fantees as carriers. He promised to try, but thought it would not be possible to obtain so many.

Evening drew in by the time we had done packing, and we all sat round in the open court with the black prisoners; several of these expressing decided hopes that our surrender might lead to a suspension of hostilities, and restore liberty to all the other captives. Palm and his wife (our nurse) alone remained deeply depressed.

It was past nine o'clock when the messenger appeared who was to accompany us, and after another season of weary waiting, we were led through eight courts of the palace into a smaller one, where the king sat in his undress by the fire, with two chiefs. His majesty looked troubled and gloomy, as if our liberation had cost him a severe struggle. On entering the court, we had put on the new dresses; remarking this, he looked down at us and said gravely, "well Susse, so you know how to wear the national dress." Feeling sorry to see him so miserable, M. Bonnat and I again assured him that we would do everything to bring about peace with the general; the result would shew whether we kept our word. He smiled and dismissed us with the words "yes; it is all right, go, and do as you say."

While we were still in the yard, Owusu Kokoo told us that we might have ten Fantees, but not Mrs. Palm, as she must wait until her husband was set at liberty. Thus the king had really *given us up:* We could not fully believe it, however, until we fairly reached the English camp. We now saw Mr. Dawson again, and took charge of his letters and messages. I obtained one more bearer from Owusu after some trouble; of course all the Fantees wished to be included among our "eleven," but we were obliged to give the preference to those sent to meet us a year before, by prince Ansa, and these poor fellows heard the decision with loud cries of joy.

At length we were ready to start, and our farewells were accomplished by about eleven o'clock, after which a few friends accompanied us to the market-place, where we went through a second parting, and then laid ourselves in our hammocks. The whole thing seemed like a dream. The night was peculiarly dark, only a few stars being visible, and our road lay through a deep forest. We progressed but slowly, for the bearers had to feel their way, creeping over numberless roots and stones, and once they let me fall into the bush. However this mattered little, for were we not travelling towards the liberty for which we had longed all these years?

In two hours we arrived at the village of Kaase, three miles from the city, where we remained for the rest of the night, not sleeping much however. Early next morning (January 22nd), we started, hoping to reach Akankawase, a distance of from twenty to thirty miles. On our way we met two chiefs with a small retinue,—Kwame Agyapong, and the interpreter Apea, a cunning man who had always opposed our freedom; they now, however, saluted us kindly. One of the royal messengers accompanying us had already disappeared, going as he said to communicate the king's message to the chief of Mampong, who was in camp near Kaase. This struck us as rather strange.

At four o'clock in the afternoon we reached Amoaforo, where a fierce battle was yet to take place (January 31st), and here it transpired that we could go no further; so we visited the chief, who "in consequence of our liberation at the intercession of the Mampong chiefs and of

THE RELEASE OF THE REST. 283

the queen mother," had been officially ordered to board us. The sword-bearer went out after whispering to the chief that if the enemy approach he was to retire. The chief now sent us some game and yams; he could not give a sheep, for "Amankwa's army had devoured everything." We were just sitting in the twilight at our "fufu," when our first messenger returned. He had really visited the camp of Dsomo, the chief of Mampong, and brought an interpreter back with him, whom the friendly prince offered us as an escort. Little did I think that this brave Dsomo would so soon meet his death in the battle-field. I was glad that my presentiment of treachery was unfounded; still we knew that at any moment the king's decisions might be altered, and thus we were glad when the sword-bearer proposed an early move.

In the morning (January 23rd) I awoke my people betimes, bidding them boil rice for the whole party, and adding that we should not rest till we had reached the white men, so no one was to buy anything on the road. All must resolve to exert themselves to the utmost. When we reached Akankawase, not a woman was to be seen; this showed us the near approach of the enemy, but the men met us there as everywhere else, in a friendly spirit. Our freedom seemed to lighten all hearts, for in their eyes we were the only cause of the war.

Meanwhile we heard by Dawson's boy, that Obeng, who had been obliged to flee from Fomana and was now stationed near Adubiase, intended to meet us on the road and bring us a parting salutation. A curious idea, this seemed to us, for we certainly felt we had seen quite enough of Obeng already. I walked the greater part of the way in spite of my lameness, inciting, urging, and hurrying the whole company; encouraging everyone by the prospect of freedom within two hours, my heart beating wildly all the time.

About half-past nine we reached the first deserted village; not a creature was to be seen. Four and a half years before such empty dwellings spoke to us only of imprisonment, want and misery, now they were signs that the deliverer was at hand. After we had passed several small villages, we suddenly came upon Dompoase, scarcely three miles from the British army. But the streets swarmed with black soldiers, and under the tree in front of the chief's house stood Obeng, with three hundred and fifty warriors. Was he going to afford us his protection to the border, or to attack the English army, under cover of giving us up? It was the last anxious hour we were to spend in Ashantee.

After sitting a long time, we were obliged to go in procession to the proud man, who thirteen months previously had plundered us. He was, however, studiously polite, as were also his subordinates. Sitting under the shadow of a tree we received their return greetings, a solemnity which had never before seemed so dreadfully tedious, and then appeared before Obeng once more with our escort, so that he might be duly informed of the royal message to the general. He appeared pleased, and together with all his followers, begged that we would say a good word for them, as the Ashantees had no quarrel with the white men. Altogether, he said, war was a bad thing. "Look at this village, it is quite deserted; does it not make one's heart ache?" I could but think it really served the Ashantees right, after having burnt so many villages, to be forced now to tremble for their own homes.

Half an hour had elapsed with these ceremonies, and various messengers came up, all begging us to advise the general to come to terms. We broke away at last, and had gone some forty steps when we were again stopped, as a further escort had been despatched to accompany us to the general. We burned with impatience; what did we want with fresh men? But politeness on our part was inevitable, for were we not still prisoners, and likely to remain so for at least the next three-quarters of an hour! So we waited patiently, till allowed to resume our journey, wondering whether we were to be stopped any more. It seemed not, for we now lost sight of the band of soldiers, and every step of the journey carried us on to freedom. No one wished to linger; no one felt fatigue. M. B. formed the vanguard, while I as rearguard hurried on the bearers, with promises of rest when we should all be free. This inducement winged the steps of all, as may be readily imagined. With rapid tread, and yet noiselessly, like fugitives, we fled past the majestic trees of the ancient forest.

Suddenly our procession halted. "What is it?" I asked. "Here are your countrymen," was the glad response! I ran forward, and found standing beside M. Bonnat two hussars and a young officer, whose weapons were two revolvers and a carbine. He welcomed us with much emotion; but I cannot describe the feelings that overwhelmed us at this moment! We grasped his hands, as one can only grasp the hand of a deliverer: when I tried to speak, my tongue failed, and tears were all the thanks I could offer.

Our net was broken at last, and with the sense of freedom, the whole world was given back to us. Lieutenant Hart sent word immediately to his superiors, and in a few minutes Major Russell and other officers appeared, greeting us cordially, wishing us every happiness, and inviting us to their table.

But here we had to learn that we were ignorant of the strictness of military discipline. If, before leaving Coomassie, we had hoped to do something for our Ashantee guides, we now found ourselves unable to carry out these intentions. The poor lads were not a little frightened on being at once parted from us, and conducted to a separate house, there to be guarded till they might be sent home. We could not even visit them, and never saw them again.

The officers conducted us through a number of outposts, along a well lighted path, where hundreds of West Africans were at work felling trees, and levelling the ground. Their joy was great; "welcome, sir," "good morning, sir," sounded on all sides, in the Tschi and Akra dialects. In the superabundance of our joy, we thought we must shake hands with all the Europeans who were employed; but this soon became impossible, for there were whole companies of them. The major felt great pleasure in offering us the first cup of welcome on free soil, for it seems that for the last two days they had given up all hope of our release. They were greatly astonished at our children, and made themselves very merry with little Rosie. How strange all the surroundings, in which we were so suddenly placed appeared to us. The whole thing was like a vision of joy and wonder. We could hardly swallow any of the plentiful food that was set before us, our hearts were much too full.

After resting some hours with our kind friends, we again started for the Monse camp, to appear before Sir Garnet Wolseley. Our way led through the never-to-be-forgotten town of Fomana. From thence a beautiful road stretched to the Monse mountain, past Kwisa; hundreds being still at work on it, while others constructed bamboo huts. What a bustle, and what haste! Carriers and loads of all kinds, cows and horses abounded everywhere. Dawson's boy, who conducted brother Kühne, had on his return to Coomassie, broken out in the cry, "Europe is come to Africa!" This we now saw confirmed, for how wonderful was the appearance of so many white faces in the old African forest.

But we soon began to feel very footsore, and before us

rose the steep Adanse mountain, 1,600 feet in height. It was no trifle for such tired wanderers to have to climb it, yet the word "liberty" acted like a spell, even on the bearers of my wife and children. Thus we reached the summit (though not without some heavy sighs), and were refreshed with a glass of wine and water, and even a cup of tea was offered by friendly hands.

Here it seems the newspaper correspondents had set up their own little camp, and their choice of residence was not by any means a bad one; for the Adanse mountain, with its cool, fresh breezes and splendid view, is about the most healthy spot in the whole of Ashantee. We would willingly have conversed with the correspondents, but Lieutenant Grant, who accompanied us, had impressed upon us the general's orders not to answer any questions. So we passed on, descended the southern side of the mountain, which we found quite as steep as the other, and at last reached the camp, with aching feet, about half-past five o'clock. A battalion of English had arrived in the morning, and formed an imposing sight, while their military music sounded beautifully in our ears.

As soon as we had taken possession of our quarters (which the staff-officers had cleared for us), we were introduced to his excellency. Our first desire was to give thanks for our freedom; for next to God, we certainly owed it to the English army. The general expressed his joy at having been the instrument of our release, although this was not the primary aim of the expedition. Sir Garnet gave us the honour of an invitation to dine in the evening with his staff, and showed us much kindness besides. The sympathy which all those gentlemen seemed to feel in every circumstance of our deliverance was most hearty, and the remembrance of that evening will always be a happy one.

On the morning of the 24th, when his excellency had

gone very early to Fomana, M. Bonnat and I followed him in order to speak a word for the Fantees and others who were still in Coomassie. We had another pleasant conversation with Sir Garnet, in which he asked me about many things, and I commended the Fantees to his care. Here I parted with our faithful fellow-sufferer, who had begged to be allowed to remain with his excellency, while I returned to Monse alone, thenceto set out (January 25th) on our journey to the Coast.

It was with a strange feeling that on the morning of the 2nd February we entered Cape Coast, and had to run the gauntlet, as it were, between men of all colours and costumes, and receive the greetings and welcomes of an ever increasing multitude. Far too many wanted to shake hands, while little Rosie stared at the crowds with most comical placidity, and seemed to think they had all gone mad together.

We were kindly welcomed in the Wesleyan mission house by Mr. and Mrs. Picot, and the missionary Lawerac, and here again I embraced our dear Kühne, who was overjoyed to see us, as he had suffered much anxiety on our account. After he had become composed, I found him more cheerful than in Coomassie, but the physician who attended him said that half of the right lung was gone, which he attributed to the privations he had endured. Captain Lees, the provisional administrator, received us most obligingly, and communicated to us a telegram just received of the battle at Bekwae and Amoaforo, and we also had great pleasure in meeting old Mr. Freeman, the founder of the Wesleyan mission in Coomassie.

That we made purchases of clothes, shoes, and other necessaries of civilized life, it is not necessary for these pages to relate, nor that warm-hearted ladies loaded us with gifts, nor that we ventured out to sea and inspected the magnificent hospital ship, one of the great fleet that

THE RELEASE OF THE REST. 289

lay at anchor here. The mail steamer arrived on the 6th, and conveyed us to Christiansborg the next day, where we stepped (still as if in a dream) into the midst of our brethren and their people.

Thus were we rescued!—not through a ransom, as Adu Bofo had sworn, but by means of an army which the Lord Himself had sent to deliver us.

And looking back on the chain of wonders through which our lives were preserved, and we ourselves restored to our friends, even the heathen natives expressed astonishment, greeted us with deep emotion, and confessed that they were now forced to believe in our Lord as a living, almighty, and merciful God; for on hearing of our capture, they had all decided that prayer was useless, and we should never return from Ashantee.

CHAPTER XXXI.

THE JUDGMENT.

A FEW facts must yet be added to complete this narrative. The British forces had hitherto been sufficient for the defence of the coast towns only, and to keep back the raids of such Ashantees as dared to come within reach of their ships. The whole of the western Protectorate was occupied by them, when on the 2nd October, 1873, Sir Garnet Wolseley landed with his staff of twenty-nine chosen officers at Cape Coast.

He first cleared the neighbourhood of Elmina of the enemy's soldiers, which induced their general, Amankwa Tia, to write a letter declaring he had not marched against the British, but against the kings of Akem, Abora, Denkjera, and Wasa. Sir Garnet replied to this by ordering Kofi Kari to clear the Protectorate immediately, and this order was carried out by the retreat of the Ashantee army. The retiring troops were however to be prevented approaching Abakrampa, the residence of the Abora king, who had been chosen head of the Fantee confederation,—which place was occupied and successfully defended by a small British force against the attack of several thousand Ashantees. On this occasion Amankwa Tia's sedan chair fell into the hands of the British, but he and his army managed safely to effect the passage of the Prah.

The first British troops landed at the opening of the year 1874. They were to undertake the "engineers and doctor's campaign," which Sir Garnet had planned, so that the European troops might be released from duty in two months. A road to the Prah was already made, and at the chief stations the necessary shelter could be afforded. The camp was fixed in Prasu, from thence the boundary stream was to be crossed.

Two Ashantee ambassadors arrived at this place on January 2nd, bringing letters and negotiations of peace from Kofi Kari. The general would not receive them, but ordered that all the preparations for war should be shown them, and a Gatling mitrailleuse was fired off, which caused one of them to remark to his companion, that now every hope of defence must disappear. His comrade taunted him with cowardice, and threatened to complain of him to the king, upon which he shot himself in the night. He was buried, by his companion's wish, on the Ashantee side of the river. The rest of the party were dismissed by the general over the now completed bridge (January 6th), whilst he insisted upon the conclusion of peace in the capital.

The Prah was then crossed by the troops, who marched to Asiaman, and found on their route many corpses of Ashantee soldiers, who seemed to have died of starvation. Kühne entered the camp at Asiaman on the 14th, and remained there a week. On the 23rd the other white captives arrived in Fomana and Monse.

The Monse mountain (1,500 feet in height) had already been ascended on the 17th by Lord Gifford and his Asen scouts, although a Fetish priest and several companions came forward to meet him, with a warning to go no further, as death stood in the way. But Gifford found only a Fetish thread across his path—near which lay a mangled human sacrifice. A wooden gun and dagger were placed by its side pointing backwards. Of course the English were not deterred by this for a moment.

Another reminder was sent to the king from Fomana (January 25th), to the effect that he was to set *all* his prisoners free (Mr. Dawson excepted), to send the half of the 50,000 ounces of gold, and to give up as hostages prince Mensa, the queen mother, and the heirs of the princes of Dwaben, Kokofu, Mampong, and Bekwae; upon which the general would come himself to Coomassie with a small escort, and there conclude peace. To give the king time, he promised to approach very slowly during the following days. This promise, by the way, was an easy one, because of the ever-recurring difficulty of procuring necessary provisions, and a convenient halt could be made in the healthy district of Fomana.

Here the general heard a wonderful story from M. Bonnat. On the 6th of January the great Fetish tree in Coomassie suddenly fell, and the king then sought to learn from the priests what were the prospects of this war. Two men being pierced through the cheek with knives, were bound to trees in the wood and left to die. The priests declared that if their death soon ensued, Ashantee would be victorious. But the poor creatures lived long; one five, the other nine days!

Amankwa had stationed himself on the heights between Bekwae and Amoaforo, about twenty-four miles south of Coomassie, whilst a second army under the prince of Adanse held the towns of Adobiase and Borborase. These latter were taken on the 29th with little loss, and the chief commander's umbrella was captured. The British had not known till then how near they were to this general, Asamoa Kwanta, an old man, who was considered a great master in the art of war, in which he is said to have instructed Amankwa Tia. It was still hoped that the king might wish for peace; and thus in each encounter the English troops waited for the fire of the Ashantees before commencing proceedings on their own account.

But though letters were received from his majesty professing desire for peace, no guarantees accompanied them, and Mr. Dawson, who had to write a few lines of thanks for a present of gold from the general, added as date* " 2 Cor. ii. 11." A significant warning!

By 8 A.M. on January 31st the British troops pushed forward, discovering an ambuscade in the neighbourhood of Amoaforo, where the native camp had in the previous night been visited and explored by a scout, whose reward was £20. It now became evident that the king had done his utmost to raise an overwhelming force; he succeeded in engaging the English, and a sharp struggle took place in this primeval forest. The British troops, amounting to three thousand only (European and African combined), were badly covered, and had to fight an invisible enemy, numbering at least twenty thousand.

Happily the Ashantees were ill provided with bullets, and obliged to make use of pieces of metal; but it was almost impossible to take aim at them, so that rockets and small shell had to be resorted to. They kept up with much spirit till the afternoon, when they fled before a bayonet charge, and in the evening they again threatened the English right wing and rear. Asamoa Kwanta seems to have planned and commanded with much insight, yet he lost the battle. Among the many slain were Amankwa Tia, who fell on the left wing, and the brave and worthy prince of Mampong on the right, whilst Apea lost his life in the centre. The English only lost seven men at the time, but over two hundred were carried off the field wounded. They also buried more than a hundred Ashantees after the majority had been taken away by their country people.

On the following day the stately town of Bekwae was

* "Lest Satan should get advantage of us, for we are not ignorant of his devices."

stormed, Fomana being meanwhile attacked (February 2nd) by the Ashantees under their "Moltke," and almost burnt down. The small English garrison could not attempt more than to hold the custom house, hospital, and the magazine. Sir Garnet, amidst constant fighting, now advanced rapidly along the western road, from Adjuman towards the Oda (Da) river, where a letter from the king reached him (written by Mr. Dawson), begging that he would remain where he was, and promising that the demanded sum should certainly be paid. The general again asked for hostages, and proceeded without delay to throw a bridge over the Oda. On the morning of February the 4th the king disputed the passage of the river, and the struggle was maintained seven hours near Odaso, Kari-Kari looking on, seated on a golden footstool under his red umbrella. When defeat was certain, he fled to his villa at Amanghyia.

The British forces now pressed on without delay past Akankawase and Kaase, and marched into Coomassie in the evening amidst the sounding of bagpipes; there were only a thousand Europeans and four hundred black troops. The inhabitants (many of them with arms in their hands) gazed with great curiosity on the many white faces, but displayed neither fear nor hatred in their own appearance. The troops on their part entirely refrained from plunder, but the mob of the town, with some Fantees and other blacks, attacked the houses of princes and nobles, and took various liberties.

The imprisoned Fantees, and among them Mr. Dawson, had been set free, but many were found still bound to large trees, or in the stocks. They all withdrew, most taking with them a suspicious amount of property. The troops who had advanced so far, had again to retreat for want of provisions, heavy rains having also set in. An offer was made to the king (February 5th) to save his palace on condition of his accepting the terms of peace; in the meanwhile, however, the Ashantees endeavoured to remove from the town as much powder and as many arms as possible.

In the night a dreadful storm occurred, which threatened to make the rivers impassable; the palace was therefore undermined (Feb. 6th), notice having been given to the inhabitants, and the houses in Coomassie were fired; no great spoil came to light, but many curious things were found in the stone palace, which were afterwards sold at high prices in London.

The main army speedily retreated; wading through the rivers, up to the chin in water (the Da bridge being flooded knee-deep), and reached the Prah without any great sacrifice of health. The fact of the Mausoleum of Bantama ("the Louvre and Tower of Ashantee") not being destroyed, was complained of by many Englishmen as a great mistake; but a delay of two days would have endangered many valuable lives, and the burning of Coomassie was sufficient to announce the fall of Ashantee to the tribes of the gold coast. Everywhere the odour of blood predominated over every other; and no European would have willingly encountered a longer stay in Coomassie than was absolutely necessary.

Meanwhile, Captain Sir John Glover, with a small detachment, had entered Ashantee from the Volta. He took the town of Obago (Agnago ?) January the 16th, just in time to save the lives of forty slaves who were to fall at a funeral festival. When Dwaben, the second capital of the kingdom, surrendered on February the 11th, Captain Sartorius, sent by Sir John, and accompanied by twenty mounted men, rode through the streets of burnt Coomassie without finding a single sign of life in the whole town. He was to inform the general that Glover was at a distance of eight hours from him.

All this forced Kofi Kari to yield, for the allegiance of many among the minor princes began to totter. He therefore (February 13th), sent an entreaty for peace to Fomana, accompanied by a thousand ounces of the purest gold, as first installment of the war costs. Peace was signed on condition that he should pay fifty thousand ounces more, and open the way for free trade and communication with the Coast, which was to be carried on by a road fifteen feet broad, reaching from Cape Coast to the Prah. He gave up his rights to five vassal states, and also promised that in order to prove his friendship for Queen Victoria, he would strive to do away with the practice of human sacrifices, with a view to the total abolition of a custom so repugnant to all christian nations.

By a subsequent arrangement, the eastern boundary of the Protectorate was extended to Keta, and thus the river Volta ceased to be an apple of discord to the surrounding tribes, while the importation of arms was rendered increasingly difficult to the Ashantees.

When Sir Garnet Wolseley laid before the Geographical Society the particulars of his short but successful campaign (May 10th, 1874), he began by describing the primeval forest, where he scarcely ever saw either the sun or the enemy, although the latter certainly managed to make himself uncomfortably felt.

Scarcely anything beyond a snail-hunt was possible, and although this species of game reached a considerable size, food of that sort was hardly agreeable to European tastes. "When we landed in Cape Coast," says he, "the name of England stood in poor reputation, but now I believe it will be more than ever honoured, and it is almost certain that the interior of Africa will thus open itself to our explorers in an unexpected manner. A further result of the war will be the abolition of human sacrifices—a practice which forty years ago was as firmly rooted at Cape Coast as in Ashantee. One of my military doctors was billeted in the house of the head executioner" (no doubt Agja Kese, alluded to in the journal) "and heard from him that during last year from two to three thousand human beings had been slain." "We slay," said he, in the tone of a butcher who speaks of his trade, "somewhere about from five to ten a day, and on every day of the week except Friday." It was a terrible sight, that deep pit (Apetisini) filled with human corpses, in all stages of decomposition.

The last reports from the Gold Coast announce that the king has promised to do all in his power to abolish human sacrifices, and that he had sent one of his sons to the Coast to be educated there.

Respecting this son, whom the king even wished to send to England for further instruction, a negotiation was commenced with the Colonial government, inasmuch as the latter wished to know first, whether the prince had any prospect of ascending the throne; an embarrassing question, for the aforesaid throne has lately become very tottering, as might well be expected under the circumstances. Ashantee owed much of its power to the close alliance of the neighbouring kingdoms, Dwaben, Kokofu, Bekwae, Mampong, and Adanse, whose princes paid tribute in Coomassie, stationed soldiers there, and themselves assembled at all the great festivities and important meetings of the Ashantee council. Now, of course, there is a loosening of all these connections, if indeed they are not entirely broken up.

In February last the prince of Adanse, "the customhouse officer" (Obeng), begged the British general to allow him and his people to emigrate to the Protectorate, that they might be able to appeal in future to Cape Coast instead of to Coomassie, where one was never sure of his head. He swore the great oath to unite and form one nation with the Wasa people. Other tribes also sought to place themselves under British protection, or aimed at completely freeing themselves from the Ashantee yoke; the old jealousy on this subject especially showed itself again at Dwaben.

The British administrator, captain Lees, went himself to Coomassie in July, in order to effect an arrangement of these affairs. He was received in the barely restored town with manifestations of joy and respect. The king and the queen mother coming to meet him, and everyone dancing around him. No definite public information has yet reached us as to the result of the negociations, but it is said, that the king seemed willing to acknowledge the independence of Dwaben. Lees refused to help the king to subdue the revolted princes of Dwaben and Bekwae, and even visited both of them, and was welcomed with great cordiality. This was a tempting example for the other tributaries, and Okwau, where it may be remembered the prisoners were welcomed with so much sympathy, has also expressed a wish to ally itself to the Protectorate; both Okwau and Dwaben has requested the erection of a missionary station in their towns, and David Asante finds people from these two districts among the most attentive of his hearers at his street preaching in Akem.

From the latest reports we learn that the queen mother, who had long striven against the deposition of her son, had at last herself suggested a change of sovereign, so that the kingdom might at least be preserved for the dynasty, Adu Bofo appears to have rebelled against the king; thus it seems that the continuance of the kingdom will only be possible under very limited and altered circumstances.

Such a change as the abolition of the old national custom of human sacrifices would be a difficult matter for a popular and prosperous king; for the humiliated Kofi Kari-Kari it would be simply impossible. In any case, a turning point has arrived in the history of the kingdom, which augers happier prospects in the future, if the right men are found ready to step into the gap, and to sow seeds of Christian culture in the blood-stained soil of Ashantee.

APPENDIX.

APPENDIX I.

THE ADAE.

BESIDES the week of seven days, which were apparently appropriated to seven persons, and gave names to every boy and girl, and which were also used by neighbouring tribes in their various languages, the Tshies have twelve months of thirty or thirty-two days, named according to the seasons or the situation of the plantations, but these are different in different places, and are not in general use.

More frequently time was reckoned by the Adae. This feast fell on every fortieth or forty-second day. The great Adae was always celebrated on a Sunday, the little Adae on a Wednesday. According to a peculiar mode of reckoning, the Adae began at different hours of the day.

This manner of dividing the time is also found in other nations, as in Malabar in India, where the doctors reckon the "Mandalam" of forty days, divided into half and quarter circles, as a method of measurement:—

18th December, 1869,	Sunday,	Great Adae.
11th January, 1870,	Wednesday,	Small ,,
29th ,, ,,	Sunday,	Great ,,
22nd February, ,,	Wednesday,	Small ,,
12th March, ,,	Sunday,	Great ,,
5th April, ,,	Wednesday,	Small ,,

23rd April 1870,	Sunday,	Great Adae.
26th ,, ,,	Wednesday,	Small ,,
4th June, ,,	Sunday,	Great ,,
28th ,, ,,	Wednesday,	Small ,,
16th July, ,,	Sunday,	Great ,,
9th August, ,,	Monday,	Small ,,
27th ,, ,,	Sunday,	Great ,,
20th September, ,,	Monday,	Small ,,
8th October, ,,	Sunday,	Great ,,
1st November, ,,	Monday,	Small ,,
19th ,, ,,	Sunday,	Great ,,
13th December, ,,	Monday,	Small ,,
31st ,, ,,	Sunday,	Great ,,

APPENDIX II.

THE WEIGHTS OF GOLD IN ASHANTEE.

The most extraordinary weights of gold may be compared with English money as follows :—

	£	s.	d.
1 pesewa	0	0	1¾
1 dama	0	0	3
1 kokoa (3 pesewa)	0	0	5¼
1 taku (4 pesewa)	0	0	7
1 sua	0	6	9
1 suru	1	0	3
1 asia	1	7	0
1 osua	2	0	6
1 ounce (½ benna)	3	12	0
1 benna	7	4	0
1 peredwane	8	2	0

The following list contains further names :—

1 soafa (½ soa)	6 taku	
1 fiasofa (½ fiaso)	6½ ,,	
1 domafa	7 ,,	
1 borowofa	8 ,,	1 dollar (ackie)
1 agirakwefa	9 ,,	
1 soansafa	10 ,,	
1 bodommofa	11 ,,	
1 soa	12 ,,	
1 fiaso	13 ,,	
1 doma	14 ,,	
1 borowo	16 ,,	2 dollars
1 agirakwe	16½ ,,	
1 soansa	20 ,,	
1 bodomme	22 ,,	

1 nnomanu	-	-	-	24 taku,	3 dollars	
1 nsano	-	-	-	26 ,,		
1 dyoasuru	-	-	-	28 ,,		
1 amamfisuru	-	-	-	32 ,,	4 dollars	
1 suru	-	-	-	36 ,,	£1 0 3	
1 peresuru	-	-	-	40 ,,	5 dollars	
1 takimansua	-	-	-	44 ,,	5½ ,,	
1 asia	-	-	-	48 ,,	6 ,,	
1 dyoa	-	-	-	56 ,,	7 ,,	
1 namfi	-	-	-	60 ,,	7½ ,,	
1 nansua	-	-	-	64 ,,	8 ,,	
1 sua	-	-	-	72 ,,	9 ,,	
1 asuanu	-	-	-	1 oz.	2 acki (dollars)	
1 asuasu	-	-	-	1 ,,	11 ,,	
1 peredwane	-	-	-	2 ,,	4 ,,	
1 tesuanu	-	-	-	3 ,,	6 ,,	
1 ntanu	-	-	-	4 ,,	8 ,,	
1 ntansa	-	-	-	6 ,,	12 ,,	

In Akem, an agiratschifa = 1 ackie or 1 dollar; an agiratsche = 2 dollars; a bodoma = 2½ dollars; a dyoa = 8 dollars. Doma, usano, and asia differ in the two countries; soa, suru, osua, benna, and peredwane are the same in both.

An ounce of gold (£3 12 6d—£4) is divided by the merchants on the Coast into 16 ackie; 1 ackie = 1 Spanish or American dollar, 4s 6d,—in England, 4s 2d.

APPENDIX III.

THE GOVERNMENT OF ASHANTEE.

As it has been easy to perceive by the reading of these pages, that the reins of the Ashantee government are not exclusively in the hands of the king, nor does he possess unlimited power, but shares it with a council which includes, besides his majesty, his mother, the three first chiefs of the kingdom, and a few nobles of Kumasi (Coomassie). This council is called " Asante Kotoko," or the Ashantee porcupine, which means that like the animal of that name, nobody dare touch them. The principal drum in Coomassie has as its peculiar strain or motto, " Asante Kotoko, wokum apem, apem reba," which means " if thousands are killed, thousands are coming up again."

It is this Kotoko council which rules the entire kingdom, and deals with the people, who must obey, whatever their own wishes or inclinations may be, in the most despotic way. In case of war the people have no voice, and to enforce obedience they must be ever under the consciousness that the king and his council are the arbitrators of their life or death. In important matters all the other chiefs of the kingdom are called together to discuss the case, but they are sure to vote in accordance with the view of the council, for who would dare to oppose the Kotoko?

At the Yam festival, usually held in October, all the chiefs of the kingdom meet at Coomassie, and have to report the events of the year in the parts under their jurisdiction. The chiefs belonging to the household of his majesty have in important matters no voice in court, but they have nevertheless great influence, and lose no opportunity of advising the king privately.

In court and in ordinary meetings the king takes his place in his skilfully carved and gold ornamented chair on a kind of platform at the bottom of the court, and over him is held his state umbrella (now in South Kensington Museum), while around him stand some of his swordbearers and other satellites. On his right and left side are the two state swords, and suspended from each is a large gold nugget. One of these is the war sword. If the king has taken it in his hand, the war is decided.

On the platform near his majesty are seated his mother and the nobles of Coomassie. A little lower down the court, on his right, we find the linguists and some other chiefs, surrounded by under chiefs and servants. On the left are the chiefs belonging to the royal household. In front of his majesty, placed so as to allow a free though narrow passage, are the court criers in great numbers, and lastly the executioners, whose business it is to praise his majesty, " to give him names," as they say, *i.e.*, to cry out his titles, as for instance, " ode tuo tia gyina mpreno ano "—" with a little gun he is standing at the mouth of the canons." " Pam'bo "—" he sews stones together—he tears and binds together again." " Bore " (the name of a venomous serpent) " you are most beautiful but your bite is deadly."

According to court etiquette, the speaker has to address himself to the linguists, who place the case before the king in more eloquent language.

If an accused person is brought before the court the linguists have to discuss the case, to find him guilty, and to pronounce the sentence, which, alas! is too often a sentence of death. The king can ratify the judgment or mitigate it, by changing it into a fine, or to the mutilation of any prominent part of the face, but in some cases the king is obliged to give way to the will of his chiefs.

The rank of the chiefs can be seen by the different insignia or emblems of their dignity, which always follow them. The three first dukes of the kingdom have large silk umbrellas topped with gold, a large band of elephant tusk blowers, and several drums. They are also allowed to have sandals ornamented with silver and gold, like those of the king. The duke or king of Dwaben has his own keteband.

Chiefs of the second rank have silk umbrellas topped with carved wood, and a very nicely carved arm-chair, ornamented on each side with brass nails. They are preceded by a party of about twelve boys, each of whom carries an elephant's tail; they have also horn-blowers and drummers.

The dukes of the third rank have a carved arm-chair, and servants who carry elephants' tails, but their umbrellas are made of cotton. The chiefs of the fourth rank have the same, but in place of elephants' tails their boys carry horse tails.

Those of the fifth rank have a large portly umbrella, but their arm-chair is common and less ornamented. All the principal captains have their special strains or motoes for their horns and drums. For instance, Amankwatia's drums say, "piridu, piridu"—go on, push forward. Boakje Tenteng's drums say, "don kofo didi in atem ene sen," or the donkos (negresses from the interior), insult me for what? Bobie's horn has for a motto, "Bobie annac o five agyaman agyaman ne nsam ade wo"—Bobie keeps watch for the king, there is something in the king's hand.

In the following lists we give the names of the dignitaries and the more influential chiefs and captains of

Coomassie and the kingdom of Ashantee. The Roman numbers indicate their rank.

(Coffee) Kari-Kari the king.
Afera Osuwa Kobe, king's mother, Kwakoo Dooah's neice.

THE THREE DUKES OF THE KINGDOM.

I. Yaw Agyei, king or duke of Dwaben.
I. ? ,, ,, Bekwae.
I. Djomo ,, ,, Mampong

CHIEFS OF PROVINCES.

II. Chief of Kokofu.
II. ,, Korausa.
II. ,, Nsuta.
II. ,, Abessin.
III. Oben of Adanse (Fomana).

CHIEFS AND CAPTAINS OF COOMASSIE.

II. Barempa, brother of prince Ansa. ⎫
II. Adonten Boaten.   ⎬ King's councillors.
II. Asamoa Kwanta.   ⎪
II. Abenkwa Osei (commander of the army). ⎭
II. Amankwa Tia (chief of Bantama). ⎫ In absence of the king they
II. Asafo Boakje.   ⎭ have charge over the town.
III. Karapa.
III. Agyapon.
III. Anyin.
III. Opoku (head of the linguists, minister ⎫
    of foreign affairs).   ⎪
III. Boakje Tenteng, linguist, husband of ⎬ Very influential men,
    the queen mother.   ⎪ so far as they are re-
IV. Yaw Nantshi, linguist.   ⎪ presentatives for the
IV. Apea. ,,   ⎪ provinces.
IV. Amoatin ,,   ⎭

Besides these a good number of under captains.

KING'S HOUSEHOLD.

II. Akjampong, the king's uncle, and chief over his household.
II. Adu Bofo, keeper of the keys, treasurer, eventual commander of the army.

III. Kwasi Domfu, head of the Tasumankwa (priests of the protectors and physician of the Fetishes).
III. Agya Kese, head of the executioners.
IV. Nkra Shene, brother of prince Ansa.
IV. Bobie,   ,,   ,,   (superintendent of police and of the buildings.)
IV. Owosu Kwabena ,,   ,,   (head of the king's hammockmen.)
IV.   ?   head of the court-criers.
IV.   ?   head of the eunuchs.
V. Kwami Mensa, king's brother (heir apparent).*
V. Bosommuru Tia. } Chamberlains and private councillors.
V. Bosommuru Dwira.
V. Mensa. Kukua, honorary king's soul.
V. Saben.
V. Onyame Dusei,
    And some other under captains.

In reference to the king it may be observed that during the lifetime of his predecessor, Kwakoo Dooah, an ill feeling had sprung up between him and the family of his sister, which increased during the latter years of his reign, and at length ripened into hatred. Kofi Kari sometimes said that his ascendancy to the throne of Ashantee was like a dream to him. It is said that in a moment of excitement, Kwakoo Dooah once sent to his sister a silken band, with a message to the effect, that the best thing she could do was to hang herself. She accepted the brotherly suggestion, and committed suicide. Her son Opoku was then accused of aspiring to the throne, and was sacrificed, with the honour due to his rank, viz., by having his neck broken with an elephant's tusk. Afua Kobe, the mother of king Kofi Kari, is the daughter of Kwakoo Dooah's sister, who committed suicide. It is said that in his last days Kwakoo deeply regretted his conduct towards her.

In reference to the chiefs, &c., of Coomassie, who have

* Present king.

been so often alluded to in the journal, no further explanation seems necessary. Of one, however, we may make the statement which follows.

The old "ruler of the battles," Asamoa Kwanta, is not mentioned in this list, although in reality he was the commander of the whole Ashantee army, when the prince of Mampong was not present. There are peculiar circumstances connected with this man, which the following facts, drawn from Mr. Ramseyer's and prince Ansa's letters, will elucidate.

In the year 1853 Asamoa Kwanta was commander-in-chief during the campaign against the Coast; but, having succeeded in getting the heads of the Assin chiefs who had provoked the anger of the king, he was recalled with the army by king Kwakoo Dooah before it came to a serious struggle. When this peace-loving monarch died, in 1867, a dreadful émeute broke out in the palace, and a nephew of the great marshal's was slain, prince Boakje Asu being implicated in the murder.

Although custom in Ashantee permits a prince to take the life of any subject on the death of his father, yet the aged Asamoa Kwanta took arms, and with his chiefs threatened to destroy Coomassie. This insurrection was only quelled by the entreaties of Ansa's two brothers, Owusu Sakiri and Owusu Intobu; they soothed the old man, who however would not be pacified till he had slain the Audawous prince and two of his sisters; he also demanded the life of the mother of the criminal, but it was ransomed with eighty ounces of gold.

After this the commander-in-chief kept aloof from the palace. The campaign to Krepe in 1869 was confided to Adu Bofo, although his rank was far below that of Asamoa. The prince of Bantama, Amankwa Tia, envied Adu Bofo for the large number of slaves which he had stolen and brought with him from the Coast; on this

account he intrigued against him, and with the help of
his followers succeeded in December 1872 in gaining the
command in the new campaign. This was against the
law, which confided to him and Asafo Boakje the defence
of Coomassie; it also offended the troops, who despised
Amankwa as a dreadful drunkard. But now that he was
at the head of the army the chiefs of Mampong and
Asamoa were obliged to be content with an unrecognised
but influential position.

After the defeat of Amankwa and his retreat, in January 1874, the command of the army was taken from
him and given to the prince of Mampong, with co-ordinate
rank as first general to Asamoa Kwanta. He was an old
grey-headed man, but full of energy and intelligence, and
as far as we could judge, opposed to the war, for he
knew all the difficulties and risks it involved. He always
behaved kindly to us, and certainly had something to do
with our release; he showed too in his last interview with
Mr. Dawson (January 17th), that he saw the state of
affairs more clearly than any one else. There are only
three chiefs superior to him in rank, the princes of Dwaben, Bekwae and Mampong, also the near relations of the
king.

APPENDIX IV.

A LETTER OF PRINCE ANSA.

It will not be regarded as an indiscretion if we give here an extract from a letter of prince Ansa, dated June 21st, 1871, in order to explain the accusation brought against him. It proves better than anything else the feelings of the prince towards his countrymen; it also expresses the king's view of the Elmina acquisition; and besides this it gives an insight into the head and heart of a civilised and christianised Ashantee.

On the 30th of May, the prince wrote to the prisoners thus—"A very serious accusation has been brought against me respecting the letter which I wrote to the administrator by the king's order, with regard to the right of the king to the town and fort of Elmina. The people of Elmina accuse me of having added the following sentence on my own responsibility: 'The king of Ashantee says that the king of Holland is his subject.' The reason why the Dutch governor sends that young man (the commissioner Plange) is simply this, he wishes to make sure whether the king commissioned me to write that letter or not. The Elminers and the Dutch dispute most emphatically that the king has any rights in Elmina. Now, if the king deny having authorised me to write that letter, I shall hardly come up (to Coomassie). I believe I showed you the copy of the letter which I have now given to Mr. Crawford, in order to justify myself before the king."

APPENDIX. 313

On June the 21st, he writes again—" When I last wrote I had not time to go into particulars about the accusation. You know that shortly before you went from Ebenezer to Coomassie,* the king authorised me to write to the administrator, that Elmina and the Fort had belonged to his ancestors for ages past, and that therefore they belonged to him. If, then, the British Government took possession of the Gold Coast, the town and fort were not to be included, as they were his. The administrator of course sent this letter to England, and the English government communicated it to the Dutch Government. When the Dutch heard that the king had sent his chief, Akjampong, to Elmina, they were angry, and ordered the governor to banish Akjampong; he was therefore ordered to leave Elmina, but he refused to do so. The governor, wishing to prove to him that Elmina did not belong to the Ashantee king, caused him to be shut up in the Fort. Then the Elminers and Akjampong accused me of having written that letter without the king's knowledge, and especially that the sentence, that 'the king of Ashantee regarded the king of Holland as his subject,' had been added by me. I am sorry to say that my friends who accompanied me as ambassadors (Afirifa, &c.), have taken part against me, and supported Akjampong and the Elminers. However, the Dutch governor and the administrator are on my side; and what is more, the Lord is for me.

"Now I expect to prove how far the king and his council are conscientious, by their owning or denying that I was fully authorised by them to write that letter. The governor of Elmina has decided not to deliver the usual yearly payment unless he apologises with regard to it.

"I am waiting to see whether the king really will beg pardon in order to receive that payment (four hundred

* November 24th, 1870, is the date of that foolish letter.

dollars a year) and my dear brothers, my sense seems to dictate to me that it is best I should stay here and await the end of all this before I take any further steps. I know my countrymen well enough to be sure that it is advisable for me to be careful. I assure you that if they withdraw themselves from me in this affair, it will be all the worse for them.

"You have the sympathy of all my friends, from the governor to the trades-people, particularly Mr. Blankson, Mr. Grant, Mr. Cleaver, and your brethren, the missionaries.

"But I prize most the sympathy of our Lord for His people. (Isaiah xlix. 14-16, lxiii. 9). Wherefore take courage, my brethren, do not despair, for

> 'Of every sorrow which *our* hearts can move,
> Half is supported in God's heart of love.'

The Lord is with His own people! Look alone to Him, and your release is certain!

"I have been privately informed that the Prussians think of you with as much earnest anxiety as the British felt for the poor prisoners in Abyssinia. A certain prince Bismarck is particularly interested in you. The Lord is working for you, and who can hinder Him? O trust in Him and you will be safe! I entreat poor Mrs. R. to take courage, she has the deepest sympathy from every one.

"I am sorry to tell you that Paris is in flames; all is dreadful there, the streets swimming in blood; the whole town with its splendid palaces is destroyed. France lies in ruins, more from civil war and their own dissensions than from the Prussians. I will try to send you a few newspapers.

"As some compensation for this sad news, I am pleased to hear from Mr. Schrenk that your house in Anum is not destroyed; some of your teachers and pupils came from there to the war, and brought this news; your people too assembled in safety. Joseph has not yet shown himself. I only hope he has not confided the goods I sent by him to my country people. If you see my cousin tell him he is not to trust any one; if he do so he will lose my confidence for ever. Write to me all news, particularly what you hear about me. I must conclude with sincere regards, in which my wife and all my family unite.—I remain,

"Ever your sincere friend,

"ANSA.

"P.S.—The exchange of the Dutch possessions is not yet completed. Some say it *will* take place; others that it *will not*. We shall hear the truth by the next despatches from England."

On August 1st 1871.—The prince again sent a letter by Asengro's messenger (who had formerly shown kindness to the prisoners), and he writes thus :—

"I ordered a piece of material to be given to Asengro as a present from you, and introduced him to his excellency the administrator (T. Salmon), to whom I related how kind he had been to you when you stayed in his village. In consequence of this his excellency presented him with two pieces of material, and the provisions which he required. I am only sorry that my best friends are not in the town just now, or he would go away laden with presents, and all for your sakes. At any rate I will certainly mention him to all my friends.

"I have written to Mr. Schrenk to tell him that I have determined to take a journey to Coomassie, and that one of your brethren was to go also. My wife thanks Mrs. R. for her letter, and begs me to say, that when the time comes, if she is in good health, she will be very glad to go to Coomassie and make her acquaintance.

The king had thought fit to recal the letter which had been written by prince Ansa to Mr. Ussher as having contained vague and clumsy expressions, and this recall had been given in writing to Mr. Plange.* His Majesty had never pardoned this young man for the injury which he alleged had been done to him by the wording of this letter. On May 6th, 1872, after twenty-three and a half years of Dutch government, Elmina was formally made over to Mr. Pope Hennessy, the Dutch governor, at the same time handing to him the staff of office (ivory inlaid with gold), which had passed through the hands of a hundred successive plenipotentiaries, and now came into the possession of the British. But before this time, in December 1871, prince Ansa really made the promised visit to Coomassie at great risk to himself, and without obtaining the results he had hoped for.

From the case of this prince, who had become so much of an Englishman in his ideas, it may be proved that it is possible for something good to come out of Ashantee; and we may be permitted to mention another Ashantee, who through civilisation became more like a German. He was thus designated by the German Oriental Company more than twenty years ago.—"His royal highness Aguarie Boachin prince of Ashantee, royal Dutch moun-

* The terms of the recall (August, 1871), were as follows :—"Herewith it is announced, that the terms of letter of November 24th, 1870, addressed to his Excellency, H. T. Ussher, the administrator of the British settlement on the Gold Coast, through me Coffee Calcalli (Kofi Kari), King of Ashantee in Coomassie, were entirely misrepresented by those persons employed in the writing and dictating thereof. I therefore declare, in the presence of your Excellency's ambassador, Mr. Plange, Government writer of St George in Elmina, and before my chiefs, that I only meant board wages or salary, and not tribute by right of arms on the part of the Dutch Government." Of course, this declaration did not in the least deter the king, a year later (March, 1873), from claiming Elmina, Denkjera, Akem, and Asen, from the British Government, and the people as his slaves.

tain engineer, for service in Surubagu, East Indies." He was the son of the reigning sovereign, and by his father's wish was taken to Amsterdam at nine years of age, and there educated. He became a convert to Christianity, and was baptized, so that his return to Coomassie seemed impossible. He therefore went to Frieburg to study mining; and there becoming intimately acquainted with many German families, he formed such an attachment to that nation, that he sent from Java, where he was residing, a contribution of one thousand florins for the wounded during the last war, to the editor of the *Gartenlaube* (a German periodical). He was first director of mines in Java, but has now a coffee plantation.

These two instances are sufficient to prove the kind of material for civilsation which exists in Ashantee, even in the palaces of Coomassie; and they also show how little those modern reports are to be depended on, which, while they allow the negro to have as much common sense and more cunning than the Caucassians, yet make him out to be thoroughly heartless.

APPENDIX V.

A WORD ON THE POLITICS OF THE COLONIAL GOVERNMENT IN THE YEAR 1872.

The captives feel in duty bound to return sincere thanks to all the officers of state, who have shown themselves in any way interested in their welfare. They can well understand the difficulty of men in their position passing judgment on the actions and motives of the authorities, and they refrain from any expression of criticism on the colonial politics of that period.

But the case is different with the English press. A history of the campaign, which embodies all the events recorded in the preceding pages ("From Cape Coast to Coomassie," *Illustrated London News*), subjects the two facts mentioned in the journal, to severe criticism.

"Mr. Pope Hennessy would not condescend to pay British government money for the ransom of the European prisoners, but he was not above suggesting that the Missionary Society to which Mr. Ramseyer and Mr. Kühne belonged might perhaps be disposed to give £1000 on this account. At the same time our governor actually released a son of Adu Bofo who had been prisoner at Cape Coast, and defrayed his travelling expenses home to Coomassie. The king of Ashantee and his kidnapping general had a mind to get the £1000 which the Basle Mission, we are ashamed to say, had been invited by our government to offer."

The circumstances connected with this son (or nephew) of Adu Bofo were as follows :—

After the invasion of Anum, the British colonial government were perplexed about the steps to be taken. The missionaries in Odumase meanwhile persuaded the friendly king of Krobo to interpose on behalf of their brethren who had been carried off. The latter sent three successive messages by his brother to the camp of the United Ashantees and Akwarmers, demanding that the missionaries should be given up. But they were continually put off by excuses.

When however in October, 1869, Dompre had beaten the Ashantee army, and the tribes in the eastern part of the Protectorate were preparing for an armed attack, the king of Akwarme became so frightened that he sent the king of Krobo hostages who were to answer for the life of the captive missionaries. Adu Bofo, realizing the difficulty of his position, sent his son with these hostages, hoping by this means to keep the people in Krobo from rising.

King Kari-Kari was also impressed with the dangers by which his general was surrounded, so that on November 2nd, 1869, he expressed to the Colonial government his readiness to exchange the missionaries for the Ashantee prisoners.

If therefore Mr. Ramseyer and Mr. Kühne were astonished, when in March 1871 an exchange of prisoners had been made without themselves having been taken into consideration, how much more were they surprised, when in July, 1872, these hostages appeared in Coomassie, set free without any equivalent! This fact shows more than anything the conciliatory disposition of the British government.

The Ashantees themselves mistook this peaceful policy for weakness, and it is therefore not surprising that

APPENDIX.

Stanley (in his book, "Coomassie and Magdala") states that the ambassador Plange wrote in October, 1872, from Coomassie, "The chiefs here are in hope that in return for the release of the prisoners, they will have the whole Gold Coast."

The same conciliatory policy was followed in the release of Akjampong. The above named work ("From Cape Coast to Coomassie," *Illustrated London News*), relates this in the following manner :—

"Akjampong, with seven hundred followers, was arrested in October, 1872, in Apollonia, and brought to Cape Coast to be set free in the course of a month or two, and sent to Coomassie. This was done without taking into consideration the ransom of the European captives, or the fact that in Akjampong they were sending back to Kari-Kari's council the greatest intriguer and the chief of the war officers, which just signified throwing a spark among a heap of shavings. He came to Coomassie at the great death festivities, and decided for 'war!'"

The missionaries' journals prove that the latter was not the case. War was decided upon before Akjampong's arrival in Coomassie. But thus much is clear from these facts, that *the British Government did not provoke the last Ashantee war.*

www.ingramcontent.com/pod-product-compliance
Lightning Source LLC
Chambersburg PA
CBHW031855220426
43663CB00006B/628